AMERICA

Ready-to-Use
INTERDISCIPLINARY
LESSONS & ACTIVITIES
for Grades 5-12

VOLUME I

DWILA BLOOM

**THE CENTER FOR APPLIED
RESEARCH IN EDUCATION**
West Nyack, New York 10994

Library of Congress Cataloging-in-Publication Data

Bloom, Dwila
      Social studies curriculum activities library : ready-to-use interdisciplinary lessons &
      activities for grades 5–12 / by Dwila Bloom ; Amy Craig, social studies consultant ;
      Dianne Trujillo, media specialist consultant ; Vincent Walter, photographer.
            p.   cm.
      Includes bibliographical references.
      Contents: v. 1. America—v. 2. Africa, Europe & Asia
      ISBN 0-87628-589-2 (v. 1). — ISBN 0-87628-590-6 (v. 2)
      1. Social sciences—Study and teaching (Elementary)—Activity programs—United States.
   2. Social sciences—Study and teaching (Secondary)—Activity programs—United States.
   3. Interdisciplinary approach in education—United States.   I. Craig, Amy (Amy Ann)
   II. Trujillo, Dianne.   III. Walter, Vincent.   IV. Title.
   LB1584.B658   1997   97-25321
   300'.71'073—dc21   CIP

© 1997 *by* The Center for Applied Research in Education

Every effort has been made to ensure that no copyrighted material has been used without permission. The author regrets any oversights that may have occurred and would be happy to rectify them in future printings of this book.

Printed in the United States of America

10 9 8 7 6 5 4 3 2 1

ISBN 0-87628-589-2

ATTENTION: CORPORATIONS AND SCHOOLS

The Center for Applied Research in Education books are available at quantity discounts with bulk purchase for educational, business, or sales promotional use. For information, please write to: Prentice Hall Career & Personal Development Special Sales, 240 Frisch Court, Paramus, New Jersey 07652. Please supply: title of book, ISBN, quantity, how the book will be used, date needed.

Illustrations used in this book are from the following sources:
—Corel Print House User's Manual, Version 1.0 Corel ClipArt
—IMSI 101,000 Master Clips, Premium Image Collection
—Dover Publications, Mineola, New York
—Dwila Bloom

Front cover photograph courtesy of Plimouth Plantation, Plymouth, MA
Gary Andrashko, photographer

 **THE CENTER FOR APPLIED RESEARCH
IN EDUCATION**
West Nyack, NY 10994
A Simon & Schuster Company

On the World Wide Web at http://www.phdirect.com

Prentice Hall International (UK) Limited, *London*
Prentice Hall of Australia Pty. Limited, *Sydney*
Prentice Hall Canada, Inc., *Toronto*
Prentice Hall Hispanoamericana, S.A., *Mexico*
Prentice Hall of India Private Limited, *New Delhi*
Prentice Hall of Japan, Inc., *Tokyo*
Simon & Schuster Asia Pte. Ltd., *Singapore*
Editora Prentice Hall do Brasil, Ltda., *Rio de Janeiro*

DEDICATED

To Bruce . . . in loving memory

ABOUT THE AUTHOR

Dwila Bloom has over 20 years of art education experience in the Tippecanoe School Corporation, Lafayette, Indiana. She has taught classes in elementary through ninth grade as well as special, gifted, and adult art programs. Mrs. Bloom earned an undergraduate degree from Purdue University in Art Education as well as a Master of Arts specializing in Art History and Curriculum Planning. She is the author of *Multicultural Art Activities Kit,* also published by The Center for Applied Research in Education, 1994.

Additional studies in Europe and America sparked Mrs. Bloom's interest in cooperative educational experiences for students. As a result many projects were developed integrating art into the social studies classroom. With the encouragement of social studies teachers, an interdisciplinary program was initiated incorporating activities in language arts, mathematics, physical education, music, and home economics into the social studies program. *Social Studies Curriculum Activities Library* emerged from all these experiences.

ABOUT THE SOCIAL STUDIES CONSULTANT

Amy Craig has 13 years of experience teaching Social Studies in the Tippecanoe School Corporation, Lafayette, Indiana. She has taught elementary and middle school social studies as well as basic and gifted classes. Amy received Bachelor of Arts and Master's of Science degrees from Purdue University. She believes that students learn social studies best by being totally submerged into the cultures. Amy has promoted many exciting extra-curricular activities locally, regionally, and nationally. She has also sponsored several social studies excursions for living history experiences and has been nominated for the *Golden Apple Award* for excellence in teaching.

ABOUT THE MEDIA SPECIALIST CONSULTANT

Dianne Trujillo has 28 years of teaching experience in the Benton Community Schools, Oxford, Indiana, and the Tippecanoe School Corporation, Lafayette, Indiana. The last 16 years, Dianne has been a Media Specialist with experience in elementary, middle, and high school media centers. Ms. Trujillo earned her undergraduate degree from Chicago State University in elementary education and a Master's Degree in Media Science from Purdue University. Dianne believes that technology has changed the role of the media specialist in many ways. However, she also believes that reading will never become obsolete and the greatest gift we can instill in children is to read. She especially encourages reading and book talking with students of all ages.

ACKNOWLEDGMENTS

There are many people who helped produce this library. These educators, students, professionals, friends, and family deserve acknowledgment for all their contributions and support.

First and foremost, I want to thank Amy Craig for her enthusiasm for teaching Social Studies and for her intense interest in making history come alive for students. Without her belief in and dedication to interdisciplinary and cooperative education, this book would never have been written.

Close behind, I want to thank Dianne Trujillo, Media Specialist, who spent many hours helping with the Language Arts activities and reading the manuscript with supportive and insightful suggestions.

A large thank-you to the students at Klondike Middle School. They were always eager to participate in the activities and displayed genuine interest in the lessons and projects as they developed.

Special appreciation goes to Connie Kallback, my editor at The Center. What a treat to work with an editor with the supportive, warm, and positive energy she projects.

Sincere thanks to Win Huppuch and all the people at The Center who helped put this project together. Everyone involved with this series was professional, cooperative, and enthusiastic about working on it.

Finally, to the most important people of all, thank you to my family—Don, Brian, and Betty—for their unending patience with and interest in the writing of this series during the last three years.

ABOUT THIS RESOURCE

The *Social Studies Curriculum Activities Library* presents a unique approach to teaching. It is based on the concept of *interdisciplinary* teaching which brings a broad range of *across-the-curriculum* subjects into the social studies classroom. Although each section begins with social studies lessons, it also includes activities for mathematics, language arts, physical education, music, art, and consumer and family living. All activities for each discipline were chosen as they pertain to social studies for the purpose of helping students better understand the culture they are studying.

The *Library* was designed to enhance and compliment the social studies curriculum. It was developed for you, the classroom teacher, to bring a broad range of cultural experiences into the social studies classroom. The library includes *over 240 reproducible, ready-to-use lessons and activities*. All of the lessons are accompanied by worksheets and all of the activities include step-by-step directions or ideas for active participation.

The *Library* is a two-volume series briefly described as follows:

- **Volume 1—America** is divided into three units that chronicle the development of the United States as Europeans settle the new land. Unit 1 follows the new Americans of **The Thirteen Colonies** as they settle along the Atlantic coast. Unit 2 journeys with the pioneers of **An Expanding Nation** as they cross the Appalachian Mountains into **The Midwest and Great Plains.** The unit also follows the expansion of **The Mississippi Valley** in the south central region. Unit 3 directs students to **The Beckoning West** as the new Americans fight for independence from Mexico in **The Southwest.** They follow others as they journey to **The Northwest** along the Oregon Trail or to **The West** along the California Trail.

- **Volume 2—Africa, Europe & Asia** covers eight countries in three continents. Unit 1, **Africa,** travels to the ancient civilization of **Egypt,** which represents one of the north African nations closely associated with cultures of the Middle East. South of the Sahara Desert, the eastern country of **Kenya** is part of this unit as well. Unit 2, **Europe,** focuses on the ancient civilization of **Greece,** the Medieval era in **England,** and the Renaissance in **Italy.** In Unit 3, **Asia,** the cultures of **China, Japan,** and **India** are explored.

FEATURES OF THE BOOK

The *Social Studies Curriculum Activities Library* was developed to provide you with a variety of day-to-day cultural experiences. The lessons and activities are designed to spark students' interest in learning about the traditions and values of many cultures. In essence, they *bring the sounds, sights, and smells of cultures around the world* right into the classroom. This approach will provide students with an in-depth cultural experience.

Each unit in the *Library* includes:

- quiet participation lessons in Social Studies, Mathematics, and Language Arts with *reproducible worksheets* and a *minimum amount of preparation*

- active participation activities or projects in Physical Education, Art, or Consumer and Family Living with *easy-to-follow directions* and/or a list for *easy-to-obtain materials*
- in Music there is a list of suggestions for *cultural listening*
- many *Extended Activity ideas* that include inside- and outside-the-classroom participation
- a bibliography for additional information
- *Glossary of Terms* for vocabulary words

GOALS OF THE LIBRARY

Learning about the cultural values of others is an important part of education. Differences in cultural values bring about conflict in some areas of the world. Therefore, understanding the values of others may help us gain important insight into these differences. The goals of the *Library* are to:

- acquaint students with various traditions and customs from cultures around the world
- encourage a respect for the values of others
- allow direct experiences with a wide range of cultural activities
- encourage cooperative and interdisciplinary education
- prepare students for responsible citizenship

CONCERNING BOOK AND FILM SUGGESTIONS

Throughout the books are suggestions for introducing students to various reading material as well as ideas for viewing films related to different cultures. It should be emphasized that all of these listings should be carefully considered by you in their final selection. What reading material may seem inappropriate to some may be acceptable to others. That is true with viewing films as well. Some of the films suggested have a G or PG rating while others have no rating. In all cases, the discretion of the teacher is advised along with parental consent whenever necessary.

ART IN THE SOCIAL STUDIES CLASSROOM

One of the goals of the *Library* is to develop an *awareness* of various art forms around the world. Effort was made to select art activities that the classroom teacher would feel comfortable presenting. In these projects, emphasis is placed on cultural awareness rather than accomplished artwork. For those wanting a more in-depth study, there are suggestions in every section for interdisciplinary projects with the art teacher.

In addition, most of the activities selected include the use of *basic materials only* with emphasis on inexpensive and easy-to-obtain supplies. A word about safety! It is important to stress safety in the classroom at all times; however, it is particularly important when using materials that have harmful potential built into them—such as sharp-pointed scissors or needles.

CONSUMER AND FAMILY LIVING IN THE CLASSROOM

Another goal of the *Library* is to develop an *awareness* of the various culinary customs in regional America as well as around the world. Like the art activities, effort was made to select recipes that the classroom teacher would feel comfortable presenting. Special care was taken so that the recipes were kept as simple as possible, often in one-bowl steps. In addition, three options for participation are suggested: (1) classroom demonstration, (2) an outside-the-classroom assignment, or (3) an interdisciplinary activity with the Consumer and Family Living teacher.

Finally, it is important to remember that a few of the foods enjoyed by specific regions in America or countries around the world may seem strange or peculiar to the tastes of some. Hopefully, students will be able to keep an open mind while sampling the culinary customs of various regions or cultures.

A FINAL WORD

The projects and activities in the *Social Studies Curriculum Activities Library* provide all the information you need to learn about a variety of cultures. However, it is you, the classroom teacher, who will make the lessons come to life. Each of you will present the lessons in your own unique way, and your own area of expertise will help you provide additional knowledge to the presentations. Your guidance and direction will challenge students to better understand themselves and their cultural heritage.

Dwila Bloom

CONTENTS

UNIT TWO   AN EXPANDING NATION

Section 4 The Midwest and Great Plains   136

Section 5 The Mississippi Valley   180

UNIT THREE   THE BECKONING WEST

SECTION 6 THE SOUTHWEST   224

UNIT ONE

THE THIRTEEN COLONIES

Section 1, The New England Colonies included the present-day states of Connecticut, Massachusetts, New Hampshire, and Rhode Island. Maine was part of Massachusetts and Vermont was claimed by both New Hampshire and New York. Later, Maine and New Hampshire became states.

Although you will learn about all of the New England Colonies in Section 1, it will feature **Plimoth Plantation at Plymouth, Massachusetts**—the second permanent English settlement in America and the first permanent settlement in New England. The English Pilgrims sailed to America on the *Mayflower*. After 67 days at sea, they chose to land in a harbor near present-day Plymouth. Within a few weeks the Pilgrims began to erect a village they called Plimoth Plantation. The Pilgrims at Plimoth Plantation endured many hardships. Nevertheless, with the help of the Native Americans, they survived and cleared the land. In a few short years many colonists came to America for a new life.

Section 2, The Middle Colonies included Delaware, New Jersey, New York, and Pennsylvania. Today this region is often referred to as **The Middle Atlantic.**

In Section 2 you will learn about all the Middle Colonies; however, it will feature the **Pennsylvania Dutch** from Lancaster County. The Pennsylvania Dutch have maintained many traditions and customs they brought to America in the 1700s. In some ways visiting Lancaster County is stepping back into history.

Section 3, The Southern Colonies included Virginia, Maryland, North Carolina, South Carolina, and Georgia. Today this region is called **The South**. There is debate on what states are considered to be a part of the present-day south. This book includes all of the original southern colonies (now states) plus West Virginia, Alabama, and Florida.

Even though you will learn about all of the Southern Colonies, the focus will be on **Jamestown, Virginia**—the first permanent settlement in America, and **Williamsburg**—the colonial capital of Virginia from 1699 to 1780.

THE NEW ENGLAND COLONIES

Below is an outline of the interdisciplinary activities included in this section. They are designed to bring a broad range of hands-on cultural activities and projects into the social studies classroom. Pick and choose the ones that best fit into your program.

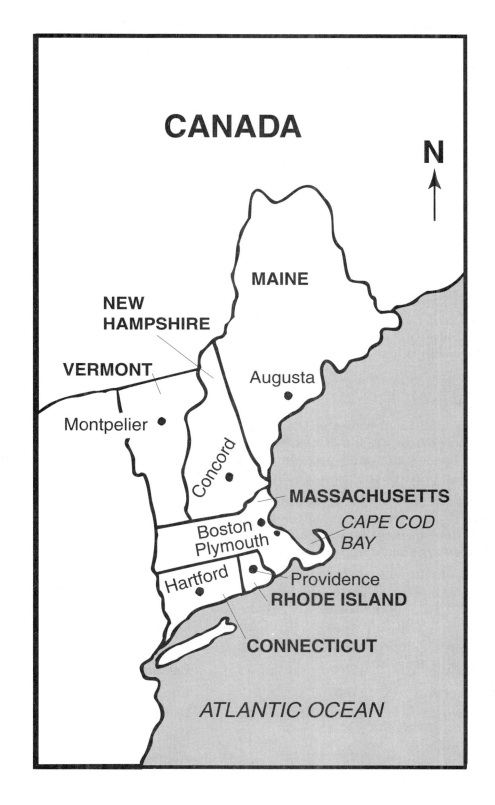

1-1 GETTING TO KNOW NEW ENGLAND

For the Teacher

Materials Needed:

- copies of Activity 1-1
- labeled map of New England (enlarged on opaque projector)
- copies of unlabeled map of New England
- (colored) pencils

Teacher Preparation:

- Reproduce Activity 1-1, *Getting to Know New England*, as needed. Also reproduce copies of the unlabeled map of the New England Colonies as needed.

- Pass out the activity and map to each student. Then allow time for students to locate and label New England as outlined in the activity. When they are finished, review the geography with them.

Extended Activities:

- Reproduce additional copies of the unlabeled map and have students identify other features of the New England Colonies, such as population distribution, land use, or climate. PC Globe® computer program can provide much of the information needed for this activity. Consult your school's media person for assistance, too.

- Reproduce the chart of *The Fifty States* (at back of book) as needed. Pass out the chart and have students make a list of the New England Colonies, the date each entered the Union, order of entry, capital, and largest city. *List states in order they entered the union*. Answers should appear as follows:

State	Date Entered Union	Order of Entry	Capital	Largest City
Connecticut	1788	5	Hartford	Bridgeport
Massachusetts	1788	6	Boston	Boston
New Hampshire	1788	9	Concord	Manchester
Rhode Island	1790	13	Providence	Providence
Vermont	1791	14	Montpelier	Burlington
Maine	1820	23	Augusta	Portland

Name _____ **Date** _____ **Period** _____

1-1 GETTING TO KNOW NEW ENGLAND

Use the map provided to locate and label the following colonies (now states) as well as Maine and Vermont, their capitals, and bordering bodies of water.

State: Connecticut

Capital: Hartford

State: Maine

Capital: Augusta

State: Massachusetts

Capital: Boston

Early settlement: Plymouth

Body of water: Cape Cod Bay

State: New Hampshire

Capital: Concord

State: Rhode Island

Capital: Providence

State: Vermont

Capital: Montpelier

Bordering body of water: Atlantic Ocean

Neighboring country: Canada

1-1 GETTING TO KNOW NEW ENGLAND

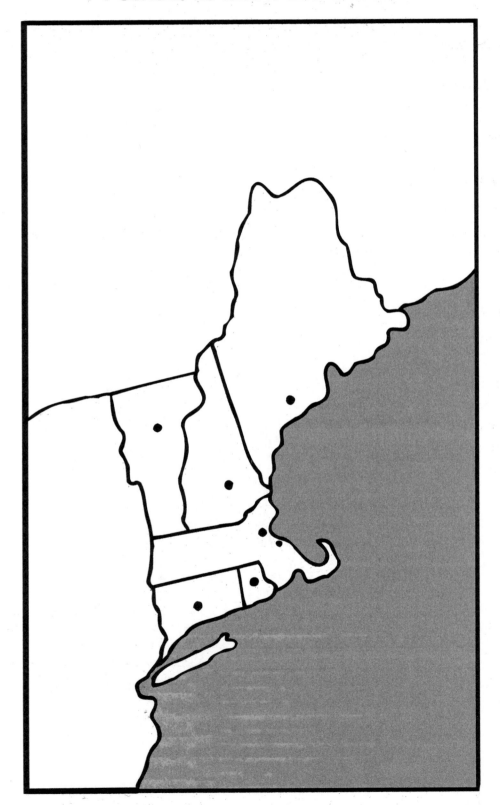

1-2 THE EARLY NEW ENGLAND COLONISTS

For the Teacher

Materials Needed:

- copies of Activity 1-2
- pencils

Teacher Preparation:

- Reproduce Activity 1-2A and 1-2B, *The Early New England Colonists*, as needed.
- Pass out Activity 1-2A and allow time for students to read the information. Then distribute Activity 1-2B and have students complete the word puzzle. When they are finished, review the answers (given below) with them.

Answer Key:

1. Mayflower
2. Separatists
3. Pilgrim
4. Massachusetts
5. Plimoth
6. William Bradford
7. Samoset
8. Squanto
9. Thanksgiving
10. charter
11. Massachusetts Bay Colony
12. Puritans
13. John Winthrop
14. Great Migration
15. Thomas Hooker
16. Hartford
17. Roger Williams
18. Providence

Extended Activities:

- Encourage students to learn more about the early New England colonies by writing research papers and assign extra credit for those who participate. Appropriate titles include The Pilgrims at Plymouth, Squanto, The First Thanksgiving, The Massachusetts Bay Colony at Boston, or Early Settlements in Rhode Island, New Hampshire, Maine or Vermont. Consult your school's media person for assistance, too.
- Films have been made about the early New England colonists. Select one and show it to your classes.

1-2A THE EARLY NEW ENGLAND COLONISTS

THE PILGRIMS AT PLYMOUTH

In 1620 a group of English settlers sailed to America on board a small ship called the *Mayflower*. Some of the people were seeking religious freedom. They were called Separatists because they wanted to separate from the Church of England. Later the Separatists were called Pilgrims. The term "pilgrim" has come to be used as the general term for all of the early colonists to Plymouth.

The Pilgrims were headed for the northern part of Virginia. However, the Mayflower sailed off course and landed in New England in the present state of Massachusetts. After exploring the area the Pilgrims decided to settle in Plymouth, Massachusetts where they set up a community they called *Plimoth Plantation*.

William Bradford was an early governor of the plantation. He wrote about the many difficulties and hardships endured by the Pilgrims and settlers during their first winter. However, the Pilgrims had strong religious beliefs and refused to give up.

One day a Wampanoag Indian named Samoset walked into the plantation and welcomed the Pilgrims. He had learned English from earlier fishermen from England. Samoset also introduced the Pilgrims to another Indian named Squanto. Squanto gave the Pilgrims good advice on how to raise corn and fish. By the fall of 1621 the Pilgrims had learned to survive and raise good crops in the new land.

Because the Pilgrims believed that God had helped them, they set aside a day of giving thanks for the good harvest. This celebration was called The Harvest Feast of 1621 and included both the colonists and the Wampanoag leader Massasoit, with some ninety of his men.

The later New England colonists celebrated good harvests by declaring Days of Thanksgiving. Over time New Englanders concluded their Thanksgiving Day with an elaborate dinner and the celebration began to look more like our modern holiday.

©1997 by The Center for Applied Research in Education

THE MASSACHUSETTS BAY COLONY AT BOSTON, MASSACHUSETTS

In 1629 a group of English people called Puritans obtained a charter from the King of England. A charter is a written document that grants rights and privileges. The charter gave the settlers land in New England and allowed them to form The Massachusetts Bay Company. Puritans were Protestants who wished to purify The Church of England by opposing traditional practices. The Puritans were searching for religious freedom as well as a better life.

The next year, in 1630, a group of about 1,000 men, women, and children sailed from England in several ships to settle The Massachusetts Bay Colony in present-day Boston. John Winthrop was a leader and first governor of the colony. Unlike the Pilgrims who landed earlier, the Puritans were successful from the start. The settlers arrived in America early in the spring so there was time to plant crops and build homes before winter arrived. Encouraged by the success of the colony, many others left England and came to America for a chance to improve their lives or enjoy religious freedom. Between 1630 and 1640 more than 20,000 new colonists arrived in Massachusetts. The movement was called The Great Migration.

ADDITIONAL COLONIES

Trouble grew among The Massachusetts Bay Colonists as religious and political conflict arose. In the 1630s Thomas Hooker, a minister, left the colony with about 100 supporters. The small group of Puritans settled in present-day Hartford, Connecticut.

Additional differences grew among the Puritan colonists in Massachusetts. Roger Williams, another minister, challenged the authority of John Winthrop. Williams believed that church and state should be separate. He also believed England had no right to give land in America to Puritans or anyone else. The land, after all, belonged to the Indians. The leaders of The Massachusetts Bay Colony wanted to put Williams on a ship to return to England. However, Williams, along with several followers, escaped. Later the group established a settlement in Providence, Rhode Island.

Some settlers moved north of Massachusetts to present-day New Hampshire, Maine, and Vermont. Many moved because of the strict rules set down by The Massachusetts Bay Colony. Others were simply searching for good farm land.

1-2B THE EARLY NEW ENGLAND COLONISTS

Read the information in Activity 1-2A. Then complete the word puzzle about the people from Europe who settled the New England Colonies during the 1600s.

1. ship that brought the Pilgrims to America
2. name given to English who wanted to separate from The Church of England
3. general term for all early colonists
4. state where Pilgrims landed in 1620
5. name of plantation the Pilgrims built
6. early governor of Plimoth Plantation
7. Wampanoag Indian who welcomed Pilgrims
8. Indian who showed Pilgrims how to raise corn
9. name of modern holiday that emerged from early harvest feast
10. a written document with certain privileges
11. colony formed by Puritans of England
12. name given to Protestants who wanted to purify The Church of England
13. leader of The Massachusetts Bay Colony
14. movement in 1630s when many settlers came to Massachusetts
15. leader who founded Connecticut
16. name of early colony in Connecticut
17. leader who founded Rhode Island
18. name of early colony in Rhode Island

©1997 by The Center for Applied Research in Education

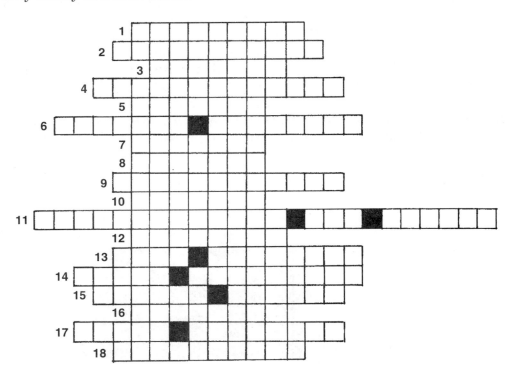

1-3 LIFE IN A NEW ENGLAND VILLAGE

For the Teacher

Materials Needed:

- copies of Activity 1-3
- pencils

Teacher Preparation:

- Reproduce Activity 1-3, *Life in a New England Village*, as needed.
- Pass out the activity. Then allow time for students to complete the story. When they are finished, review the answers (given below) with them.

Answer Key:

(1)	villages	(11)	crops
(2)	common	(12)	gardens
(3)	meetinghouse	(13)	bread
(4)	God	(14)	cloth
(5)	wood planks	(15)	candles
(6)	thatch	(16)	Sunday
(7)	fireplace	(17)	read
(8)	corn	(18)	write
(9)	beans	(19)	hornbook
(10)	squash	(20)	primer

Extended Activity:

- There are many historic sites and landmarks in New England worth visiting. Two outstanding Massachusetts ones include **Plimoth Plantation** near Plymouth and **Old Sturbridge Village** in Sturbridge. Plimoth Plantation is a recreation of the original Pilgrim village as it was in the early 1600s. Old Sturbridge Village, on the other hand, depicts a typical New England village of the 1800s. Show a film or develop an exhibit on one or both places. Contact the Visitor Information Center in Plymouth and in Sturbridge for specific orientation materials and programs.

1-3 LIFE IN A NEW ENGLAND VILLAGE

Read the story slowly. Then make a selection from the word bank that best completes the blank. Look carefully at the sentences that follow the blanks for helpful hints or descriptions. **Hint:** Each dash in a blank represents one letter. Therefore, if there are five dashes, choose the best word for the sentence that has five letters.

WORD BANK

primer	villages	hornbook
common	write	read
meetinghouse	God	Sunday
wood planks	candles	thatch
cloth	bread	gardens
fireplace	crops	squash
beans	corn	

Many New England families of the 17th century lived in small towns called (1) _ _ _ _ _ _ _ _. At the center or end of the village was an open area. This area was called the (2) _ _ _ _ _ _. The most important building on the common was the (3) _ _ _ _ _ _ _ _ _ _ _ _. The meetinghouse served two purposes. It served as a church where Puritans could meet to worship and give thanks to (4) _ _ _. It also served as a place where town meetings were held to make important community decisions.

Houses lined the narrow streets of New England villages. They were made of (5) _ _ _ _ _ _ _ _ _ _ and the roofs were covered with (6) _ _ _ _ _ _. Thatch refers to a style of roof made from grasses and other plants. The center of every home was the (7) _ _ _ _ _ _ _ _ _. The fireplace was very important because it was the place where family meals were prepared. It also kept families warm during the cold winters.

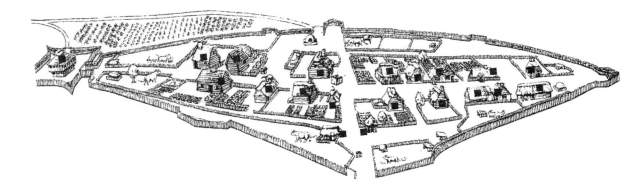

©1997 by The Center for Applied Research in Education

1-3 LIFE IN A NEW ENGLAND VILLAGE (continued)

Although most New England families lived in villages, they went outside the town each day to work in fields. The climate of the area was quite harsh and the soil was not very fertile. Families worked hard to grow food. Crops consisted mainly of (8) _ _ _ _, (9) _ _ _ _ _, and (10) _ _ _ _ _ _. Everyone in the family was expected to work. Fathers planted and harvested (11) _ _ _ _ _ in the field. Mothers planted and tended vegetable (12) _ _ _ _ _ _ _. They also baked (13) _ _ _ _ _, wove (14) _ _ _ _ _ for clothing, and dipped (15) _ _ _ _ _ _ _ for light during long winter evenings. Older children were expected to help their parents in all tasks and help care for the younger children.

Religion was an important part of life in New England. The people often gave thanks to God for their blessings. (16) _ _ _ _ _ _ was a day of rest and worship. No work, travel, or recreation was permitted on this day. Instead the people spent Sunday attending church services.

Education was also very important to the Puritans. They believed that all children should learn to (17) _ _ _ _ and (18) _ _ _ _ _ so they could learn their prayers and study the Bible. Students' first reading lessons were on a (19) _ _ _ _ _ _ _ _. A hornbook was a wooden shaped paddle. The letters of the alphabet were placed on paper and attached to the paddle. After learning some basics on the hornbook, students moved up to a book called the (20) _ _ _ _ _ _. The primer contained prayers and other religious writings.

Although life was difficult New Englanders were generally happy with their life in America. The Pilgrims had learned to adapt to a new way of life; in the process they acquired something very important to them—religious freedom.

1-4 TAKE A TRIP TO NEW ENGLAND

For the Teacher

Materials Needed:

- copies of Activity 1-4
- travel agency pamphlets
- travel books (such as *Mobil Travel Guides*)

Note:

The original New England Colonies included Connecticut, Massachusetts, New Hampshire, and Rhode Island. Later the New England states also included Maine and Vermont. Travel books may vary somewhat on what states constitute the New England States. This book includes Connecticut, Massachusetts, New Hampshire, Maine, Rhode Island, and Vermont.

Teacher Preparation:

- Reproduce Activity 1-4, *Take a Trip to New England*, as needed and organize reference materials.
- Divide classes into small groups and assign specific states or regions of New England for students to visit. Encourage groups to center their trips around historical places and events, when possible.
- Pass out travel materials and the journal activity. Then allow time for students to complete the activity. Encourage the inclusion of photographs or illustrations, if possible. When students are finished, allow groups to share their journeys with the rest of the class.

Extended Activities:

- Show classes a travel video on one or more of the New England states. Sources for travelogue tapes include educational channel television, video stores, or libraries.
- Encourage students to learn more about the economy of the state they are visiting. What products or services does the state make or provide? What are the major types of jobs in the state? Information on state economy can be found in encyclopedias.

1-4 TAKE A TRIP TO NEW ENGLAND

DESTINATION _____

For each day, describe the location, place visited, and special activity (such as art, music, food, or holiday).

DAILY ITINERARY

Day 1 _____

_____

_____

Day 2 _____

_____

_____

Day 3 _____

_____

_____

Day 4 _____

_____

_____

Day 5 _____

_____

_____

Day 6 _____

_____

_____

Day 7 _____

_____

_____

1-5 WHAT WILL IT COST?

For the Teacher

Materials Needed:

- copies of Activity 1-5
- travel books
- pencils or pens

Teacher Preparation:

- Reproduce Activity 1-5, *What Will It Cost?*, as needed.
- Pass out the activity and allow time for students to solve the problems. When they are finished, review the answers (given below) with them.

Answer Key:

1. $58
2. $15.75
3. $37
4. $15
5. $30.80; $4.62; $35.42
6. $5
7. $58; $15.75; $37; $15; $35.42; $5; $166.17

Extended Activity:

- Have students estimate the costs for one day of *their* destination for a family of four (2 adults and 2 students). Approximate hotel and dining costs can be found in most travel books. Other expenses can be estimated. Although Activity 1-5 can be used as a guide, encourage students to make other selections on how the family will spend the day.

1-5 WHAT WILL IT COST?

A family of four (2 adults and 2 students) are visiting New England. One of their stops is Plymouth, Massachusetts. Listed below are some places they will visit. Solve the problems to see how much money they will spend for the day.

1. The first place the family visits is Plimoth Plantation, a recreation of the early 16th-century English settlement. Admission charge to Plimoth Plantation is $15 for adults and $11 for students. In addition, tickets for the *Mayflower* ship is $2 for adults and $1 for students. The family needs 2 adult and 2 student admissions.

   What is the total cost for all admissions? $_____

2. The family eats lunch at the Plimoth Plantation cafeteria. Lunch expenses are $5.50, $3.75, $4.25, and $2.25.

   What is the total cost for lunches? $_____

3. After lunch the family purchases the following items at the Plimoth Plantation gift shop: a book of 16th-century games for $5; 2 marble games totaling $8; a clay bowl for $18; and a package of dried cranberries, $6.

   What is the total cost for all items? $_____

4. During the afternoon the family visits The New Bedford Whaling Museum. Cost is $4.50 for adults and $3 for students.

   What is the total cost for museum tickets? $_____

5. The family eats dinner at one of the restaurants at Village Landing Marketplace overlooking historic Plymouth Harbor. The restaurant specialty is seafood. Two dinners are $8.95 each; a third dinner is $6.95; and a fourth dinner is $5.95.

   What is the cost for 4 dinners? $_____

   Add 15% tip. $_____

   What is the total cost for the dinners? $_____

6. After dinner the family visits Cranberry World, then buys dessert at the Plymouth Bakery. There is no charge at Cranberry World and the bakery expenses are as follows: 2 cranberry scones at $1.25 each; 1 slice pumpkin bread at $1.00; and 1 apple crisp at $1.50.

   What is the cost for desserts? $_____

7. Add all the expenses to see how much money the family has spent:
   Total cost for #1. $_____
   Total cost for #2. $_____
   Total cost for #3. $_____
   Total cost for #4. $_____
   Total cost for #5. $_____
   Total cost for #6. $_____
   Total cost for the day. $_____

1-6 NEW ENGLAND TERMS

For the Teacher

Materials Needed:

- copies of Activity 1-6
- copies of *Glossary of Terms* (at back of book)

Teacher Preparation:

- Reproduce Activity 1-6, *New England Terms*, as needed. Also reproduce copies of the *Glossary* as needed.

- Pass out the activity and allow time for students to complete the matching definitions. When they are finished, review the terms (answers given below) with them.

Answer Key:

g.	bay	h.	Separatists
k.	immigrant	b.	Pilgrim
e.	hornbook	i.	Mayflower
r.	charter	j.	Sabbath
d.	colony	a.	Thanksgiving
l.	freedom	n.	Puritans
q.	tolerance	f.	Mayflower Compact
o.	witch hunt	m.	mountain
c.	Indians	p.	Appalachian

Extended Activity:

- Use some of the terms in the activity as topics for further research. Appropriate titles include The Eastern Woodland Indians, The Pilgrims of Plymouth, The Mayflower Compact, The Massachusetts Bay Colony, and The Salem Witch Hunts.

1-6 NEW ENGLAND TERMS

Expand your vocabulary by learning some terms associated with
the New England colonies or states. Match the correct definitions
to the words.

_____bay

_____immigrant

_____hornbook

_____charter

_____colony

_____freedom

_____tolerance

_____witch hunt

_____Indians

_____Separatists

_____Pilgrim

_____Mayflower

_____Sabbath

_____Thanksgiving

_____Puritans

_____Mayflower Compact

_____mountain

_____Appalachian

a. a holiday resulting from the Pilgrims' harvest celebration of 1621

b. a person who journeys to a foreign land often for religious freedom

c. Native Americans who lived in America before the Europeans arrived

d. a settlement developed by a country beyond its borders

e. a wooden shaped paddle that serves as a tool for learning to read

f. an agreement made by Pilgrims to consult each other about the laws of the Plymouth Colony

g. an inlet off of a larger body of water

h. a group of people who wanted to separate from The Church of England, later called Pilgrims

i. the small ship that brought the Pilgrims to America

j. a day set aside for rest and worship

k. a person who leaves his or her country to live elsewhere

l. the power of acting without restraint

m. a land mass that projects high above its surroundings and is bigger than a hill

n. a group of Protestants who wanted to purify The Church of England and founded The Massachusetts Bay Colony

o. the searching out and persecution of those who hold unpopular views or practice witchcraft

p. a mountain range in the eastern part of the United States extending from Canada to Georgia

q. the capacity to accept the beliefs or practices differing from one's own

r. a written agreement granting privileges from a sovereign power or country

1-7 FOLKTALES AND LITERATURE

For the Teacher

Materials Needed:

- copies of Activity 1-7
- practice paper and pencils
- drawing paper and pens
- (*optional*) black markers and/or colored pencils

Teacher Preparation:

- Reproduce Activity 1-7, *Folktales and Literature*, as needed and organize materials.

- Pass out the activity and allow students time to read the story. When they are finished, have students write a Thanksgiving story of their own. It may develop around a family Thanksgiving that has special traditions or a Thanksgiving tale around another family (people or animal).

- Using drawing paper and pens, have students rewrite their story in their best printing or writing.

- (*optional*) Encourage students to illustrate their stories with markers and/or colored pencils.

Extended Activity:

- Set aside time for reading folktales or stories that relate to New England in the 17th and 18th centuries. Contact the media person in your building or community for assistance in gathering appropriate materials. A brief list follows that will help you get started. **Note:** Remember, this is merely a list of some options that are available. Regional differences may vary, so use whatever is available in your area.

FOLKTALES

Native American Stories by Joseph Bruchac (Golden, CO: Fulcrum, 1991) and *Native American Animal Stories* by Joseph Bruchac (Golden, CO: Fulcrum, 1992). These two books are a collection of Native American tales and myths from various tribes throughout the United States.

American Tall Tales by Mary Pope Osborne (New York: Random House, 1991). This book is about America's folk heroes. From New England there is Stormalong, a folk hero who sailed on clipper ships from New England ports to China and the West Indies.

CHILDREN'S LITERATURE

Squanto and the First Thanksgiving by Joyce K. Kessel and Lisa Donze (Minneapolis: Carolrhoda Books, 1983). The story of Squanto, the Indian who helped the Pilgrims at Plymouth survive, and how they all celebrated the fall harvest with a feast. There are several books on the adventures and life of Squanto.

The Pilgrims of Plimoth by Marcia Sewell (New York: Simon & Schuster Children's, 1986). Describes the life at the Plimoth Plantation during the 1600s.

N. C. Wyeth's Pilgrims by Robert San Souci (San Francisco: Chronicle Books, 1991). There are many excellent books about the adventurous saga of settling the Plymouth Colony and Thanksgiving. This one is exceptionally well done because it was illustrated by N. C. Wyeth, a member of the extraordinarily talented family of artists.

Pilgrim Voices by Connie and Peter Roop (New York: Walker & Co., 1995). Nearly 400 years after the Pilgrims' first year, their own writings still tell the most accurate account of their adventure in the New World. The authors take passages from their diaries to reveal the flavor of their experience.

A Gathering of Days by Joan Blos (Newbery Award Book) (New York: Simon & Schuster Children's, 1979). The setting is New England, 1830–1832. Thirteen-year-old Catherine Cabot Hall keeps house for her widowed father until he remarries and her best friend dies. This book is written in short journal form.

A Journey to the New World: The Diary of Remember Patience Whipple, Mayflower by Kathryn Lasky (Dear America Series) (New York: Scholastic, 1996). A fictional diary account of a twelve-year-old girl and her family making the trip on the *Mayflower* to the New World.

An Old-Fashioned Thanksgiving by Louisa May Alcott (various editions available). At the Bassett farm in New Hampshire Thanksgiving preparations are being made for a splendid feast. Suddenly there's news that Grandmother is ill, so Mr. and Mrs. Bassett set out for Grandma's house. The girls decide to go ahead with the Thanksgiving feast on their own.

Thanksgiving at Our House by Wendy Watson (Boston: Houghton Mifflin, 1991). Come celebrate Thanksgiving with some traditions of a family whose house is filled with the activity in preparation for the harvest holiday.

CLASSIC LITERATURE *(suggested for older students)*

The House of Seven Gables and *The Scarlet Letter* by Nathaniel Hawthorne (various editions available). These novels are set against the harsh background of Puritanism in the colonies. They depict the cruelty that can be enforced in the name of righteousness.

POEMS

The Courtship of Miles Standish by Henry Wadsworth Longfellow (various editions available). This beloved American poet dramatizes historical events in poems. Although his poems bend facts to suit his tastes, they remain popular.

1-7 FOLKTALES AND LITERATURE

The following is an adaptation of *Squanto and the First Thanksgiving* as told by Joyce K. Kessel and Lisa Donze.

SQUANTO AND THE FIRST THANKSGIVING

Squanto was an Indian from the Patuxet tribe that lived in the present-day state of Massachusetts near Plymouth. They were a friendly tribe that grew corn and hunted wild animals.

In the early 1600s English explorers came to America in search of gold or silver. Instead they found Indians and corn. Since they found no gold, they captured some of the Indians to sell as slaves. Squanto was among the braves who were returned to England and sold into slavery.

In England Squanto escaped from his original captors and lived with a group of Catholic monks. They were kind to him and taught him English. They also taught him about the Christian faith. But Squanto was very sad because he missed his freedom and his family. The monks felt sorry for Squanto and helped him board a ship to return home to America.

Sadly, when Squanto returned to his tribe, he found the Patuxets were dead. They had been killed by smallpox, a disease the English had brought from England. Squanto was very sad that he had no family or home. Soon he moved in and lived with a neighboring tribe.

In 1620 the Pilgrims landed in Massachusetts. The Pilgrims were a group of English people looking for a new home where they could worship God as they chose. It was winter and the Pilgrims did not have much to eat. In addition, they were people from towns and did not know how to plant crops or build homes. By the spring of 1621 many had died and the surviving ones were frail and sickly.

Squanto and other Indians had watched the Pilgrims from a distance but had not approached or bothered them. By the spring Squanto decided to help the Pilgrims. Squanto knew English and had learned about Christianity from the monks. After Squanto's first visit to the Pilgrims' colony, he never left them.

©1997 by The Center for Applied Research in Education

1-7 FOLKTALES AND LITERATURE *(continued)*

During the spring and summer of 1621 Squanto taught the Pilgrims how to hunt animals for meat and build warm homes. He also taught them how to plant and cook corn and fish in nearby waters. Squanto and the Pilgrims worked very hard and by the fall had a good harvest.

The Pilgrims wanted to have a celebration and give thanks to God. They sent Squanto to invite Massasoit, an Indian chief. He accepted the invitation and brought many braves with him. The Pilgrims spent days preparing for the feast. They baked breads and puddings. They prepared stews and roasted turkeys, geese, and deer. It was a big feast for the Pilgrims and the Indians. After dinner they all played games and held contests. What a joyful day for the first Thanksgiving. None of it would have been possible without the help from Squanto.

1-8 17TH-CENTURY PASTIMES AND SPORTS

For the Teacher

Materials Needed:

• copies of Activity 1-8

• items mentioned in "Teacher Preparation"

Teacher Preparation:

• Reproduce Activity 1-8, *17th-Century Pastimes and Sports*, as needed.

• Pass out the activity and go over the pastimes outlined. If possible, *allow students to help make choices on which activities will be selected. Then set aside some time for participation.*

• If marble games are selected, ask for volunteers to bring in marbles to share with classes.

• If participating in sports is possible, contact the Physical Education person in your building well in advance and organize games of *lacrosse.*

The photograph of the young people was taken at Plimoth Plantation as they recreate the pastimes of the early New England colonists. Marble games, especially *Ring Taw* and *Blow-out,* were favorites.

Photo 1-1   Recreation of 17th-Century marble games

1-8 17TH-CENTURY PASTIMES AND SPORTS

PASTIMES

The early settlers had little time for games or amusements. Nevertheless young people did spend *some* time at play. There were few items of luxury so the activities were simple with little or no equipment. Listed below are a few games played during the 17th century. How many have you played? Which ones would you like to play?

BLIND MAN'S BLUFF (4 TO 12 PLAYERS)

One player is blindfolded. The other players form a circle around the blindfolded person within a confined area. One of the players turns the blindfolded person around three times, then takes a position within the circle. The blindfolded person moves about to catch one of the players—who are not allowed to move. The first person caught by the blindfolded person becomes the next blindfolded person.

HUNT THE SLIPPER (6 TO 18 PLAYERS)

Players sit in a circle. One player (the hunter) leaves while the others hide a slipper or other object. When the hunter returns, the other players pass the object around secretly while the hunter is not looking. The hunter is allowed to ask questions and has three guesses on the whereabouts of the object. When the slipper is located, the hunter exchanges places with the player who has the object and the games starts over.

BLOW-OUT (2 PLAYERS)

This is one of the oldest marble games known where two players try to win marbles from each other. The first player tosses a marble on a smooth surface. The second player tries to hit the marble by tossing another marble at it. If successful, the second player wins the marble. If not, the first player has a turn to hit the second player's marble.

RING TAW (4 TO 6 PLAYERS)

Two circles are drawn on the ground. The inner circle is about two feet in diameter. Each player places four to six marbles in the inner circle. Then the outer circle, called the "taw," is drawn about seven feet in diameter. The players take turns to roll their marble from the outer circle (taw) into the inner circle. The object is to touch one of the marbles in the inner circle. If the player is successful, he or she wins the marble and has a chance to win another one. However, the player may not hit the same player's marble twice in a row. If the player is unsuccessful, the next player gets a turn.

SPORTS

Native Americans enjoyed competitions of all kinds. One particular favorite was *lacrosse*. The lacrosse stick is long with a net at the end. The net is used to catch then fling the ball into a specified goal. The New England settlers learned this game from the American Indians. It is still popular today, especially in Canada.

1-9 SOUNDS OF NEW ENGLAND

For the Teacher

Materials Needed:

- CD or cassette
- audio equipment

Teacher Preparation:

- For the early colonists at Plymouth, Massachusetts, Psalms were the only type of music permitted. Psalms were sung at church by the entire congregation without accompaniment. Later, the practice of "lining" psalms was practiced. In lining, each psalm is sung by the Pastor, then repeated by the group.

  In the 1800s many religious hymns were introduced. The dominant composer was Lowell Mason (1792–1872), who compiled more than 1,200 hymns and five major collections of church music. His most successful work includes **The Boston Handel** and **Haydn Society Collection of Church Music**. Encourage your students to become familiar with this music.

- There are cassettes and CDs available that provide an opportunity to listen to music from or relating to early New England. Check your local library or record store for specific titles and use whatever resources are available in your community. Listed below are a few titles that will give you an idea of what is available. Regional options may vary.

  Trav'ling Home, American Spirituals 1770–1870
  (Warner Music Mfg., Germany, 1996).

  Make a Joyful Noise, Mainstreams and Backwaters of American Psalms 1770–1840
  (New World Records, New York, 1996).

  The Flowering of Vocal Music in America 1767–1823
  (New World Records, New York).

  Early Shaker Spirituals
  The United Society of Shakers, Sabbathday Lake, Maine
  (Rounder Records Corporation, Cambridge, MA, 1996).

  Brave Boys, New England Traditions in Folk Music
  (New World Records, New York, 1995).

1-10 DRIED PEPPER HANGINGS

For the Teacher *(This activity makes an excellent out-of-class assignment for extra credit.)*

Materials Needed:

- copies of Activity 1-10

Teacher Preparation:

- Reproduce Activity 1-10, *Dried Pepper Hangings*, as needed.

- Pass out the activity and go over the information with your students. Make an out-of-class assignment for students to make dried peppers at home and assign extra credit for those who participate. Finished dried arrangements make attractive hangings around the room while learning about the Thirteen Colonies.

Extended Activity:

- Another 17th-century craft was making dried-flower bouquets. Students might want to choose this activity in place of dried vegetable hangings or along with it. Both dried vegetables and flowers make attractive hangings.

Colonial women spent most of their energies providing food, clothing, and shelter for their families, but somehow they saved a little time and space for a patch of flowers. Bouquets of dried flowers often hung in 17th-century homes to serve as air fresheners.

You need:

- flowers and plants that will air-dry (baby's breath, bittersweet, heather, milkweed pods, bayberry, straw flowers, thistle, corn, goldenrod, cattails, wheat, hydrangea)

- scissors

- heavy string

Steps to making dried bouquets:

1. Pick and cut the flowers or plants when they are in bloom.

2. Sort and arrange bouquets, then tie with heavy string.

3. Make sure there are no insects on the bouquets. Then hang them upside down by the string in a warm, dry place.

Photo 1-2 *Dried flowers, collection of the author.* Gathering and drying flowers was a popular fall activity during the colonial era in America. The bouquets added a touch of color to the drab dwellings and provided pleasant smells as well. Drying flowers is still enjoyed by many Americans during modern times.

1-10 DRIED PEPPER HANGINGS

Having enough food to eat was a constant concern for the early New England colonists. They feared hunger and starvation, especially during the last weeks of winter. In the fall season they prepared and stored as much food as possible for the coming months.

One common colonial method of food preservation was air-drying fruits and vegetables. The Indians taught the Pilgrims what foods to preserve and how to sun-dry them. When winter came, the fruits and vegetables were soaked in water and cooked. In the meantime strings of dried fruit and vegetables hung in many colonial homes. They not only helped feed the colonists during the winter months, but they also decorated homes and created pleasant scents.

Two common vegetables that were hung and dried included peppers and corn. Some of the easiest and most attractive hangings can be made using red or green peppers. Try making a pepper hanging by following the easy directions below.

Materials Needed:

- sharp knife
- needle and strong thread
- scissors
- green and/or red peppers

Steps to Dried Pepper Hangings:

1. Wash and dry several red and/or green peppers.
2. String peppers with a needle on a piece of strong thread. The illustration below shows how the peppers look.
3. After stringing the peppers, hang them in a high place where they will receive good ventilation.
4. (optional) You may want to string the peppers in clusters instead of in a row as shown in the illustration. For a touch of brightness, tie a yarn bow at the top of the cluster. Dried Pepper Hangings add an attractive decoration to any room and make delightful gifts.

©1997 by The Center for Applied Research in Education

1-11 PAPER WEAVINGS

For the Teacher

Materials Needed

- copies of Activity 1-11
- 12" × 18" colored construction paper
- rulers
- scissors
- school glue

Teacher Preparation:

- Reproduce Activity 1-11, *Paper Weavings*, as needed and organize materials. Regular school-grade colored construction paper is suggested for this activity because it is inexpensive and readily available. Choose colors that were popular to the early colonists; these include naturals (cream, off-white, tan), all shades of blue, yellow, pink, orange, and purple.

- Pass out the activity and go over the information with your students.

- Distribute materials and allow time for students to make a weaving. Encourage variations to the basic weaving pattern as outlined and suggest limiting color selections to three or four choices.

- When students are finished, display the weavings around the room.

- (*optional*) Laminating the weavings will preserve them and turn them into usable placemats.

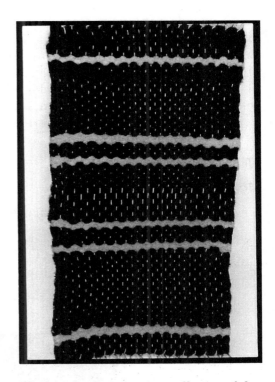

Photo 1-3 *Rag weaving, collection of the author.* The rag rug weaving was done by an eighth-grade student during the time classes were learning about the Thirteen Colonies. The weaving was made from scraps of fabric torn into rags. Before the fabric strips were woven, they were twisted. As a result no torn edges can be seen.

Extended Activity:

- Contact the art teacher in your building well in advance and coordinate a fabric or rag weaving activity while your classes are learning about the New England colonies.

1-11 PAPER WEAVINGS

Most women living in the early New England colonies were expected to weave lengths of cloth. The fabrics were used to make homespun clothes and household items such as bedding and linens. The process of making cloth was long and tedious. First, the colonists had to spin and dye the yarn in preparation for the weaving process.

The women took great pride in preparing plant dyes to create attractive colors. One of the favorite colors was all shades of blue made from the indigo plant. They also made yellow from goldenrod flowers, pink and orange from boiled sassafras bark, and purple from iris petals. Leaving the yarns in their natural shades of creams and tans was also common.

When the preparation of the fibers were finally complete, the women spent many hours weaving the yarn into cloth. Children loved to watch the weaver and begged for bits of yarn to make small items. Girls created hat bands, hair pieces, and shoestrings. Boys made suspenders to hold up their trousers and garters to keep their stockings in place.

To develop an appreciation for what the early colonists needed to do in order to have something to wear or keep warm, create easy-to-make paper weavings. Can you imagine living in a community where there were no department stores?

STEPS TO PAPER WEAVING

Making the paper loom

1. With a ruler and pencil measure a 2-inch border on both ends of a 12" × 18" sheet of colored construction paper.

2. Fold the paper in half so that you can see the pencil marks.

3. Measure and cut 1/2-inch lines from the fold to the pencil marks.

4. Cut out every other line to the edge of the 2-inch border.

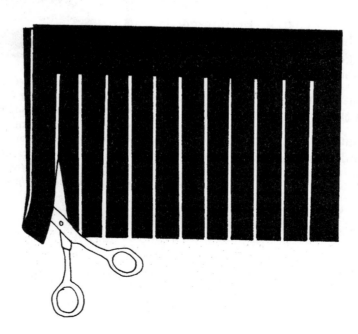

1-11 PAPER WEAVINGS *(continued)*

Weaving into the paper loom

5. Using contrasting colors, cut a variety of 12-inch strips (to weave into the paper loom). For variety cut some narrow and some medium widths. For additional variety, cut some curved, pointed, or torn strips.

6. Weave the strips into the loom. Row 1 will be *under one, over one*. Row 2 will reverse and be *over one, under one*. Repeat rows 1 and 2 until the loom is full.

7. When finished weaving, carefully glue every other strip edge to the edge of the loom (on both sides).

1-12 BASICS OF NEW ENGLAND COOKING

For the Teacher

Materials Needed:

- copies of Activity 1–12
- pencils

Teacher Preparation:

- Reproduce Activity 1-12, *Basics of New England Cooking*, as needed.
- Pass out the activity and allow time for students to read the information and complete the worksheet. (Answers are given below.) When they are finished, review the food basics of New England.

Answer Key:

Three earliest foods: corn; pumpkin; beans

Meats: deer; duck; turkey; rabbit; geese; pigeon

Seafood: lobster; clams; oysters; cod fish

Breads: cheate; cornbread

Vegetables: onions; artichokes; carrots; turnips; cabbage; beets

Fruits: blueberries; cranberries; blackberries; raspberries; gooseberries; apples

Nuts: walnuts; chestnuts; hickory nuts

Desserts: Indian pudding; pumpkin pie

Sweeteners: molasses; maple syrup

Common meat dish: New England boiled dinner

Common seafood dish: fish chowder

Extended Activity:

- Encourage students to collectively develop a New England cookbook. Divide classes into pairs or groups and assign specific topics to each group. Appropriate topics include Soups, Breads, Vegetables, Seafood, Meats, and Desserts. **Note:** The emphasis of this writing revolves around the foods of the early settlers in Massachusetts. Students can expand beyond that time to include cuisine from all the New England states. After they have collected and submitted their recipes, duplicate them and allow each person to organize a cookbook of his or her own.

1-12 BASICS OF NEW ENGLAND COOKING

The problems the early New England colonists faced were many. They had to struggle for survival in the midst of a land of plenty. Despite grueling hardships, within a short period of time homes were built, fields were cleared and sowed, and orchards and gardens were planted.

Although their food supplies were limited at first, colonial cooks learned to make some very tasty dishes. As soon as they began to receive such imported items as baking powder, yeast, and sugar, many delicious recipes developed. Some of the finest cooking in American history has come from Colonial New England.

BASIC FOODS

Everyone who arrived during the early 1600s had to become accustomed to three foods available in this new land. These foods included *corn, pumpkins*, and *beans*. For the early colonists, corn and pumpkins were often the difference between survival and starvation. Colonial cooks learned how to use them in ingenious and inventive ways.

Meat, fish, and bread were an important part of the early settlers' diet, as well.

Meat: The early colonists were surprised by the abundance of game. In England hunting was a privilege reserved for the rich. The Indians taught the colonists how to hunt game and catch fish. Some of the animals eaten were *deer, duck, turkey, rabbit, geese*, and *pigeon*. A common meat dish was *New England boiled dinner*, a one-pot meal that simmered all day over an open fire. It consisted of vegetables cooked with meat and broth. Common vegetables included turnips, carrots, onions, and cabbage. Later potatoes were added.

Seafood was plentiful in New England waters, especially *lobster, clams, oysters*, and *cod fish*. A popular soup made from seafood was *fish chowder*. New England fish chowder consists of some kind of seafood in a thick, creamy soup flavored with salt pork and diced potatoes.

Breads: The most common bread was known as *cheate bread*, a thick sourdough version, and *cornbread*, made from cornmeal, flour, and water.

Vegetables: The term "vegetable" was not used in the 16th century. Edible plants were called "sallets." The most widely used sallets included *onions, artichokes, carrots, turnips, cabbages*, and *beets*.

Fruits: The Pilgrims found a number of native fruits that included *blueberries, cranberries, blackberries, raspberries*, and *gooseberries*. As soon as they could, they planted *apple* orchards. In addition, the colonists also found *walnuts, chestnuts*, and *hickory nuts*.

Desserts: Puddings and pies were two basic types of desserts made by early cooks. Especially popular was *Indian pudding*, an authentic American treat made from cornmeal, milk, and molasses. In the fall season, *pumpkin pies* were a favored treat. Fruit pies, made from native fruits, were also baked. During the early years in America, an apple pie was rare because apples were unknown in America at that time and needed to be imported from England. Sweeteners included *molasses* and *maple syrup*.

Name _____ **Date** _____ **Period** _____

1-12 BASICS OF NEW ENGLAND COOKING *(continued)*

Use the boxes below to outline some of the
basics of early New England foods.

Three earliest foods:	_____	_____
	_____	
Meats:	_____	_____
	_____	_____
	_____	_____
Seafood:	_____	_____
	_____	_____
Breads:	_____	_____
Vegetables:	_____	_____
	_____	_____
	_____	_____
Fruits:	_____	_____
	_____	_____
	_____	_____
Nuts:	_____	_____
	_____	
Desserts:	_____	_____
	_____	_____
Sweeteners:	_____	_____
Common meat dish: _____		
Common seafood dish: _____		

1-13 17TH-CENTURY NEW ENGLAND FEASTS

For the Teacher

Hint: It is helpful to complete Activity 1-12, *Basics of New England Cooking*, before participating in this one.

Materials Needed:

- copies of Activity 1-13
- pencils or pens

Teacher Preparation:

- Reproduce Activity 1-13, *17th-Century New England Feasts*, as needed.
- Pass out the activity. Then allow students time to read the menus and make their dinner selections. When they are finished, lead a discussion to compare the food items offered during the 17th century in New England with those at a modern-day Thanksgiving dinner. What are the similarities? What are the differences?

Extended Activity:

- Ask students to bring to class some simple foods that the New England Pilgrims might have enjoyed and set aside time for a food-tasting party. Choices may include dried cranberries, pumpkin seeds, pumpkin pie, cornbread, and cranberry juice.

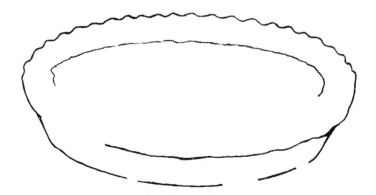

1-13 17TH-CENTURY NEW ENGLAND FEASTS

You are at Plimoth Plantation in the fall and have the opportunity to choose from one of three feasts presented. Look at the menu items carefully. Then make your dinner selections on the activity sheet. **Note:** The menu items have been adapted for 20th-century functions. Although not totally accurate to the period, they give guests a good sampling of what the Pilgrims ate. (*The menus are compliments of **Plimoth Plantation, Harvest Feasts & Thanksgiving Dining.***)

HARVEST

FEASTS

&

THANKSGIVING

DINING AT

PLIMOTH

PLANTATION

Harvest Feasts & Thanksgiving Dining at Plimoth Plantation

EXPERIENCE A BIT OF AMERICA'S PAST

Our modern Thanksgiving holiday is a blend of three earlier traditions: the harvest festival, the Separatist Day of Thanksgiving and Praise, and the commemoration of the 1620 landing known as Forefather's Day. As it developed in New England in the 17th and 18th centuries, Thanksgiving Day was a blend of the first two as residents attended church services followed by family or community dinners. Thanksgiving Day took on its modern form when interest shifted from the Pilgrims' landing to the Pilgrims' 1621 harvest celebration, and when Abraham Lincoln declared the first annual, national Thanksgiving Day in 1863.

MAKE PLIMOTH PLANTATION A PART OF YOUR FAMILY'S THANKSGIVING

THE HARVEST FEAST OF 1621
popularly known as
"The First Thanksgiving"

In the early fall of 1621, the Plymouth colonists and the Wampanoag Indians enjoyed a feast which became known as the "First Thanksgiving." They dined for three days on wild fowl — ducks, geese and turkeys brought by the colonists, and venison from five deer, provided by Chief Massasoit's men, as well as other foods. Join us now for a bill of fare, representing the bounty of New England's forests and shores, as Plimoth Plantation's costumed interpreters bring to the table a re-creation of the 1621 Pilgrim harvest feast for your dining pleasure.

MENU

FIRST COURSE
- Sallet of Spinage
- Seethed Lobster
- Goose with a Pudding
- Boyled Turkie
- Fryed Coney (Rabbit)

SECOND COURSE
- Indian Pudding
- Fricase of Cod
- Roasted Duck
- Stewed Pompion
- Roasted Venison
- Savory Pudding of Hominy
- Charger of Cheese & Fruit
- Beer and Ciderkin

17TH-CENTURY HARVEST FEAST

October 12,13   5:30 pm
November 9,10,16,23,24,27,29,30   5:30 pm

Your 17th-century host, Master Cole, invites you to dine on this deliciously authentic bill of English fare. Costumed performers will enliven your evening with the music and songs which the Pilgrims knew and enjoyed.

MENU

Grand Sallet of Watercress
Carrot Sallet
Mussels Steamed in Beer
Cheate Bread
Turkish Dish of Meat
Seethed Cod
Charger of Cheese & Fruit
Stewed Sweet Potatoes & Apples
Spit Roasted Turkey
Indian Pudding
Boiled Spinage & Colewort Sallet
Ciderkin
Roast Fillet of Beef

VICTORIAN THANKSGIVING DINNER

Thanksgiving Day, November 28
Seatings at 11 am, 2:30 and 6 pm

Celebrate the quintessential American Holiday at our Victorian Thanksgiving Dinner. Victorian hosts will take you back to the mid-19th century, during Lincoln's presidency, to experience a delightfully familiar holiday feast. Enjoy the sweet harmonies of period singers and remember your Thanksgiving experience with a complimentary posy and souvenir program. Join us for an unforgettable taste of the good old days.

MENU

Fall Harvest Fruits, Assorted Nuts, Victorian Relish Tray, Split Pea Soup, Escalloped Oysters

MAIN COURSE

Roast Native Turkey with Giblet Gravy and Traditional *Bell's Seasonings* Stuffing
Mashed Potatoes, Butternut Squash
Steamed Cape Cod Turnip
Harvard Beets, Creamed Onions
Cranberry Relish
Hot Crusty Rolls, Cider Cake,
Ginger Bread, Wood Pressed Cider

DESSERTS

Indian Pudding
Homemade Pumpkin Pie
Apple Pie

1-13 17TH-CENTURY NEW ENGLAND FEASTS *(continued)*

Look over the three menus offered: *The Harvest Feast of 1621, 17th-Century Harvest Feast,* and *Victorian Thanksgiving Dinner.* In the spaces provided on the left, make your selections from one of the three menus. Make as many selections as you like, but stay with the menu selected.

In the spaces provided on the right, list the items your family eat at Thanksgiving. When you are finished, compare the Harvest or Victorian feasts to our modern-day versions.

17th-Century Menu Items

(choose as many as you like,
but from one menu only)

Present-day Thanksgiving Menu Items

(choose as many as you like)

_____ _____

_____ _____

_____ _____

_____ _____

_____ _____

_____ _____

_____ _____

_____ _____

_____ _____

_____ _____

_____ _____

_____ _____

_____ _____

_____ _____

1-14 INDIAN PUDDING

For the Teacher

Equipment Needed:

- copies of Activity 1-14
- 2-quart saucepan
- spoon
- measuring spoons
- measuring cup
- small mixing bowl
- hand mixer
- 1-quart baking dish

Supplies Needed:

- milk
- molasses
- yellow cornmeal
- egg
- sugar
- butter or margarine
- cinnamon
- ginger
- salt
- (*optional*) vanilla ice cream

Teacher Preparation:

- Reproduce Activity 1-14, *Indian Pudding*, as needed and organize equipment and supplies.
- Give a demonstration on making Indian Pudding as students follow along with the recipe.
- **ALTERNATIVE:** Go over the recipe with students. Then make an out-of-class assignment for students to make the pudding at home and bring it to school for a special New England treat day. Encourage students to ask for adult supervision when making the pudding.

Extended Activity:

- Contact the Consumer and Family Living teacher well in advance to coordinate a New England or Thanksgiving lunch-lab activity while your classes are learning about the New England Colonies.

1-14 INDIAN PUDDING

The first year the Pilgrims spent in America was difficult and harsh. They quickly learned to depend on the foods available in the land, which included corn, beans, and squash. When times were hard, it was quite common for them to eat corn in some manner three times a day. The resourceful colonial women learned to make a wide variety of breads, puddings, and pies from cornmeal. The Indians taught them how to create a pudding that featured cornmeal with molasses as a sweetener. It became known as Indian Pudding. This version includes two colonial luxuries—eggs and sugar. Today the pudding is still served, but modern versions often top it with vanilla ice cream. This recipe serves 6.

You need:

1	tablespoon margarine or butter
3	cups milk
1/3	cup molasses
1/3	cup cornmeal
1	tablespoon margarine or butter
1	egg
1/4	cup sugar
1/2	teaspoon cinnamon
1/2	teaspoon ginger
1/4	teaspoon salt
	(*optional*) vanilla ice cream

What to do:

1. Preheat oven to 300°.
2. Grease the bottom and sides of a baking dish with 1 tablespoon margarine or butter.
3. In a saucepan, combine milk and molasses. Then gradually stir in cornmeal.
4. Cook and stir over medium heat until mixture thickens. This will take about 10 minutes.
5. Remove pudding from heat and stir in 1 tablespoon margarine or butter.
6. In a small mixing bowl, beat egg. Then add sugar, cinnamon, ginger, and salt.
7. Gradually add egg mixture to hot cornmeal pudding.
8. Pour in greased baking dish and bake, uncovered, for about 1-1/2 hours or until pudding has thickened.
9. (*optional*) Serve topped with scoops of vanilla ice cream. Note: The pudding is especially tasty when served warm.

1-15 CRANBERRY-NUT BREAD

For the Teacher

Equipment Needed:
- copies of Activity 1-15
- large mixing bowl
- spoon
- measuring spoons
- measuring cup
- hand mixer
- 8-1/2" × 4-1/2" × 2-1/2" bread pan
- cooling rack

Supplies Needed:
- egg
- vegetable oil
- orange juice
- flour
- sugar
- baking powder
- baking soda
- salt
- cranberries, fresh or frozen
- chopped walnuts

Teacher Preparation:
- Reproduce Activity 1-15, *Cranberry-Nut Bread*, as needed and organize equipment and supplies.
- Give a demonstration on making Cranberry-Nut Bread as students follow along with the recipe. Follow up with a bread tasting treat.
- **ALTERNATIVE:** Go over the recipe with students. Then make an out-of-class assignment for students to make the bread at home and bring it to school for a special New England treat. Encourage students to ask for adult assistance when baking the bread.

1-15 CRANBERRY-NUT BREAD

The forests of New England provided the early colonists with an assortment of berries such as cranberries, blueberries, blackberries, and gooseberries. The fruits were eaten plain, with cream, dried, or in baked goods.

Cranberry bread would not have appeared on the table of the first colonists who settled in the New England Colonies because they had no baking powder. However, as soon as shipments arrived to provide them with a few luxury items, many types of muffins, breads, and cakes were baked.

This recipe makes 1 loaf.

You need:

1	egg
1/3	cup vegetable oil
1	cup orange juice
2	cups flour
3/4	cup sugar
1-1/2	teaspoons baking powder
1/2	teaspoon baking soda
	dash salt
1	cup fresh or frozen cranberries, chopped
1/2	cup walnuts, chopped

What to do:

1. Preheat oven to 350°.
2. Grease 8-1/2" × 4-1/2" × 2-1/2" bread pan.
3. In a mixing bowl, beat egg. Then add vegetable oil and orange juice. Blend thoroughly with a hand mixer.
4. Add flour, sugar, baking powder, baking soda, and salt. Blend together until thoroughly mixed.
5. By hand, stir in chopped cranberries and nuts.
6. Spread evenly into bread pan.
7. Bake 55 to 60 minutes or until an inserted toothpick comes out clean.
8. Cool 5 minutes, then loosen sides from pan. Place bread on a cooling rack to cool completely.
9. Slice the bread and serve with margarine or cream cheese, if desired.

BIBLIOGRAPHY FOR NEW ENGLAND

Art

Hoople, Cheryl. *The Heritage Sampler: A Book of Colonial Arts and Crafts*. New York: Dial Press, 1975.

Children's Literature

Kessel, Joyce K. and Lisa Donze. *Squanto and the First Thanksgiving*. Minneapolis: Carolrhoda Books, 1983.

Children's Nonfiction

Harrington, Ty. *America the Beautiful: Maine*. Chicago: Children's Press, 1992.

Heinrichs, Ann. *America the Beautiful: Rhode Island*. Chicago: Children's Press, 1990.

Kent, Deborah. *America the Beautiful: Connecticut*. Chicago: Children's Press, 1990.

Kent, Deborah. *America the Beautiful: Massachusetts*. Chicago: Children's Press, 1987.

McNair, Sylvia. *America the Beautiful: New Hampshire*. Chicago: Children's Press, 1992.

McNair, Sylvia. *America the Beautiful: Vermont*. Chicago: Children's Press, 1991.

Cookbooks

Barchers, Suzanne and Patricia Marden. *Cooking Up U.S. History*. Englewood, CO: Teacher Ideas Press, 1991.

Editors. *Better Homes and Garden Heritage of America Cookbook*. Des Moines: Meredith Corporation, 1993.

Music

Staff. *Academic American Encyclopedia, Volume 1*. Danbury, CT: Grolier, Inc., 1996.

Pastimes

Kalman, Bobbie. *Games from Long Ago*. New York: Crabtree Publishing, 1995.

Kalman, Bobbie and David Schimpky. *Old-Time Toys*. New York: Crabtree Publishing, 1995.

Warner, John F. *Colonial American Home Life*. New York: Franklin Watts, 1993.

Social Studies

Bass, Herbert. *People in Time and Place: Our Country*. Parsippany, NJ: Silver Burdett & Ginn, 1991.

Davidson, James and John Batchelor. *The American Nation*. Englewood Cliffs, NJ: Prentice Hall, 1991.

Travel

Staff. *Mobil 1996 Travel Guide, Northeast*. New York: Fodor's Travel Publications, 1996.

SECTION 2

THE MIDDLE COLONIES

Below is an outline of the interdisciplinary activities included in this section. They are designed to bring a broad range of hands-on cultural lessons and activities into the social studies classroom. Pick and choose the ones that best fit into your program.

Social Studies

Mathematics

Language Arts

Physical Education

Music

Art

Consumer and Family Living

Bibliography for the Middle Colonies

2-1 GETTING TO KNOW THE MIDDLE ATLANTIC

For the Teacher

Materials Needed:

- copies of Activity 2-1
- labeled map of Middle Colonies (enlarged on opaque projector)
- copies of unlabeled map of Middle Atlantic Colonies
- (colored) pencils

Teacher Preparation:

- Reproduce Activity 2-1, *Getting to Know the Middle Atlantic*, as needed. Also reproduce copies of the unlabeled map of the Middle Atlantic Colonies as needed.

- Pass out the activity and map to each student. Then allow time for students to locate and label the Middle Atlantic as outlined in the activity. When they are finished, review the geography with them.

Extended Activities:

- Reproduce additional copies of the unlabeled map and have students identify other features of the Middle Atlantic states such as population distribution, land use, or climate. PC Globe® computer program can provide much of the information needed for this activity. Consult your school's media person for assistance, too.

- Reproduce the chart of *The Fifty States* (at back of book) as needed. Pass out the chart and have students make a list of the Middle Atlantic states, date they entered the Union, order of entry, capital, and largest city. *List states in order they entered the union.* Answers should appear as follows:

State	Date Entered Union	Order of Entry	Capital	Largest City
Delaware	1787	1	Dover	Wilmington
Pennsylvania	1787	2	Harrisburg	Philadelphia
New Jersey	1787	3	Trenton	Newark
New York	1788	11	Albany	New York

©1997 by The Center for Applied Research in Education

Name _____ **Date** _____ **Period** _____

2-1 GETTING TO KNOW THE MIDDLE ATLANTIC

Use the map provided to locate and label the following features:

State: Delaware
Capital: Dover

State: New Jersey
Capital: Trenton

State: New York
Capital: Albany
Major city: New York
Bodies of water: Lake Erie, Lake Ontario

State: Pennsylvania
Capital: Harrisburg
Early settlements: Philadelphia, Lancaster

Bordering body of water: Atlantic Ocean

Neighboring country: Canada

2-1 GETTING TO KNOW THE MIDDLE ATLANTIC

2-2 PEOPLE OF THE MIDDLE COLONIES

For the Teacher

Materials Needed:

- copies of Activity 2-2

- pencils

Teacher Preparation:

- Reproduce Activity 2-2A and 2-2B, *People of the Middle Colonies*, as needed.

- Pass out the Activity 2-2A and allow time for students to read the information. Then distribute Activity 2-2B and have students complete the word puzzle. When they are finished, review the answers (given below) with them.

Answer Key:

1.	The Netherlands	10.	Swedes
2.	New Netherlands	11.	New Sweden
3.	Albany	12.	Delaware
4.	New Amsterdam	13.	Berkeley, Carteret
5.	New York	14.	religious, political
6.	Dutch West Indies	15.	William Penn
7.	patroons	16.	Philadelphia
8.	Peter Stuyvesant	17.	Mennonite
9.	New York	18.	Lancaster

Extended Activities:

- Encourage students to learn more about the early Middle Atlantic colonies by writing research papers and assign extra credit for those who participate. Appropriate titles include The Dutch Settlers in New York, The Swedish Settlers in Delaware, Early Settlers of New Jersey, William Penn in Pennsylvania, Benjamin Franklin, or Philadelphia and the Birth of a New Nation. Consult your school's media person for assistance, too.

- Films have been made about the early Middle Atlantic colonists. Select one and show it to your classes.

2-2A PEOPLE OF THE MIDDLE COLONIES

NEW NETHERLANDS BECOMES NEW YORK

Some of the first Europeans who settled in the Middle Colonies were the Dutch from The Netherlands. In the early 1600s they founded an outpost in present-day Albany, New York. The Dutch named their colony New Netherlands. At about the same time the Dutch also settled on the island of Manhattan. They called the island New Amsterdam. Later, part of New Amsterdam became New York City.

The Dutch West India Company ran the New Netherlands colony. They granted large estates to a few selected families called **patroons**. The patroons encouraged settlers from all parts of the world to settle New Netherlands and farm the estates.

In 1647 Peter Stuyvesant became the governor of New Netherlands. For several years Stuyvesant was a good governor and the people of the colony became prosperous. Stuyvesant believed, however, that the colony needed strong rule to survive. Because he was so stern, he became very unpopular with the colonists. In the 1660s the English decided they wanted New Netherlands to become part of England. They demanded that Stuyvesant surrender. Because the Dutch refused to help Stuyvesant keep the colony, the English were able to take it over without firing a shot. The English changed the name of the colony from New Netherlands to New York.

DELAWARE

The first permanent European settlement in Delaware was established by a group of Swedes from Sweden. They established a settlement in Wilmington and named the colony New Sweden. The colony was a business venture to expand trade. Later the colony was seized by New Netherlands then England. Eventually the colony became the state of Delaware.

NEW JERSEY

In 1664 the king of England gave a large parcel of land in America to two of his friends, Lord John Berkeley and Sir George Carteret. These men set up a colony they called New Jersey. They encouraged settlers from many countries to come to New Jersey. Berkeley and Carteret promised them three things: religious and political freedom, and cheap land.

PENNSYLVANIA

In 1682 a Quaker from England named William Penn founded Pennsylvania. Religious freedom was important to William Penn. He invited people of all religions to come and live in Pennsylvania. Penn advertised throughout Europe for settlers to come and farm the rich land. Penn and the first settlers founded the colony's first settlement and named it Philadelphia. In a short period of time many people came to Penn's settlement. Thousands of German-speaking Protestants called Mennonites and Amish came to Pennsylvania. They were called Pennsylvania Dutch or Pennsylvania Germans. Although some of the German settlers stayed near Philadelphia, many others settled in Lancaster County near Lancaster.

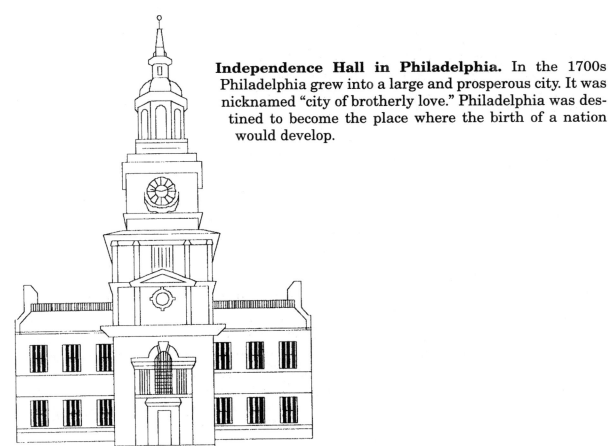

Independence Hall in Philadelphia. In the 1700s Philadelphia grew into a large and prosperous city. It was nicknamed "city of brotherly love." Philadelphia was destined to become the place where the birth of a nation would develop.

Name _____ Date _____ Period _____

2-2B PEOPLE OF THE MIDDLE COLONIES

Read the information in Activity 2-2A. Then complete the word puzzle to learn about the people who settled the Middle Colonies in the 1600s.

1. first European country to settle in the Middle Colonies
2. name given to first Middle Colony
3. early outpost in New Netherlands
4. early name given to island of Manhattan
5. present-day name of city on Manhattan island
6. name of company that ran New Netherlands colony
7. name given to families of estates in New Netherlands
8. early governor of New Netherlands
9. present-day name of state that was New Netherlands
10. group of people that settled Delaware
11. name of colony Swedes founded
12. present-day name of New Sweden
13. names of two men who founded New Jersey
14. two types of freedoms promised to New Jersey settlers
15. name of Quaker who founded Pennsylvania
16. name of first Pennsylvania settlement
17. a Protestant religious group that settled in Pennsylvania
18. county where many Pennsylvania Dutch settled

©1997 by The Center for Applied Research in Education

2-3 LIFE IN PENNSYLVANIA DUTCH COUNTRY

For the Teacher

Materials Needed:

- copies of Activity 2-3
- pencils

Teacher Preparation:

- Reproduce Activity 2-3, *Life in Pennsylvania Dutch Country*, as needed.
- Pass out the activity and allow time for students to complete the story. When they are finished, review the answers (given below) with them.

Answer Key:

(1) Germany

(2) Amish

(3) Mennonite

(4) Moravian

(5) Church of the Brethren

(6) automobiles (or televisions)

(7) televisions (or automobiles)

(8) tractors

(9) telephones

(10) farming

(11) wheat

(12) rye

(13) breadbasket

(14) cows (or pigs)

(15) pigs (or cows)

(16) sheep

(17) horses

(18) apples

(19) peaches

(20) clocks

(21) watches

(22) tools

(23) wagon wheels

(24) pots

(25) skillets

(26) hex

(27) birth

(28) marriage

Extended Activity:

- There are many historic sites and landmarks in the Middle Colonies worth visiting. Lancaster, Pennsylvania and the surrounding area is one. This region is the heart of Pennsylvania Dutch country and blends the colonial past to the present. Show a film or develop an exhibit on the Pennsylvania Dutch of Lancaster County. Contact the Visitor Information Center in Lancaster for specific orientation materials.

2-3 LIFE IN PENNSYLVANIA DUTCH COUNTRY

Read the activity carefully. Then make a selection from the word bank that best completes the sentence. **Hint**: Each dash represents one letter; therefore, if there are five dashes, choose the best word available that has five letters.

WORD BANK

watches	clocks	wheat
rye	hex	tools
breadbasket	farming	Germany
Amish	birth	marriage
telephones	Moravian	tractors
Church of the Brethren	cows	automobiles
peaches	sheep	skillets
horses	apples	pigs
pots	Mennonite	televisions
wagon wheels		

The Pennsylvania Dutch are a group of German immigrants that first came to America in the 1680s. These people are more correctly called Pennsylvania Germans because they came from (1) _ _ _ _ _ _ _. However, they were called Dutch by many colonists who mispronounced the word "Deutsch," which means German.

The Pennsylvania Dutch came to America for religious freedom. The main religions are (2) _ _ _ _ _, (3) _ _ _ _ _ _ _ _ _, (4) _ _ _ _ _ _ _ _, and (5) _ _ _ _ _ _ _ _ _ _ _ _ _ _ _ _ _. Many Pennsylvania Dutch practice the same traditional and social customs as they have for hundreds of years. Generally they reject worldly goods such as (6) _ _ _ _ _ _ _ _ _ _, (7) _ _ _ _ _ _ _ _ _ _ _, (8) _ _ _ _ _ _ _ _, and (9) _ _ _ _ _ _ _ _ _ _. They are known to be gentle, industrious people who live simply.

©1997 by The Center for Applied Research in Education

Name _____ Date _____ Period _____

2-3 LIFE IN PENNSYLVANIA DUTCH COUNTRY

The Pennsylvania Dutch have made important contributions to the development of America. They settled mainly in Lancaster and York counties in southern Pennsylvania where they made their living by (10) _ _ _ _ _ _ _. The good soil and mild climate of Pennsylvania helped the farmers produce many fine crops such as (11) _ _ _ _ _ and (12) _ _ _. Since most breads were made from these two grains, Pennsylvania came to be known as one of the (13) _ _ _ _ _ _ _ _ _ _ _ colonies. The Pennsylvania Dutch farmers also raised and sold farm animals such as (14) _ _ _ _, (15) _ _ _ _, (16) _ _ _ _ _, and (17) _ _ _ _ _ _. In addition, they grew and sold fruit such as (18) _ _ _ _ _ _ and (19) _ _ _ _ _ _ _.

During the 18th century the Pennsylvania Dutch also produced many kinds of manufactured goods. Clock makers turned out (20) _ _ _ _ _ _ and (21) _ _ _ _ _ _ _. The blacksmith manufactured needed farm items such as (22) _ _ _ _ _ and (23) _ _ _ _ _ _ _ _ _ _ _. He also made kitchen items such as (24) _ _ _ _ and (25) _ _ _ _ _ _ _ _.

The Pennsylvania Dutch were also famous for their art and crafts. They lived on beautifully tended farms that often featured a red barn adorned with brightly colored geometric designs called (26) _ _ _ signs. Another popular art form was Fractur Painting which is the art of decorating important documents such as (27) _ _ _ _ _ and (28) _ _ _ _ _ _ _ _ certificates.

2-4 TAKE A TRIP TO THE MIDDLE ATLANTIC

For the Teacher

Materials Needed:

- copies of Activity 2-4
- travel agency pamphlets
- travel books (such as *Mobil Travel Guide*)

Note:

The Middle Colonies included Delaware, New Jersey, New York, and Pennsylvania. Today's travel books that include this region are titled *Middle Atlantic States.*

Teacher Preparation:

- Reproduce Activity 2-4, *Take a Trip to the Middle Atlantic,* as needed and organize reference materials.
- Divide classes into small groups and assign specific states or regions of the Middle Atlantic for students to visit. Encourage groups to center their trip around historical places and events when possible.
- Pass out travel materials and the journal activity. Then allow time for students to complete the activity. Encourage the inclusion of photographs or illustrations, if possible. When students are finished, allow time for groups to share their journeys with the rest of the class.

Extended Activities:

- Show classes a travel video on one or more of the Middle Atlantic states. Sources for travelogue tapes include educational channel television, video stores, and libraries.
- Encourage students to learn more about the economy of the state they are visiting. What products or services does the state make or provide? What are the major types of jobs in the state? Information on state economy can be found in encyclopedias.

2-4 TAKE A TRIP TO THE MIDDLE ATLANTIC

DESTINATION _____

For each day, describe the location, place visited, and special activity (such as art, music, food, or holiday).

DAILY ITINERARY

Day 1 _____
_____
_____

Day 2 _____
_____
_____

Day 3 _____
_____
_____

Day 4 _____
_____
_____

Day 5 _____
_____
_____

Day 6 _____
_____
_____

Day 7 _____
_____
_____

2-5 WHAT WILL IT COST?

For the Teacher

Materials Needed:

- copies of Activity 2-5
- travel books
- pencils or pens

Teacher Preparation:

- Reproduce Activity 2-5, *What Will It Cost?*, as needed.
- Pass out the activity and allow time for students to solve the problems. When they are finished, review the answers (given below) with them.

Answer Key:

1. $32
2. $23.80; $3.57; $27.37
3. $64.90
4. $33.80
5. $32.00; $27.37; $64.90; $33.80; $158.07

Extended Activity:

- Have students estimate the costs for one day of *their* trip for a family of four (2 adults and 2 students). Approximate hotel and dining costs can be found in most travel books. Other expenses can be estimated. Although Activity 2-5 can be used as a guide, encourage students to make other selections on how the family will spend the day.

Name _____   Date _____   Period _____

2-5 WHAT WILL IT COST?

A family of four (2 adults and 2 children) is visiting *Pennsylvania Dutch Country* around Lancaster, Pennsylvania. Solve the problems to see how much money they will spend for the day.

1. Admission charge to Amish Village, a reconstructed Pennsylvania Dutch village, is $10 for adults and $6 for students. The family needs 2 adult and 2 student tickets.

   What is the total cost for the tickets? $_____

2. The family has lunch at a Pennsylvania Dutch restaurant. Lunches are as follows: 1 at $3.95, 2 at $6.95, and 1 at $5.95.

   How much are the lunches? $_____

   Add a 15% tip for the waitress. $_____

   What is the total cost for the lunches? $_____

3. After lunch the family visits a Pennsylvania Dutch folk craft center. The following items are purchased: Fractur painting birth certificate for $4; bag of German pretzels, $3; decorated hex sign, $18; and 2 horseshoes for $19.95 each.

   What is the total cost for the crafts? $_____

4. During the afternoon the family takes a buggy ride through the Amish farmland. The cost is $9.95 for adults and $6.95 for students. The family needs 2 adult and 2 student tickets.

   What is the total cost for the tickets? $_____

5. Add all the expenses to see how much money the family has spent:

   Total cost for #1. $_____

   Total cost for #2. $_____

   Total cost for #3. $_____

   Total cost for #4. $_____

   Total cost for the day. $_____

2-6 MIDDLE ATLANTIC TERMS

For the Teacher

Materials Needed:

- copies of Activity 2-6
- copies of *Glossary of Terms* (at back of book)

Teacher Preparation:

- Reproduce Activity 3-6, *Middle Atlantic Terms*, as needed. Also reproduce copies of the *Glossary* as needed.
- Pass out the activity and allow time for students to complete the matching definitions. When they are finished, review the vocabulary words (answers given below) with them.

Answer Key:

e.	colony	n.	mill
i.	fur trader	b.	sound
f.	Quaker	m.	Benjamin Franklin
l.	Philadelphia	a.	bay
g.	melting pot	o.	printer
r.	economy	q.	library
c.	breadbasket	j.	Conestoga
d.	cash crops	p.	statesman
k.	back country	h.	grain

Extended Activity:

- Use some of the terms in the activity as topics for further research. Appropriate titles include: The Pennsylvania Dutch, Benjamin Franklin's Philadelphia, and The Life of William Penn.

2-6 MIDDLE ATLANTIC TERMS

Expand your vocabulary by learning some terms associated with the Middle Colonies or states. Match the correct definitions to the words.

_____colony

_____fur trader

_____Quaker

_____Philadelphia

_____melting pot

_____economy

_____breadbasket

_____cash crops

_____back country

_____mill

_____sound

_____Benjamin Franklin

_____bay

_____printer

_____library

_____Conestoga

_____statesman

_____grain

a.   an inlet off of a larger body of water

b.   a long broad passage of water generally parallel to a coast line

c.   a name given to the Middle Colonies because they raised and exported so much grain

d.   crops that are raised and sold for profit on the world market

e.   a settlement developed by a country beyond its borders

f.   a religious group also known as *Friends of Society*

g.   a place where many cultures blend together

h.   the seeds of various food plants that produce food

i.   one who trades furs

j.   a type of large wagon built by the Settlers to carry goods along the road

k.   name given to the area along the Appalachian mountain range

l.   city in Pennsylvania founded by William Penn

m.   printer, author, diplomat, and statesman who spent much of his life in Philadelphia

n.   the process of grinding grain into flour

o.   a person who engages in the mass production of the written word

p.   a person who is actively engaged in conducting the business of government

q.   a place where literary and reference materials are located

r.   the concise use of resources for a specific region or country

2-7 FOLKTALES AND LITERATURE

For the Teacher

Materials Needed:

- copies of Activity 2-7
- practice paper and pencils
- drawing paper and pens
- (*optional*) black markers and/or colored pencils

Teacher Preparation:

- Reproduce Activity 2-7, *Folktales and Literature*, as needed and organize materials.
- Pass out the activity and allow time for students to read some of Ben Franklin's quips and words of advice. When they are finished, lead a discussion on Franklin's wit and humor.
- On practice paper have students develop some quips of their own.
- Using good drawing paper and pens, have students rewrite their favorite quips in their best printing or writing.
- (*optional*) Encourage students to illustrate their quips with markers and/or colored pencils.

Extended Activity:

- Set aside time for reading legends and literature from Middle Atlantic authors. Contact the media person in your building or community for assistance in gathering appropriate materials. When possible, take classes to the library for this activity. There are a number of books available that tell stories about the people of the Middle Colonies. A brief list follows that will help you get started. **Note:** Remember, this is merely a list of some options. Regional differences may vary, so use whatever is available in your area.

FOLKLORE

American Tall Tales by Mary Pope Osborne (New York: Random House, 1991). This book is about several of America's folk heroes. From the Middle Atlantic there is Mose, old New York's biggest, bravest fireman.

CLASSIC LITERATURE

Poor Richard's Almanack by Benjamin Franklin. In the 1700s Franklin gained wide popularity with his *Poor Richard's Almanack*, a pocket-sized periodical book of jokes, stories, witty sayings and advice to farmers. *Poor Richard's Almanack* is a series of some of Franklin's best jokes and stories. His bits of advice are still remembered and used today.

Little Women by Louisa May Alcott (various editions available). Alcott's most famous work, *Little Women* is an autobiographical novel of her childhood. It centers around sisters growing up in the 1800s.

The Legend of Sleepy Hollow and *Rip Van Winkle* by Washington Irving (various editions available). Under the pen name of Geoffrey Crayon, Irving wrote these two short stories set in days when New York was a Dutch colony. He also wrote a series of poems about the Passaic River and the countryside that surrounds it.

The Pioneers by James Fenimore Cooper (various editions available)

The Last of the Mohicans by James Fenimore Cooper (various editions available)

The Prairie by James Fenimore Cooper (various editions available)

The Pathfinder by James Fenimore Cooper (various editions available)

The Deerslayer by James Fenimore Cooper (various editions available)

These five popular novels make up the Leatherstocking Tales. They tell stories of frontiersman Natty Bumppo and his adventures in the American wilderness. In *The Deerslayer* and *The Last of the Mohicans*, Cooper drew on Indian legends. The 1992 movie version of *The Last of the Mohicans* starred Daniel Day-Lewis.

CHILDREN'S LITERATURE

The Winter of Red Snow: The Revolutionary War Diary of Abigail Jane Stewart by Kristiana Gregory (Dear America Series) (New York: Scholastic, 1996). This fictionalized story tells of General Washington as he prepares his troops to fight the British. Eleven-year-old Abigail writes in her diary about life in Valley Forge between December 1777 and July 1778.

2-7 FOLKTALES AND LITERATURE

The following quips and words of advice were written by Benjamin Franklin in the 1700s. Read them carefully. Are there underlying messages? If so what are they? When you are finished, develop some of your own quips or words of advice. Then illustrate them with drawings that are appropriate to the idea.

Ill customs and bad advice are seldom forgotten.

Fish and visitors stink after three days.

Eat few suppers and you'll need few medicines.

Who has deceived thee so oft as thy self?

The family of fools is ancient.

No better relationship than a prudent and faithful friend.

Well done is better than well said.

Keep conscience clear, then never fear.

Be slow in choosing a friend, slower in changing.

It is easy to see, hard to foresee.

Tart words make no friends; a spoonful of honey will catch more flies than a gallon of vinegar.

What you would seem to be, be really.

2-8 PASTIMES AND SPORTS

For the Teacher

Materials Needed:

- copies of Activity 2-8
- items mentioned in "Teacher Preparation"

Teacher Preparation:

- Reproduce Activity 2-8, *Pastimes and Sports*, as needed.
- Pass out the activity and go over the pastimes outlined. If possible, *allow students to help make choices on which activities will be selected. Then set aside some time for participation.*
- If *hoops, jacks,* or *tops* are selected, ask for volunteers to bring them in to share with classes.
- If there is interest in *Nine Pins,* you have two options. Contact the local historical society for authentic versions, or ask for volunteer owners of the modern plastic bowling sets to bring them to class (easy to set up and use indoors).
- If participating in sports is possible, contact the Physical Education person in your building well in advance and organize games of *field hockey, cricket,* or *baseball.*

2-8 PASTIMES AND SPORTS

SPORTS

Some sports and activities were introduced into America by the Dutch settlers of the Middle Colonies. Three winter activities included *sledding, skating*, and a game called *Shinny*. Shinny was a fast-paced game played in open fields with a stick and a ball. It was the forerunner of field hockey.

As children grew older, team sports for boys gained favor. Especially popular were *cricket* matches and games of *rounders*. Cricket was played much like it is today. The game uses a ball and bat, and is played by two teams on a large field centering on wickets at each end. Rounders was an early form of baseball.

PASTIMES

A popular activity introduced by the Dutch of the Middle Colonies was a game called *Nine Pins*. In this game nine pins were set up in a pattern on a lawn. Players rolled balls to knock down pins. This game was the forerunner of bowling.

At school, during recess and lunch, children played games of *hoops, jacks,* and *tops*. Are these pastimes still popular today?

HOOPS (2 TO 14 PLAYERS)

Contests using hoops were organized to test participants' rolling skills. Any wooden or metal hoop will work. One version selects teams to guide hoops through obstacle courses. Another contest has two to four players rolling two or more hoops at once on a designated course.

JACKS (2 TO 6 PLAYERS)

The game of *jacks* known during colonial times is still enjoyed today. The game is played with six-pronged objects called jacks and a small rubber ball. Player #1 starts the game by tossing the jacks on the ground. The player then bounces the ball. The player picks up one jack and catches the ball before it touches the ground—all with one hand. If the player succeeds, he or she stays in the game and the next player takes a turn. In the next rounds, players try to grab two, then three, then four jacks in the same manner. The player who wins is the one who can bounce the ball, then pick up the most jacks and catch the ball—always with one hand. As you can see, this game requires good reflexes.

TOPS (2 TO 6 PLAYERS)

During colonial times, tops were favorite toys with boys and girls. They came in many sizes, shapes, and styles. Several versions of top competition were played. In one version competitors would spin their top onto a flat surface and see whose top could spin the longest. In another version, two competitors spun their tops against each other. The top that spun the other one over while staying upright was the winner.

2-9 SOUNDS OF THE MIDDLE ATLANTIC

For the Teacher

Materials Needed:

- CD, cassette, or film
- audio-visual equipment

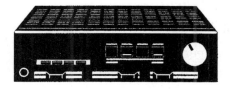

Teacher Preparation:

- Religious music was well known among the Middle Colonies. The Moravians produced original chamber and church music of their Old World German culture. The three-string trios written in the late 1700s by John Antes were some of the first chamber works composed in the Thirteen Colonies. Encourage your students to become familiar with this type of music. Check your local library or record store for availability.

- Stephen Collins Foster (1826–1864) was an American composer from Pittsburgh, Pennsylvania. Foster's songs remain some of the most popular ever written. Among his many songs include "Oh! Susanna," "Camptown Races," "Old Folks at Home," "My Old Kentucky Home," "Jeannie with the Light Brown Hair," and "Old Black Joe." His songs are noted for their touching melodies and simple harmonies. For an opportunity to listen to some of Stephen Foster's music, check with the library or record store in your community or consider the following option:

Songs of the Civil War and Stephen Foster Favorites
(Sony Music Entertainment, New York, 1992).

- The birth of the United States of America took place in Philadelphia. For opportunities to listen to music or view a film relating to these historical events, consider the following options:

Music of the American Revolution, The Birth of Liberty (CD)
(New World Records, New York, 1996).

1776 (musical film produced by Columbia Pictures, G rating)
This delightful musical celebration tells the story of the First Continental Congress in Philadelphia, Pennsylvania and the founding of the United States of America. It is highly recommended for those interested in the birth of a nation. The story centers around John Adams (William Daniels), Ben Franklin (Howard DaSilva), Thomas Jefferson (Ken Howard), and the rest of the Continental Congress as they debate the events leading up to July 4, 1776.

2-10 HEX SIGNS

For the Teacher

Materials Needed:

- copies of Activity 2-10
- practice paper and pencils
- scissors
- 8" × 8" white drawing paper
- compasses
- black markers
- colored markers or colored pencils

Teacher Preparation:

- Reproduce Activity 2-10, *Hex Designs*, as needed and organize materials. Regular school-grade drawing paper is suggested for this activity because it is inexpensive and readily available. Recommended size is 8" × 8" because it is an easy size for students to handle, although other sizes can be used as well.

- Go over the activity with your students. Then pass out the materials and allow time for students to develop hex designs.

- When students are finished, display the designs around the room.

Extended Activity:

- Contact the art teacher well in advance and coordinate a Pennsylvania art-and-craft project while your classes are learning about the Middle Colonies. One popular Pennsylvania Dutch art form is *Fractur Painting*. For assistance in showing students various types of Fractur painting designs, refer to *Pennsylvania Dutch Designs* by Judi Rettich. It contains many examples on how to create your own decorative certificates.

2-10 HEX SIGNS

WHAT ARE HEX SIGNS?

Hex signs are brightly painted, round designs that are featured on the barns of Pennsylvania German farms. These designs feature geometric, floral, and animal shapes often in repeat patterns. Hex signs are *symbolic*. Symbolic means that the design represents something else. The illustration of the *oak leaf*, for example, symbolizes strength, health, and endurance. The four large leaves represent the four seasons—spring, summer, fall, and winter.

WHY HEX SIGNS?

Traditionally, the Pennsylvania Dutch felt the hex signs brought them good luck, happiness, or love. Some believed the hex symbols would keep away evil spirits. Today the signs are created for decorative purposes. They not only hang on barns and in homes, but also decorate items for tourists, such as stationery or refrigerator magnets.

When the Pennsylvania Dutch settled in the Middle Colonies, their houses and barns were nothing more than log cabins. As the farmers became more settled, they built larger houses and even larger barns. In fact, the barns were usually larger than the houses. Painted hex signs attached to the barns became a Pennsylvania German tradition. It is a very impressive sight to drive through the rolling hills of Pennsylvania Dutch country and see the brightly colored paintings attached to the large barns.

HEX SIGN COLORS

The Pennsylvania Dutch used bright, basic colors to decorate their hex signs. Like the designs, colors are symbolic as well. Listed below are some of the colors they use along with their meaning:

RED . . . used on symbols of emotion, such as the heart, to denote love

BLUE . . . the color of water and sky to represent protection and strength

GREEN . . . associated with spring and greenery to suggest abundance and good fortune

YELLOW . . the color of the moon, flowers, and the distelfink (goldfinch) to suggest good luck and happiness

BROWN . . . associated with the earth and harvest to suggest the cycle of life

WHITE . . . symbol of purity and innocence to denote joy and strength

SYMBOLS AND THEIR MEANINGS

Look at the Pennsylvania Dutch designs and their meanings carefully. Notice how the Pennsylvania Dutch often use repeated patterns and/or mirrored images as they develop their designs. *Repeat patterns* mean that one image is drawn more than once. *Mirror images* are drawings that are exactly the same pattern repeated.

The Distelfink. The distelfink bird is actually a goldfinch. It is illustrated in a very stylized design. The single distelfink represents good luck and happiness. When two birds appear in a mirror image drawing, they symbolize friendship and happiness.

The Six-Petal Rosette. Hex designs often feature geometric drawings. A popular one is the six-petal rosette, which represents good luck. Hearts around the rosette symbolize love and affection. Generally this hex sign proclaims good luck and love for all.

©1997 by The Center for Applied Research in Education

2-10 HEX SIGNS *(continued)*

Develop a hex sign of your own by following the easy steps below. Use some of the traditional Pennsylvania designs as a starting point. Then add your own ideas to personalize your symbols.

Steps to Making Hex Signs

1. On practice paper draw several symbolic designs to create your own personal hex signs. You can use geometric designs, flowers, leaves and vines, birds, or animals for inspiration.

2. Using a compass, draw a circle on a good piece of drawing paper.

3. Pick your best drawing and *lightly* redraw it inside the circle form. Use one large single image, two repeats of the same drawing, or multiple repeated patterns.

4. Outline your hex sign with a black marker.

5. Color the design with colored markers and/or colored pencils.

   Hint: The background of a hex sign is almost always white.

Students used a variety of subjects to create their own hex signs. Many used geometric designs while others preferred to use flowers and birds for their main idea. The student-drawn hex design below represents a family. The four joining geometric shapes symbolize four members of the family. The hearts represent the love family members have for each other, and the outlining circle signifies an unending bond. What colors do you think this student used on the hex sign?

2-11 A PENNSYLVANIA DUTCH CHRISTMAS

For the Teacher

This activity is ideal during the Christmas holiday to celebrate a tradition of the settlers in the Middle Colonies.

Materials Needed:

Popcorn and Cranberry Chains

- copies of Activity 2-11
- a Christmas tree (real or artificial)
- popped corn
- fresh cranberries
- bowls
- long, thin needles
- heavy thread
- scissors

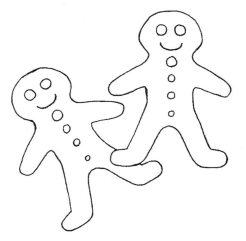

Other Pennsylvania Dutch Tree Ornaments

- apples
- white paper candles
- gingerbread cookies

Teacher Preparation:

- Reproduce Activity 2-11, *A Pennsylvania Dutch Christmas*, as needed.

- Pass out the activity and go over the information with your students. If necessary, ask for volunteers to help supply some of the materials.

- You might want to pair the classes into small groups, then put the popped corn and cranberries in bowls for each group. Also cut heavy thread in four-, five-, or six-foot lengths. Pass out the materials and allow time for pairs to make the chains.

- When students are finished, decorate the tree with the chains. If possible, also decorate with apples and paper candles.

Extended Activity:

- Gingerbread boys were a popular colonial Christmas cookie. The dough was made into many shapes. Although gingerbread boys were the most common, other shapes included angels, birds, and animals. For an extra colonial Christmas treat, make, hang, or serve gingerbread cookies. (See Activity 2-15 for the recipe.)

2-11 A PENNSYLVANIA DUTCH CHRISTMAS

The earliest colonists in America celebrated very little at Christmas because of their harsh life. As time passed, however, the spirit of the season spread throughout the colonies. In the Middle Colonies, German settlers cut down evergreen trees and brought them inside. Family members strung popped corn and fresh cranberries into chains. When the chains were finished, they decorated the tree with them along with red apples and small white candles. In kitchens, colonial cooks baked cookies and fruitcakes for special Christmas treats.

Celebrate the Christmas holiday with traditions of the colonists in the Middle Colonies. Make popped corn and cranberry chains as outlined on the next page. When the chains are finished, decorate a tree with them. Other tree adornments used by the Pennsylvania Dutch included red apples, small white candles, and gingerbread boys.

Materials for Popcorn and Cranberry Chains

- popped corn
- fresh, hard cranberries
- long, thin needles
- heavy thread
- scissors

Steps to Making Chains

1. Divide class into pairs or small groups.
2. Thread a needle with a long, heavy thread and tie a large knot at one end of the string.
3. Run the needle through the popcorn and berries lengthwise onto the heavy thread. Use various patterns to form the chains; for example, three popped corns and one berry, or five popped corns and two berries.
4. When thread lengths are filled, tie another large knot at the other end of the string.
5. String chains on a Christmas tree.
6. Also hang small red apples and white (paper) candles on the tree.
7. If possible, make gingerbread boy cookies using the recipe in Activity 2-15.

2-12 BASICS OF PENNSYLVANIA DUTCH COOKING

For the Teacher

Materials Needed:

- copies of Activity 2-12
- pencils

Teacher Preparation:

- Reproduce Activity 2-12, *Basics of Pennsylvania Dutch Cooking*, as needed.
- Pass out the activity and allow time for students to read the information and complete the worksheet. (Answers are given below.) When they are finished, review the basics of Pennsylvania Dutch cooking with them.

Answer Key:

Part One

Three German dishes: sauerbraten; spaetzle; speck un kraut

Meats: pork; chicken; beef

Meat dishes: chicken stoltzfus; chicken and dumplings

Three soup ingredients: corn; noodles; dumplings

Soups: chicken corn soup; chicken soup with homemade noodles

Vegetables: corn; cabbage; potatoes; beets

Examples of sweets: apple butter; peach marmalade; strawberry jam; ginger pears

Examples of sours: pepper relish; pickled beets; corn relish; chow chow

Desserts: shoo-fly pie; apple pandowdy; apees; lebkuchen

Breakfast treats: fastnachts; kaffee kuchen

Part Two

Sauerbraten: beef marinated in vinegar and spices

Spaetzle: dumplings

Speck un kraut: pork and sauerkraut

Chicken stoltzfus: creamed chicken served over pastry shells

Chicken corn soup: chicken, homemade noodles, and corn in a soup

Chow chow: cabbage, tomatoes, onions, and peppers in vinegar dressing

Shoo-fly pie: molasses pie with crumb topping

Apple pandowdy: deep-dish apple pie

Apees: butter cookies

Lebkuchen: lemon-cinnamon bars

Fastnachts: donuts

Kaffee kuchen: coffee cake

Extended Activity:

* Encourage students to collectively develop a Pennsylvania Dutch cookbook. Divide classes into groups and assign specific topics to each group. After students have collected their recipes, duplicate their submissions so each student can organize a cookbook of his or her own. Appropriate topics include Soups, Sweet and Sours, Vegetables, Main Dishes, Breads, and Desserts.

2-12 BASICS OF PENNSYLVANIA DUTCH COOKING

In the late 1600s many German-speaking religious groups from Europe settled in Pennsylvania. Some of these sects included Moravians, Mennonites, Amish, and Dunkards. They were hard-working people who loved good food. The blending of recipes from Europe combined with foods available in the new world produced a regional cuisine in America called Pennsylvania Dutch cooking.

TRADITIONAL DISHES FROM GERMANY

Some of the recipes used by the Pennsylvania Dutch came straight from Germany. Three favorites include *sauerbraten* (beef marinated in vinegar and spices), *spaetzle* (dumplings), and *speck un kraut* (pork and sauerkraut).

Meats: Meats used by the Pennsylvania Dutch in America included *pork, chicken*, and *beef*. Besides some old country favorites, cooks developed new traditions in the new world. An especially favorite one is called *chicken stoltzfus* (creamed chicken served over pastry shells). Another popular dish is *chicken and dumplings*.

Soups: Soups are a traditional part of the Pennsylvania Dutch style of cooking. They are sturdy soups, hearty enough to serve as a meal by themselves. Three main ingredients of soups include *corn, noodles*, and *dumplings*. Few church picnic suppers would be complete without gallons of *chicken corn soup* (chicken, homemade noodles, and corn). Another favorite is *chicken soup with homemade noodles*.

Vegetables: Although the Pennsylvania Dutch use many vegetables in their cooking, four common ones include *corn, cabbage, potatoes*, and *beets*.

Sweets and Sours: Pennsylvania Dutch are famous for serving an assortment of accompaniments to meals they call "sweets and sours." The sweets consist of various types of jams and jellies. The sours include relishes and pickled vegetables that have been seasoned with vinegar dressings. Examples of sweets are *apple butter, peach marmalade, strawberry jam*, and *ginger pears*. Examples of sours include *pepper relish, pickled beets, corn relish*, and *chow chow* (cabbage, tomatoes, onions, and peppers seasoned in a vinegar dressing).

Desserts and Sweets: Good baking is a Pennsylvania Dutch specialty. They make and serve all kinds of pies, cookies, cakes, donuts, and sweet rolls. Perhaps the most famous is *shoo-fly pie*, a molasses pie with a crumb topping. Three other dessert favorites include *apple pandowdy*, a deep-dish apple pie, *apees*, sugar cookies, and *lebkuchen*, lemon-cinnamon bars. Breakfast treats include *fastnachts* (donuts) and *kaffee kuchen* (coffee cake).

Name _____ Date _____ Period _____

2-12 BASICS OF PENNSYLVANIA DUTCH COOKING

Part One: Use the boxes below to outline some of the food basics of Pennsylvania Dutch cooking.

Three traditional dishes from Germany:	_____ _____ _____
Meats:	_____ _____ _____
Meat dishes:	_____ _____
Three ingredients of soup:	_____ _____ _____
Two favorite soups:	_____ _____
Vegetables:	_____ _____ _____ _____
Examples of sweets:	_____ _____ _____ _____
Examples of sours:	_____ _____ _____ _____
Name four desserts: **(be specific)**	_____ _____ _____ _____
Breakfast treats:	_____ _____

2-12 BASICS OF PENNSYLVANIA DUTCH COOKING *(continued)*

Part Two: Write the definitions of the foods listed below.

Sauerbraten _____

_____

Spaetzle _____

_____

Speck un kraut _____

_____

Chicken stoltzfus _____

_____

Chicken corn soup _____

_____

Chow chow _____

_____

Shoo-fly pie _____

_____

Apple pandowdy _____

_____

Apees _____

_____

Fastnachts _____

_____

Kaffee kuchen _____

_____

2-13 A PENNSYLVANIA DUTCH MENU

For the Teacher

Hint: It is helpful to complete Activity 2-12, *Basics of Pennsylvania Dutch Cooking*, before participating in this one.

Materials Needed:

- copies of Activity 2-13
- pencils or pens

Teacher Preparation:

- Reproduce Activity 2-13, *A Pennsylvania Dutch Menu,* as needed.
- Pass out the activity. Then allow students time to read the menu and make their dinner selections. When they are finished, lead a discussion to compare the food items used by the Pennsylvania Dutch to a special-occasion dinner of their family. How many dishes are familiar? Have the students ever eaten any of these regional specialties?

Extended Activities:

- Ask students to bring in some simple or ready-made foods that the Pennsylvania Dutch might enjoy. Choices may include pretzels, apple cider, apple dumplings, ginger snaps, and coffee cakes.
- Pretzels were first brought to America by the Pennsylvania Dutch. In fact, the first pretzel bakery built is in Lancaster County. Since colonial days soft and hard pretzels have gained wide acceptance in America. For a special treat, have students bring in soft pretzels and serve them with mustard, cheese, or taco sauce.

2-13 A PENNSYLVANIA DUTCH MENU

The Pennsylvania Dutch have a saying: "Kissin' wears out—cookin' don't." These German, Switzerland, and Holland descendants are a hard-working people who believe in eating hearty. Their cooking has truly become an art in America and has gained the reputation of being some of the best regional cuisine in the country.

There are many restaurants and farms in Lancaster County, Pennsylvania that offer Pennsylvania Dutch meals. Traditionally they are all placed on the table at once so that each person can choose what he or she wants. It is also customary to serve a selection of "seven sweets and seven sours" to accompany the meals. Listed below is a menu of some typical foods served in Pennsylvania Dutch country. How many food items are familiar? How many are new to you?

©1997 by The Center for Applied Research in Education

SOUPS
Chicken Corn Chowder
Chicken Dumpling

SWEETS AND SOURS
Apple Butter, Apple and Peach Marmalade, Ginger Pears,
Chow Chow, Corn Relish, Pepper Relish, Pickled Beets,
Pickled Green Beans, Sauerkraut

MEAT DISHES
Chicken Stolzfus
Lancaster County Sausages
Sauerbraten
Speck un Kraut

VEGETABLE DISHES
Corn Pudding
Peas and New Potatoes
Boiled Cabbage
Scalloped Potatoes

DESSERTS
Shoo-fly Pie
Apple Pandowdy
Lebkuchen

2-13 A PENNSYLVANIA DUTCH MENU *(continued)*

Look over the Pennsylvania Dutch menu offerings from the previous page. In the spaces provided on the left, make your selections for a Pennsylvania Dutch dinner. Since Pennsylvania Dutch meals are served family style, you may choose as many as you want.

In the spaces provided on the right, list the items your family might have for a special occasion or Sunday dinner. Compare the Pennsylvania Dutch food items to your own.

Pennsylvania Dutch Dinner (choose as many as you want)	*Special-Occasion Dinner* (choose as many as you want)
Soup	Soup
_____	_____
_____	_____
Sweets and Sours	Salad
_____	_____
_____	_____
_____	_____
Meat Dishes	Meat Dishes
_____	_____
_____	_____
_____	_____
Vegetables	Vegetables
_____	_____
_____	_____
_____	_____
Desserts	Desserts
_____	_____
_____	_____
_____	_____

2-14 SHOO-FLY PIE

For the Teacher

Equipment Needed:

- copies of Activity 2-14
- mixing bowls
- spoon
- measuring cup
- measuring spoons
- cookie sheet

Supplies Needed:

- all-purpose flour
- brown sugar
- all-spice
- cinnamon
- butter or margarine
- molasses
- baking soda
- ready-made, unbaked 9" pie shell

Teacher Preparation:

- Reproduce Activity 2-14, *Shoo-fly Pie*, as needed and organize equipment and supplies.
- Give a demonstration on making Shoo-fly Pie as students follow along with the recipe.
- **ALTERNATIVE**: Go over the recipe with students. Then make an out-of-class assignment for students to make the pie at home and bring it to school for a special Pennsylvania Dutch treat day. Encourage students to ask for adult supervision when making the pie.

Extended Activity:

- Contact the Consumer and Family Living teacher well in advance to coordinate a Pennsylvania Dutch lunch or dessert lab activity while your classes are learning about the Middle Colonies.

2-14 SHOO-FLY PIE

Shoo-fly pie is probably the most famous of all Pennsylvania Dutch desserts. It is a molasses pie sprinkled with a crumbly mixture of flour, sugar, and butter. Although there are no firm theories on how the pie was named, the most common explanation is that the sweetness of the pie drew flies around it. Because flies were always buzzing around it, cooks would shoo them away! This recipe serves 6 to 8.

You need:

1	ready-made, unbaked pie shell
	(*optional*) ice cream

For crumb mixture, you need:

1-1/2	cups all-purpose flour
1	cup brown sugar
1/2	teaspoon all-spice
1/2	teaspoon cinnamon
1/3	cup margarine or butter, softened

What to do:

1. In a mixing bowl, thoroughly mix flour, sugar, all-spice, and cinnamon.
2. Cut in margarine or butter until mixture is crumbly. Set aside.

For molasses mixture, you need:

1/2	cup molasses
1/2	cup hot water
1/4	teaspoon baking soda

What to do:

1. Preheat oven to 375°.
2. In a mixing bowl, stir molasses, hot water, and baking soda until blended.
3. Line the unbaked pie shell with half of the flour-sugar mixture.
4. Pour the molasses on top of the crumb mixture.
5. Top with remaining crumb mixture.
6. Place pie on the middle shelf of oven and bake for about 40 minutes or until golden brown.
7. Cool and serve with ice cream, if desired.

2-15 GINGERBREAD BOYS

For the Teacher

Equipment Needed:
- copies of Activity 2-15
- mixing bowl
- measuring cup
- measuring spoons
- spoon
- hand mixer
- cookie sheets
- gingerbread boy cookie cutter

Supplies Needed:
- brown sugar
- butter or margarine
- egg
- all-purpose flour
- all-spice
- baking soda
- (*optional*) cinnamon candies
- (*optional*) decorator icing in tubes

Teacher Preparation:
- Reproduce Activity 2-15, *Gingerbread Boys*, as needed and organize equipment and supplies.
- Give a demonstration on making the cookies as students follow along with the recipe.
- **ALTERNATIVE**: Go over the recipe with students. Then make an out-of-class assignment for students to make the cookies at home and bring them to school for a special American tradition treat. Encourage students to ask for adult supervision when making the cookies.

2-15 GINGERBREAD BOYS

Making gingerbread cookies and houses has become an American tradition, especially around the Christmas holidays. Both gingerbread boys and houses are made from a rolled ginger-cookie recipe. For variety, other shapes of cookie cutters can be used as well. Whether celebrating the holiday in a colonial way, or simply enjoying the flavor of the custom, it is fun to participate in making ginger cookies. This recipe makes about 2 dozen cookies.

You need:

1	cup brown sugar, packed
3/4	cup margarine or butter, softened
1	egg
2	cups all-purpose flour
1-1/2	teaspoons allspice
1/2	teaspoon baking soda
	(*optional*) cinnamon candies
	(*optional*) decorator icing in tubes

What to do:

1. Preheat oven to 350°.
2. In a mixing bowl, cream sugar, margarine, and egg until light and fluffy.
3. Add flour, all-spice, and baking soda to creamed mixture and mix well.
4. Cover and chill dough for about 2 hours.
5. On a lightly floured surface, roll dough to 1/8-inch thickness.
6. Cut gingerbread boy shapes with a cookie cutter. *Note:* If using cookies as tree ornaments, use a toothpick to pierce a hole at the top of the head before baking.
7. Place on ungreased cookie sheet and bake for 8 to 10 minutes or until lightly browned.
8. Cool cookies on cooling rack.
9. (*optional*) Decorate cookies with cinnamon candies and icing.

BIBLIOGRAPHY FOR THE MIDDLE COLONIES

Art

Costabel, Eva Deutsch. *The Pennsylvania Dutch Craftsmen and Farmers*. New York: Atheneum, 1986.

Mauer, Walt. *Hex Signs and Their Meanings*. Gettysburg, PA: Garden Spots Gifts, 1996.

Rettich, Judi. *Pennsylvania Dutch Designs*. Mineola, NY: Dover Publications, 1983.

Children's Nonfiction

Kent, Deborah. *America the Beautiful: Delaware*. Chicago: Children's Press, 1991.

Kent, Deborah. *America the Beautiful: New Jersey*. Chicago: Children's Press, 1987.

Kent, Deborah. *America the Beautiful: Pennsylvania*. Chicago: Children's Press, 1988.

Madison, Arnold. *How the Colonists Lived*. New York: David McKay Company, 1981.

Stein, Conrad. *America the Beautiful: New York*. Chicago: Children's Press, 1989.

Cookbooks

Editors. *Better Homes and Gardens Heritage Cookbook*. New York: Meredith Corporation, 1985.

Editors. *Pennsylvania Dutch Cooking*. Paradise, PA: Will Char's Amish and Dutch Books, 1996.

Music

Staff. *Academic American Encyclopedia, Volume 1*. Danbury, CT: Grolier, Inc., 1996.

Pastimes

Kalman, Bobbie. *Games from Long Ago*. New York: Crabtree Publishing, 1995.

Kalman, Bobbie and David Schimpky. *Old-Time Toys*. New York: Crabtree Publishing, 1995.

Warner, John F. *Colonial American Home Life*. New York: Franklin Watts, 1993.

Social Studies

Bass, Herbert. *People in Time and Place: Our Country*. Parsippany, NJ: Silver Burdett & Ginn, 1991.

Davidson, James and John Batchelor. *The American Nation*. Englewood Cliffs, NJ: Prentice Hall, 1991.

Travel

Staff. *Mobil 1995 Travel Guide, Mid-Atlantic*. New York: Fodor's Travel Publications, 1995.

THE SOUTHERN COLONIES

Below is an outline of the interdisciplinary activities included in this section. They are designed to bring a broad range of hands-on cultural lessons and activities into the social studies classroom. Pick and choose the ones that best fit into your program.

MAP OF THE SOUTHERN COLONIES

3-1 GETTING TO KNOW THE SOUTH

For the Teacher

Materials Needed:

- copies of Activity 3-1
- labeled map of Southern Colonies and the South (enlarged on opaque projector)
- copies of unlabeled map of Southern Colonies and the South
- (colored) pencils

Teacher Preparation:

- Reproduce Activity 3-1, *Getting to Know the South*, as needed. Also reproduce copies of the unlabeled map of the Southern Colonies as needed.
- Pass out the activity and map to each student. Then allow time for students to locate and label the South as outlined in the activity. When they are finished, review the geography with them.

Extended Activities:

- Reproduce additional copies of the unlabeled map and have students identify other features of the southern states, such as population distribution, land use, or climate. PC Globe® computer program can provide much of the information needed for this activity. Consult your school's media person for assistance, too.

- Reproduce the chart of *The Fifty States* (at back of book) as needed. Pass out the chart and have students make a list of the Southern Colonies, date they entered the Union, order of entry, capital, and largest city. *List states in order they entered the union.* Answers should appear as follows:

State	Date Entered Union	Order of Entry	Capital	Largest City
Georgia	1788	4	Atlanta	Atlanta
Maryland	1788	7	Annapolis	Baltimore
South Carolina	1788	8	Columbia	Columbia
Virginia	1788	10	Richmond	Virginia Beach
North Carolina	1789	12	Raleigh	Charlotte
Alabama	1819	22	Montgomery	Birmingham
Florida	1845	27	Tallahassee	Jacksonville
West Virginia	1863	35	Charleston	Charleston

Name _____ Date _____ Period _____

3-1 GETTING TO KNOW THE SOUTH

Use the map provided to locate and label the following features:

State: Maryland
Capital: Annapolis

State: Virginia
Capital: Richmond
Early settlement: Jamestown
Early capital: Williamsburg
Bordering body of water: Chesapeake Bay

State: North Carolina
Capital: Raleigh

State: South Carolina
Capital: Columbia

State: Georgia
Capital: Atlanta

State: West Virginia
Capital: Charleston

State: Alabama
Capital: Montgomery

State: Florida
Capital: Tallahassee

Bordering bodies of water: Gulf of Mexico, Atlantic Ocean

3-1 GETTING TO KNOW THE SOUTH

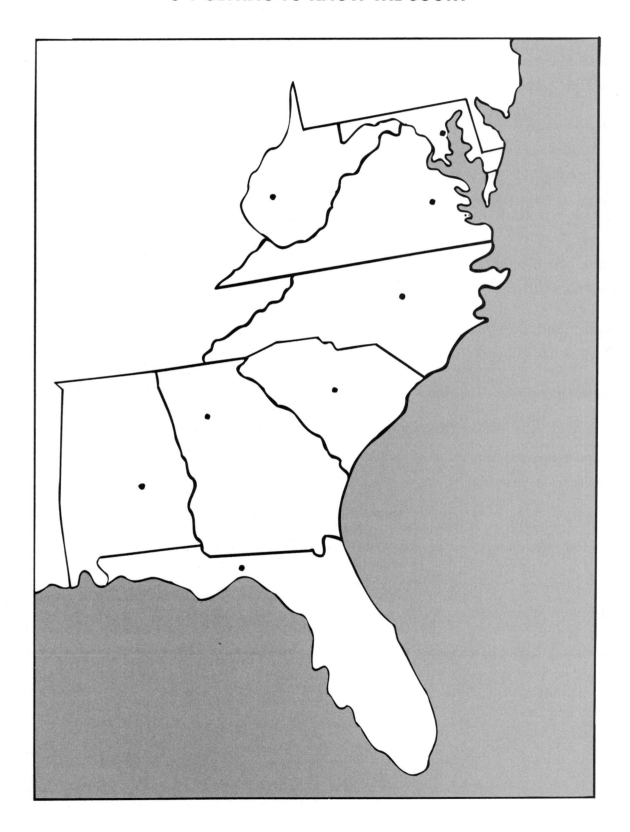

3-2 THE EARLY SOUTHERN COLONIES

For the Teacher

Materials Needed:

- copies of Activity 3-2
- pencils

Teacher Preparation:

- Reproduce Activity 3-2A, and 3-2B, *The Early Southern Colonies*, as needed.
- Pass out Activity 3-2A and allow time for students to read the information. Then distribute Activity 3-2B and have students complete the word puzzle. When they are finished, review the answers (given below) with them.

Answer Key:

1. Jamestown
2. Virginia
3. gold
4. John Smith
5. Powhatan
6. Pocahontas
7. tobacco
8. John Rolfe
9. Williamsburg

10. St. Marys
11. George Calvert
12. Charles Town
13. Anthony Ashley Cooper
14. rice, indigo
15. New Bern
16. Savannah
17. James Oglethorpe
18. cotton

Extended Activities:

- Encourage students to learn more about the early southern colonies by writing research papers and assign extra credit for those who participate. Appropriate titles include The Jamestown Colony, Pocahontas, Williamsburg, The Early Colonists in Maryland, The Early Colonists in South Carolina, The Early Colonists in North Carolina, or The Early Colonists in Georgia.
- Show a film on *Pocahontas*. One version was produced by Walt Disney in 1996 which gained wide acceptance by children of all ages.

3-2A THE EARLY SOUTHERN COLONIES

THE JAMESTOWN COLONY

In 1607 a group of English colonists sailed across the Atlantic Ocean and settled in a place they called *Jamestown*. Jamestown, Virginia became the first permanent English settlement in America. The Englishmen came to America in search of gold. Unwisely they spent all of their days searching for gold instead of planting crops. As a result, they nearly failed their first year and they never did find gold.

Captain *John Smith*, the son of a farmer, saved the colony from disaster. He visited nearby Indian tribes in search of food. *Powhatan*, an Indian chief, took Captain Smith prisoner and ordered him put to death. However, Powhatan's daughter *Pocahontas* begged her father to spare Smith's life. Powhatan agreed and ended up feeding the hungry colonists at Jamestown.

The Jamestown colony spent several years dealing with starvation and disease. Eventually the colonists learned to grow crops and raise tobacco. One colonist, *John Rolfe*, developed a blend of tobaccos that became popular in Europe. By the late 1600s tobacco growers in Virginia were making sizable profits from crop sales.

Pocahontas begged her father, Chief Powhatan, not to kill Captain Smith. The chief could not deny the request of his beloved daughter, so he set Smith free.

3-2A THE EARLY SOUTHERN COLONIES (continued)

Jamestown Festival Park (near Williamsburg, Virginia) is an authentic recreation of the early Jamestown village. It ranks among one of the popular historical attractions in America.

Jamestown Settlement in Virginia (near Williamsburg) was established in 1607. It was sponsored by a group of English investors who hoped to profit from wealth found in the New World. In the early years, many settlers died from disease and hunger. The colony was eventually saved by growing and selling tobacco. By the end of the 17th century, the colony was well established.

Near Jamestown Settlement is *Powhatan Indian Village* where costumed staff demonstrate and present a view of daily life of 17th-century American Indians. Visitors are encouraged to participate and ask questions during their visit.

Photo 3-1 Recreated dwelling from Jamestown Settlement.

Photo 3-2 Recreated Powhatan Indian Village near Jamestown Settlement.

3-2 THE EARLY SOUTHERN COLONIES *(continued)*

In 1698 Jamestown statehouse burned to the ground. The capital was rebuilt in nearby Williamsburg, Virginia. From 1699 to 1780 Williamsburg served as the capital of Virginia. The colonial capital was the scene of many social and political events. Today Williamsburg is an authentically restored 18th-century capital, as shown in the photograph. Like Jamestown Festival Park, it remains one of America's most popular historical attractions. Costumed staff and businessmen converse with visitors in 18th-century language.

Photo 3-3 Capital Building, Williamsburg, Virginia

3-2A THE EARLY SOUTHERN COLONIES (continued)

ST. MARYS, MARYLAND

In 1634 two hundred English colonists arrived in Maryland and settled in a village they named *St. Marys*. The colony was set up by a man named *George Calvert* who promised settlers religious and political freedom. The nearby Virginia colonists taught the new settlers how to grow tobacco. Like their neighbors from Virginia, the Maryland colonists profited from tobacco sales. Today St. Marys has been rebuilt and visitors may see how people lived and worked in the 1600s.

CHARLESTON, SOUTH CAROLINA

In 1670 the first permanent settlement in the Carolinas was established by an English nobleman named *Anthony Ashley Cooper*. At first the colony was named Charles Town but eventually became Charleston. The early colonists tried to raise grapes. When the crops failed, they grew rice and indigo which soon became major crops. By the early 1700s large plantations were developed in the south. Early on an aristocratic nobility was established that still exists today. *Charles Towne Landing* in Charleston is a reconstruction of the state's first permanent English settlement in the Carolinas.

NEW BERN, NORTH CAROLINA

One of the first settlements in North Carolina was established in 1710 by Swiss settlers seeking religious and political freedom. They named their settlement *New Bern* after their home town in Switzerland. Today many buildings that were built during the colonial days are open to the public at special times of the year.

SAVANNAH, GEORGIA

The last of the thirteen colonies was established in Savannah, Georgia. In 1733 *General James Oglethorpe*, along with 120 settlers, came to Georgia to establish a new colony. Oglethorpe was concerned about people in England who were imprisoned for debt. He wanted to help the debtors by paying for their passage to Georgia where they could make a new start. He also wanted the new settlers to serve as part-time soldiers to fight the attacks from the Spanish in nearby Florida. In the late 1700s Georgia became a colony with large cotton plantations and Savannah became a major shipping port. Today many architecturally significant buildings have been restored in Savannah's historic area. The Victorian district offers some fine examples of 19th-century architecture.

3-2B THE EARLY SOUTHERN COLONIES

Read the information in Activity 3-2A. Then complete the word puzzle to learn about the people who settled the Southern Colonies.

1. first permanent settlement in America
2. colony (now state) of first permanent settlement
3. reason early settlers came to America
4. Jamestown leader
5. Indian chief who captured Captain Smith
6. Indian maiden who saved Captain Smith
7. major source of profit for Jamestown colonists
8. man who developed a popular blend of tobaccos in Virginia
9. colonial capital of Virginia from 1699–1780
10. first permanent settlement in Maryland
11. founder of first permanent settlement in Maryland
12. first permanent settlement in South Carolina
13. founder of Charles Town
14. two major crops in South Carolina colony
15. early settlement in North Carolina
16. early settlement in Georgia
17. founder of Savannah
18. major crop in Georgia

©1997 by The Center for Applied Research in Education

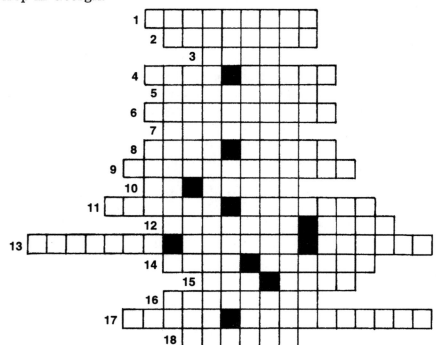

3-3 LIFE ON A PLANTATION

For the Teacher

Materials Needed:

- copies of Activity 3-3
- pencils

Teacher Preparation:

- Reproduce Activity 3-3, *Life on a Plantation*, as needed.
- Pass out the activity and allow time for students to complete the story. When they are finished, review the answers (given below) with them.

Answer Key:

(1)	tobacco	(13)	soap
(2)	plantations	(14)	dances
(3)	rice	(15)	card games
(4)	indigo	(16)	fox hunts
(5)	cash crops	(17)	horse races
(6)	indentured servants	(18)	tutors
(7)	slaves	(19)	piano
(8)	Great House	(20)	needlepoint
(9)	barn	(21)	folktales
(10)	tool shed	(22)	singing (or dancing)
(11)	storage house	(23)	dancing (or singing)
(12)	candles		

Extended Activity:

- There are many historic sites and landmarks in the Southern states worth visiting. Two outstanding places are *Jamestown Festival Park,* the site of the first permanent English settlement in America, and *Williamsburg, Virginia,* the colonial capital from 1799 to 1871. Show a film or develop an exhibit on one or both places. Contact the Visitor Information Center at each place for specific educational materials.

3-3 LIFE ON A PLANTATION

Read the activity carefully. Then make a selection from the word bank that best completes the sentence. **Hint**: Each dash represents one letter; therefore, if there are five dashes, choose the best word available that has five letters.

WORD BANK

slaves	indentured servants	cash crops
Great House	indigo	barn
tobacco	plantations	candles
rice	tool shed	dances
singing	dancing	soap
card games	storage house	tutors
piano	horse races	needlepoint
fox hunts	folktales	

Settlers in the Southern Colonies developed a different life style from the New England or Middle Colonies. The Virginia settlers learned that the climate and soil were well suited for growing (1) _ _ _ _ _ _ _. Soon large tobacco farms were established in Virginia, Maryland, and North Carolina. They were called (2) _ _ _ _ _ _ _ _ _ _. South Carolina and Georgia did not grow tobacco. Instead they produced (3) _ _ _ _ and (4) _ _ _ _ _ _. Indigo is a plant that produces a dark blue color suitable for dyes. The tobacco, rice, and indigo crops were shipped to England for profit. Therefore, they were called (5) _ _ _ _   _ _ _ _ _.

The plantations needed many workers to raise and harvest their crops. There were two main groups of laborers. One type included people who agreed to work for several years in return for their passage to America. They were called (6) _ _ _ _ _ _ _ _ _ _   _ _ _ _ _ _ _ _. However, plantations replaced indentured servants with a second group of worker called (7) _ _ _ _ _ _. Slaves are people who were brought from Africa in bondage to work for plantation owners. It is impossible to describe the horrors of the slave trade.

Many of the plantations were quite large and served as small villages. The main building was called the (8) _ _ _ _ _   _ _ _ _. It was where the planter's family lived. Behind the Great House were vegetable gardens. Further away were a number of other buildings that included a (9) _ _ _ _, (10) _ _ _ _   _ _ _ _, and a (11) _ _ _ _ _ _ _   _ _ _ _ _. There were also smaller buildings used to produce necessary household items such as (12) _ _ _ _ _ _ _ (for light) and (13) _ _ _ _ (for washing). At the back part of the plantation were one-room cabins that served as the slaves' quarters.

3-3 LIFE ON A PLANTATION (continued)

Plantation families in the south lived very comfortable lives. They had a very busy social life. Much of the social life revolved around visits with other plantation families. Popular forms of entertainment included (14) _ _ _ _ _ _, (15) _ _ _ _ _ _ _ _ _, (16) _ _ _ _ _ _ _ _, and (17) _ _ _ _ _ _ _ _ _ _. The plantation owners hired private teachers to educate their children. They were called (18) _ _ _ _ _ _. The tutor lived in the Great House and taught the white children on the plantation. The girls learned to read, write, play the (19) _ _ _ _ _, or develop stitches for (20) _ _ _ _ _ _ _ _ _ _ _. On the other hand, after a basic education, the boys were often sent to England to complete advanced studies.

Slaves were not permitted to leave the plantation. They had no chance for education. After long days in the fields, the slaves returned to their quarters. Here they created their own community. They told and retold stories handed down from one generation to another. These stories are called (21) _ _ _ _ _ _ _ _ _. They also developed a unique style of (22) _ _ _ _ _ _ _ and (23) _ _ _ _ _ _ _. These musical contributions of the early slaves are the basis of the modern-day African-American culture.

Photo 3-4, Carter's Grove Plantation Just a few miles from Colonial Williamsburg is *Carter's Grove*. In the 1750s Robert "King" Carter built an elegant brick mansion that was a symbol of his wealth and prominence in the colony. The mansion and grounds are now open for the public to see how wealthy 18th-century Virginians lived.

3-4 TAKE A TRIP TO THE SOUTH

For the Teacher

Materials Needed:

- copies of Activity 3-4
- travel agency pamphlets
- travel books (such as *Mobil Travel Guides*)

Note:

The Southern Colonies include Maryland, Virginia, North Carolina, South Carolina, and Georgia. Present-day travel books vary on what states constitute the South. This version includes all of the Southern Colonies plus Alabama, Florida, and West Virginia.

Teacher Preparation:

- Reproduce Activity 3-4, *Take a Trip to the South*, as needed and organize reference materials.
- Divide classes into small groups and assign specific states or regions of the South for students to visit. Encourage groups to center their trip around historical places and events when possible.
- Pass out travel materials and the journal activity. Then allow time for groups to complete the activity. Encourage the inclusion of photographs or illustrations, if possible. When students are finished, allow time for groups to share their journeys with the rest of the class.

Extended Activities:

- Show classes a travel video on one or more of the southern states. Sources for travelogue tapes include educational channel television, video stores, and libraries.
- Encourage students to learn more about the economy of the state they are visiting. What products or services does the state make or provide? What are the major types of jobs in the state? Information on state economy can be found in encyclopedias.

3-4 TAKE A TRIP TO THE SOUTH

DESTINATION _____

For each day, describe the location, place visited, and special activity (such as art, music, food, or holiday).

DAILY ITINERARY

Day 1 _____

_____

_____

Day 2 _____

_____

_____

Day 3 _____

_____

_____

Day 4 _____

_____

_____

Day 5 _____

_____

_____

Day 6 _____

_____

_____

Day 7 _____

_____

_____

3-5 WHAT WILL IT COST?

For the Teacher

Materials Needed:

- copies of Activity 3-5
- travel books
- pencils or pens

Teacher Preparation:

- Reproduce Activity 3-5, *What Will It Cost?*, as needed.
- Pass out the activity and allow time for students to solve the problems. When they are finished, review the answers (given below) with them.

Answer Key:

1. $80
2. $29.80; $4.47; $34.27
3. $10
4. $73.00; $3.65; $76.65
5. $10
6. $80; $34.27; $10; $76.65; $10; $210.92

Extended Activity:

- Have students estimate the costs for one day of *their* trip for a family of four (2 adults and 2 students). Approximate hotel and dining costs can be found in most travel books. Other expenses can be estimated. Although Activity 3-5 can be used as a guide, encourage students to make other selections on how the family will spend the day.

Name _____ **Date** _____ **Period** _____

3-5 WHAT WILL IT COST?

A family of four (2 adults and 2 students) are visiting Virginia, one of the southern states. They decide to spend the day at *Williamsburg*, a reconstruction of the 18th-century colonial capital. Solve the problems below to see how much money they will spend for the day.

1. Admission charge to *Colonial Williamsburg* is $25 for adults and $15 for students. The family needs 2 adults and 2 student tickets.

   How much money for the tickets? $_____

2. The family has lunch at one of the famous eateries of Williamsburg called *Chowning's Tavern*. The lunches are as follows: 2 Brunswick Stew lunches at $5.95 each and 2 Virginia Ham lunches at $8.95 each.

   How much money for the lunches? $_____

   Add a 15% tip. $_____

   What is the total cost for lunches? $_____

3. After lunch the family takes a carriage ride through the Historic Area. The charge is $3 for adults and $2 for students. The family needs 2 adult and 2 student tickets.

   What is the cost of the carriage ride? $_____

4. The family purchases the following items at some of the colonial shops: wooden bowl, $22; pewter cup, $25; Williamsburg cookbook, $14; and colonial board game, $12.

   How much money for all items? $_____

   Add a 5% sales tax. $_____

   What is the total cost for items? $_____

5. Most exhibits and historical buildings in Williamsburg are included in the price of the ticket. Admission to the *Governor's Palace and Gardens*, however, are extra. The cost is $3 for adults and $2 for students. They need 2 adult and 2 student tickets.

   How much money for the admissions? $_____

6. Add all the expenses to see how much the family has spent for the day:

   Total cost for #1. $_____

   Total cost for #2. $_____

   Total cost for #3. $_____

   Total cost for #4. $_____

   Total cost for #5. $_____

   Total cost for the day. $_____

3-6 SOUTHERN TERMS

For the Teacher

Materials Needed:

- copies of Activity 3-6
- copies of *Glossary of Terms* (at back of book)

Teacher Preparation:

- Reproduce Activity 3-6, *Southern Terms*, as needed. Also reproduce copies of the *Glossary* as needed.

- Pass out the activity and allow time for students to complete the matching definitions. When they are finished, review the terms (answers given below) with them.

Answer Key:

b.	Jamestown	c.	Appalachian
l.	charter	e.	back country
k.	bay	f.	cash crop
m.	colony	i.	tobacco
a.	House of Burgesses	g.	plantation
j.	Williamsburg	n.	indentured servant
o.	legislature	q.	slave state
r.	Piedmont	d.	racism
p.	Tidewater	h.	indigo

Extended Activity:

- Use some of the terms in the activity as topics for further research. Appropriate titles include Jamestown, Williamsburg, George Washington, Thomas Jefferson, Mount Vernon, Monticello, and Slavery in America.

3-6 SOUTHERN TERMS

Expand your vocabulary by learning some terms
associated with the Southern Colonies or states.
Match the correct definitions to the words.

_____Jamestown

_____charter

_____bay

_____colony

_____House of Burgesses

_____Williamsburg

_____legislature

_____Piedmont

_____Tidewater

_____Appalachian

_____back country

_____cash crop

_____tobacco

_____plantation

_____indentured servant

_____slave state

_____racism

_____indigo

a. the colonial representative assembly in Virginia

b. name of first English settlement in America

c. major mountain range in the eastern part of the
U.S. extending from Canada to Georgia

d. the belief that one race is superior to another

e. thinly populated rural area along the
Appalachian Mountain range

f. a crop raised to sell for profit on the world market

g. large farms or estates worked by resident labor

h. a plant that produces blue dye and was a cash
crop for southern plantations

i. a plant cultivated as a major crop in Virginia and
used for smoking

j. colonial capital of Virginia from 1799–1870 which
has been reconstructed and opened to the public

k. an inlet off of a larger body of water

l. a written agreement granting privileges from a
sovereign power or country

m. a settlement developed by a country beyond its
borders

n. a person who agrees to work for a certain period
of time in return for travel expenses and keep

o. an organized body of people having the authority
to make laws

p. the low-lying coastal land along an ocean

q. a state in America in which ownership of a Negro
person was legal

r. the land that lies at the base of a mountain

3-7 FOLKTALES AND LITERATURE

For the Teacher

Materials Needed:

- copies of Activity 3-7
- practice paper and pencils
- drawing paper and pens
- (*optional*) black markers and/or colored pencils

Teacher Preparation:

- Reproduce copies of Activity 3-7, *Folktales and Literature*, as needed and organize materials.
- Pass out the activity and allow time for classes to read the Uncle Remus story. When they are finished, discuss the underlying message in the tale.
- On practice paper have students develop a fable of their own that uses animals to convey a story with an underlying message.
- Using good drawing paper and pens, have students rewrite their fable in their best printing or writing.
- (*optional*) Encourage students to illustrate their stories with markers and/or colored pencils.

Extended Activity:

- Set aside time for reading southern folktales and literature. Contact the media person in your building or community for assistance in gathering appropriate materials. When possible, take classes to the library for this activity. There are a number of books available that tell stories about the people from the southern colonies. A brief list follows that will help you get started. **Note**: Remember, this is merely a list of some options. Regional differences may vary, so use whatever is available in your area.

FOLKTALES

The Tales of Uncle Remus by Julius Lester (New York: Dial Books, 1987).

More Tales of Uncle Remus by Julius Lester (New York: Dial Books, 1988).

Further Tales of Uncle Remus by Julius Lester (New York: Dial Books, 1990).

The Last Tales of Uncle Remus by Julius Lester (New York: Dial Books, 1994).

The hilarious adventures of Brer Rabbit have delighted all ages for many years. Master storyteller Julius Lester carries on the black American folk tradition with the tales of Brer Rabbit and Brer Fox. Originally these tales were created by Joel Chandler Harris who observed the folktale and speech patterns of southern blacks. He used his observations to create the characters of Uncle Remus, Brer Rabbit, and Brer Fox.

The Talking Eggs by Robert D. San Souci (New York: Dial Books, 1989). The author and illustrator capture the flavor of the American South in this unforgettable story about outside and inside beauty.

American Tall Tales by Mary Pope Osborne (New York: Random House, 1991). Meet some of America's folk heroes. From the south there is John Henry, the black railroad worker with his mighty hammer.

CHILDREN'S BOOKS

A Williamsburg Household by Joan Anderson (Boston: Houghton Mifflin, 1990). The author gives a fascinating look at life in 18th-century Williamsburg, Virginia for whites as well as blacks. The story focuses on the daily events of the fictional Moody family and their slaves.

The Double Life of Pocahontas by Jean Fritz (New York: Marshall Cavendish, 1991).

Pocahontas: True Princess by Mari Hanes (Sisters, OR: Questar, 1995).

Pocahontas: Princess of the River Tribes by Elaine Raphael and Don Bolognese (New York: Scholastic, 1995).

Pocahontas: The True Story of the Powhatan Princess by Catherine Iannone (Broomall, PA: Chelsea House, 1995).

There are several books available telling the story of Pocahontas and Captain John Smith from the Jamestown colony. Choose these or others that are available in your community.

CLASSICAL LITERATURE *(for older students)*

Gone With the Wind by Margaret Mitchell (various editions available). This is an epic romance set in the south during the time of the Civil War. The story was made into a 1939 award-winning film starring Clark Gable and Vivien Leigh.

A Pocketful of Goobers: A Story about George Washington Carver by Barbara Mitchell (Minneapolis: Lerner, 1986). Carver devoted much of his life and talents to growing and developing products and recipes from peanuts.

The Gift of the Magi by O. Henry (various editions available)

The Furnished Room by O. Henry (various editions available)

Cabbages and Kings by O. Henry (various editions available)

William Sydney Porter used the pen name of O. Henry. He grew up during the Civil War and became one of America's favorite short-story writers. Many of his tales revolve around human weakness as well as the influence of chance happenings.

My Bondage and My Freedom by Frederick Douglass (various editions available). Although born as a slave, Douglass escaped to freedom. He lectured and wrote about the evils of slavery.

3-7 FOLKTALES AND LITERATURE

The following is an adaptation of one of *The Tales of Uncle Remus* as told by Julius Lester. Read the story. Then develop an animal tale of your own.

BRER RABBIT COMES TO DINNER

Brer Rabbit and Brer Fox both lived in the forest, but they did not trust one another. Brer Fox often planned schemes to get Brer Rabbit. This tale is about one of those times.

One day Brer Fox met Brer Rabbit strolling along the road near the forest where they both lived. As they met Brer Fox grinned sheepishly and told Brer Rabbit he wanted to make a confession. Brer Rabbit scratched his head a bit in somewhat disbelief but decided to listen to what Brer Fox had to say. Brer Fox told Brer Rabbit that he felt bad that they were not friends and wanted a chance to show that he was sincere. In order to show Brer Rabbit his good intentions, Brer Fox invited him to dinner that very evening.

Brer Rabbit wanted to be friends with Brer Fox so when evening came, he went to his house for dinner. No sooner had Brer Rabbit stepped in the house when he heard an awful groaning. There was Brer Fox sitting in his rocking chair with a blanket over his shoulder looking pale and lifeless. Brer Rabbit looked around but saw no supper on the stove. However, he did see a long knife and a roasting pan sitting on the counter.

Brer Rabbit asked Brer Fox what they were having for dinner. Brer Fox said, "We're having chicken with cabbage and roastin' ears." Before Brer Fox could say another thing, Brer Rabbit was out the door and into the bushes to see if Brer Fox was sho' nuf' sick.

Soon Brer Fox appeared on the porch looking as healthy as a horse. Brer Rabbit peered from behind the bushes and called to Brer Fox, "I have a cabbage right here for you to have with your chicken tonight." As soon as Brer Fox saw him, he leaped from the porch and took off after Brer Rabbit. However, Brer Rabbit was much too fast for Brer Fox. He was halfway home before Brer Fox's claws touched the ground. Once again Brer Rabbit escaped one of Brer Fox's schemes to catch him.

3-8 PASTIMES AND SPORTS

For the Teacher

Materials Needed:

- copies of Activity 3-8
- items mentioned in "Teacher Preparation"

Teacher Preparation:

- Reproduce Activity 3-8, *Pastimes and Sports,* as needed.
- Pass out the activity and go over the pastimes outlined. If possible, *allow students to help make choices on which activities will be selected. Then set aside some time for participation.*
- If *Scrabble®, dominoes,* or *croquet* are selected, ask for volunteers to bring in games to share with classes.
- If participating in sports is possible, contact the Physical Education person in your building well in advance and organize games of *badminton* or *cricket.*

3-8 PASTIMES AND SPORTS

People in the South who owned large homes often had a parlor. A *parlor* is a special room where families invited guests to visit or play games. Because games were often played in the special room, they became known as *parlor games*.

PARLOR GAMES

Parlor games often involved several players. Three popular types of parlor activities included guessing games, word games, and table games. Two types of guessing games included *charades* and *twenty questions* which are still played today. A well-known word game was *anagrams*. *Dominoes* became a favorite table game of the colonial era. In fact, it is still popular today.

CHARADES (8 TO 20 PLAYERS)

Charades is a fun game for several players. It is played in the following manner. The players are divided into two groups. Each person (in both groups) writes down the name of a song, film, or book on a piece of paper and places it in a container. Players take turns drawing from the container and acting out the mystery words within a time frame of two minutes. The team with more correct guesses wins the charade.

TWENTY QUESTIONS

The game of *twenty questions* was popular with many settlers throughout the colonies. It is still a fun game today. Each person thinks of a person, place, or thing. Then, in turns, other players try to guess what the person is thinking. The players may ask no more than twenty questions that can be answered by "yes" or "no." The game is continued until answers are discovered or twenty questions have been asked.

ANAGRAMS

A popular colonial word game was *Anagrams*. The modern version of this game is *Scrabble*®. In colonial days, players used small squares of paper with various letters of the alphabet written on one side. Squares were placed face down. Then players took turns turning over a square and trying to make a word. As words are made, new letters are turned over. The game is played until all letters on the board are used. The winner is the one with the most word formations.

DOMINOES

Dominoes has been a popular game in America for many years. As colonial children grew older they enjoyed games that were more complicated. This popular game of placing black rectangular blocks in specific arrangements remains popular during modern times. Consult the rules of the game for specific details.

GAMES AND SPORTS

Two outside games that were popular during the colonial era included *lawn bowls* and *badminton*. A modern version of lawn bowls is *croquet*. An organized team sport that gained favor during the colonial era was *cricket*.

©1997 by The Center for Applied Research in Education

3-9 SOUNDS OF THE SOUTH

For the Teacher

Materials Needed:

- sheet music, CD, cassette, or film
- audio-visual equipment

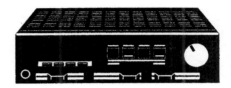

Teacher Preparation:

- *Francis Scott Key* (1779–1843) was an American lawyer and poet born in Frederick County, Maryland. During the War of 1812 he witnessed the British bombardment of Baltimore Harbor. The sight of the American flag still flying at daybreak inspired Key to write "The Star Spangled Banner." In 1931 the song became the national anthem of America. Most Americans know the first verse of the song, but how many know who wrote it or when it was written. Obtain copies of the song and encourage students to listen for a renewed awareness of the national anthem. Also encourage them to become familiar with the lesser known verses.

- *Gospel* embraces several types of song, all of which share a personal identification with the bible in rich musical vocabulary. Gospel music, particularly from the black Baptist churches in the south, is important because it has influenced white gospel forms as well as certain styles of popular music. *Mahalia Jackson*, perhaps, is most well known for her gospel-style recordings. Have the classes listen to some of her recordings. For listening to gospel music, check with your local library or record store for specific titles. Also consider the following option:

  Mahalia Jackson's Greatest Hits (Columbia Records, New York). The recording includes sixteen of Jackson's most requested songs. Jackson has several recordings and is considered a master of gospel.

- *Aretha Franklin* also has several recordings. She reproduces the vocal devices of gospel that has come to be known as *Soul*. Franklin is well known for the use of falsetto, shouts, and stretching out a single-sung syllable over several notes. For listening to Franklin, consider the following options:

  30 Greatest Hits of Aretha Franklin
  (Atlantic Recording Corporation, New York, 1996).

  Aretha Franklin, Amazing Grace
  with James Cleveland and The Southern California Community Choir (Atlantic Recording Corporation, New York, originally recorded 1972).

3-10 SILHOUETTES

For the Teacher

Materials Needed:

- copies of Activity 3-10
- practice paper and pencils
- 9" × 12" black construction paper
- 9" × 12" white drawing paper
- scissors
- glue

Teacher Preparation:

- Reproduce Activity 3-10, *Silhouettes*, as needed and organize materials. The suggested size for silhouettes is 9" × 12" because it is an easy size for students to use. However, other sizes may be used as well. School-grade construction paper is suggested because it is inexpensive and easy to attain.
- Pass out the activity and go over the information with your students.
- Distribute the materials and allow time for students to draw silhouettes of each other.
- When they are finished, display the silhouettes around the room.

Extended Activity:

- Stitchery and needlepoint were popular crafts in the South during colonial days. Contact the art teacher well in advance and coordinate a stitchery or needlepoint activity while classes are learning about the Southern colonies.

Photo 3-5 *Student stitchery, collection of the author.* The stitchery shown in the photo was done on burlap using various colors and weights of yarn. The project uses less expensive materials than many stitchery projects and is an excellent activity for beginners.

Photo 3-6 *Needlepoint sampler, collection of the author.* The needlepoint shown in this photo is called a "sampler" because students learn to make many kinds of stitches before they begin creating a needlepoint piece. Creating samplers was commonly practiced during colonial times.

3-10 SILHOUETTES

Paper crafting was a prized colonial art form. Paper is plentiful today, but in colonial times it was considered a luxury. One form of paper crafting popular during colonial times were *shadowgrams*. Shadows were produced when a person sat between a lighted candle and a piece of light paper or cloth. The shadow maker drew an outline drawing of the person from the shadows, then inked in the drawing. Most shadowgrams were portraits done with black ink on white backgrounds.

Shadowgrams were also called *silhouettes* after a French Minister, Etienne Silhouette. Instead of using shadows, the silhouette artist cut profile portraits directly from black paper. *Profile* means the drawing is done from a side view. *Portrait* generally refers to a drawing of a person's head, shoulder, and upper chest portion of the body. Another type of silhouette drawing during colonial times was figure drawing. *Figure drawing* silhouettes are outlined and filled-in drawings of the entire body.

Although portraits and figure drawings were the most common type of silhouettes produced during the 18th century, master silhouette cutters detailed pictures of other subjects as well. Nature, pets, farm animals, ships, and carriages were all used as subjects for the silhouette artist.

The profile silhouettes shown here illustrate the popularity of the colonial craft. It presented an inexpensive way of doing portraits and possessed a unique charm all its own!
Illustrations from *Silhouettes* by Carol Belanger Grafton, Dover Publications.

3-10 SILHOUETTES (continued)

The figure drawing silhouettes shown here illustrate how the outline drawings of the entire body were done during colonial times. Although the illustrations show the silhouettes of women, the craft was popular among men and children as well. **Illustrations from *Silhouettes* by Carol Belanger Grafton, Dover Publications.**

Steps to Making Silhouettes

1. On practice paper develop several profile portrait drawings using classmates as models. Concentrate on the *outline shape of the person only*. Do not attempt to make any type of detail.

2. Select the best drawing and transfer it to black paper.

3. Cut out the drawing and glue it to a white background.

   Hint: Use glue sparingly so glue will not seep out around the edges of the silhouette.

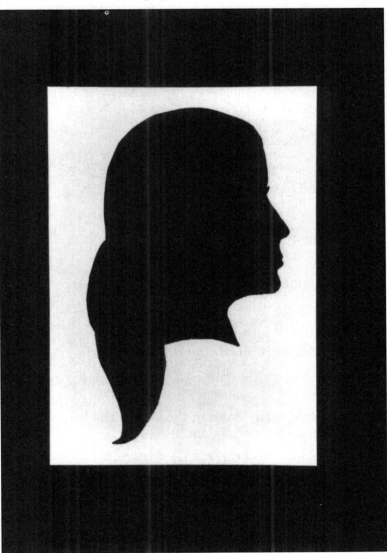

Photo 3-7 *Student silhouette, collection of the author.*
The silhouette above was done by a student during the time classes were learning about the Thirteen Colonies. Students took turns posing as models while others drew outline sketches of their faces. When they were satisfied with one of the sketches, they redrew it on black paper and cut it out. Although portraits were the most popular type of silhouette created in colonial times, sometimes artists drew outlines of their pets or nature.

3-11 POMANDER BALLS

Making pomander balls is an excellent do-on-your-own activity. **Pomander balls** are a mixture of aromatic substances that are enclosed in a cloth or bag and used to create fragrant smells for a room, dresser drawer, closet, or hand bag. Pomander balls are usually made from oranges, apples, lemons, or limes. Cinnamon and cloves provide the aromatic scents to the fruit and cheesecloth is the wrapping material. Because cheesecloth is loosely woven, the aromatic scents from the fruit and spices escape easily.

Colonial women enjoyed making fragrant pomander balls, which served two purposes: (1) they concealed unpleasant cooking odors or the strong smell of tobacco and wood smoke from the fireplace, (2) they provided attractive table decorations. A woman often tucked a spiced pomander ball into her purse when traveling so she could sniff its sweet scents. During the Christmas season pomander balls were used as gifts to friends or hung as decoration on trees. To make your own pomander balls, just follow the easy steps outlined.

Materials Needed:

- oranges, lemons, or limes
- toothpicks
- cloves
- cinnamon or allspice
- scissors
- cheesecloth
- yarn or ribbon

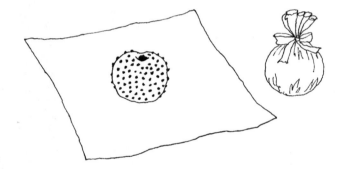

Steps to Making Pomander Balls:

1. Select firm, ripe fruit. Although oranges, apples, lemons, and limes are all used, oranges are the most common.

2. Prick many tiny holes in the skin of the fruit with a toothpick. Keep holes fairly close together and work in small areas.

3. Gently push a clove in each toothpick hole.

4. Sprinkle the fruit with cinnamon or allspice.

5. Place the fruit in the center of a cheesecloth square. The cheesecloth holds the fruit and spices together.

6. Draw the corners of the cheesecloth together at the top and tie tightly with a length of yarn or ribbon.

7. Allow the pomander ball to dry in a cool, dark place (such as a closet) for about two weeks or until the fruit has hardened.

8. Prick holes in the cheesecloth and place pomander balls in a bowl for a table arrangement or place in a dresser drawer. These spicy balls also make nice gifts to friends or serve as decorations for holidays.

©1997 by The Center for Applied Research in Education

3-12 BASICS OF SOUTHERN COOKING

For the Teacher

Materials Needed:

- copies of Activity 3-12
- pencils

Teacher Preparation:

- Reproduce Activity 3-12, *Basics of Southern Cooking*, as needed.
- Pass out the activity and allow time for students to read the information and complete the worksheet. (Answers given below.) When they are finished, review the food basics of the South.

Answer Key:

Part One:

Meats: chicken; pork

Seafood: crab; oysters; shrimp; lobster

Vegetables: sweet potatoes; rice; grits; turnip greens; spinach; green beans

Breads: biscuits; cornbread; hush puppies; Sally Lunn

Pies: sweet potato; pecan

Elegant desserts: strawberry flummery; trifle

Favorite dishes: fried chicken; baked ham; Brunswick stew; salmagundi

Part Two:

Gumbos: soups using seafood or meats and vegetables thickened with okra pods

Hush puppies: round, deep-fried breads made from cornmeal

Sally Lunn: a yeast bread

Strawberry Flummery: a pudding topped with fresh strawberries

Trifle: a dessert made from layers of sponge cake, jam or fruit, pudding, and whipped cream

Brunswick stew: a thickened one-pot meal made from meat, onions, potatoes, tomatoes, corn, and beans

Salmagundi: a salad consisting of lettuce, grapes, hard-cooked eggs, and chicken strips topped with a vinaigrette dressing

Part Three:

According to legend, hush puppies were named because they were fed to hound dogs as a way to quiet them.

According to legend, Sally Lunn was a young girl in the 18th century who sold sweet yeast bread on the streets of Bath, England.

Extended Activity:

• Encourage students to collectively develop a Southern cookbook. Divide classes into groups and assign specific topics to each group. Appropriate topics include Soups, Breads, Vegetables, Seafood, Meats, and Desserts. After students have collected and submitted their recipes, duplicate them and allow each person to organize a cookbook of his or her own.

3-12 BASICS OF SOUTHERN COOKING

For the colonists in Virginia, Maryland, and North Carolina tobacco planting became a source of great prosperity. Large plantations developed using slaves to work the fields. Two styles of cooking developed on southern plantations. One was connected to the foods served in the "Great House" on the plantation, which became closely associated with delicious food and great hospitality. The other food style, from the slaves' quarters, is called "soul food" and is connected to many inventive ways of cooking using simple ingredients.

BASIC FOODS

Meats: *Chicken* and *pork* were used in abundance in the South. In fact, southern fried chicken and smoked hams are two southern specialties that have gained wide acceptance across America.

Seafood was plentiful along the Atlantic coast and was an important part of the southern meals. *Crab, oysters, shrimp,* and *lobster* were all used. The seafood gumbos that emerged from this region are credited to the influence of the Afro-American cooks. Gumbos are soups using seafood or meats and vegetables thickened with okra pods.

Vegetables: *Sweet potatoes, rice, grits, turnip greens, spinach,* and *green beans* rank high among the favorite vegetables used in the South. The ever-popular sweet potato can be baked, boiled, fried, mashed, or candied.

Breads: *Baking powder biscuits, cornbread, hush puppies,* and *Sally Lunn* represent four popular southern breads. Hush puppies are round, deep-fried breads made from cornmeal. According to legend, hush puppies were named because they were fed to hound dogs as a way to quiet them. Sally Lunn is a yeast bread named after a young girl in the 18th century. Legend tells that Sally Lunn sold the sweet yeast bread on the streets of Bath in England.

Desserts: Delicious baked goods are specialties of the South that have gained wide acceptance. Two pie favorites are *sweet potato pie* and *pecan pie*. Elegant desserts include names like *strawberry flummery* and *trifle*. Strawberry flummery is a pudding topped with fresh strawberries. Trifle is a dessert made from layers of sponge cake, jam or fruit, pudding, and whipped cream. Both desserts offer a delightful finish to any special occasion.

FAVORITE DISHES

There are many delicious dishes and specialties that have come out of southern kitchens. A few include *southern fried chicken, Virginia baked ham, Brunswick stew* and *salmagundi*. Brunswick stew is a thickened one-pot meal made from meat, onions, potatoes, tomatoes, corn, and beans. Salmagundi is an elegant salad consisting of lettuce, grapes, hard-cooked eggs, and chicken strips topped with a vinaigrette dressing.

3-12 BASICS OF SOUTHERN COOKING

Part One: Use the boxes below to outline some of the food basics of southern cooking.

Meats: _____ _____

Seafood: _____ _____

_____ _____

Vegetables: _____ _____

_____ _____

_____ _____

Breads: _____ _____

_____ _____

Pies: _____ _____

Elegant Desserts: _____

_____

Favorite Dishes: _____ _____

_____ _____

3-12 BASICS OF SOUTHERN COOKING (continued)

Part Two: Write the definitions of the foods listed below.

Gumbo _____

_____

Hush puppies _____

_____

Sally Lunn _____

_____

Strawberry Flummery _____

_____

Trifle _____

_____

Brunswick Stew _____

_____

Salmagundi _____

_____

Part Three:

According to legend, how were hush puppies named?

_____

_____

According to legend, how was Sally Lunn named?

_____

_____

3-13 DINING IN THE COLONIAL SOUTH

For the Teacher

Hint: It is helpful to complete Activity 3-12, *Basics of Southern Cooking*, before participating in this one.

Materials Needed:

- copies of Activity 3-13
- pencils or pens

Teacher Preparation:

- Reproduce Activity 3-13, *Dining in the Colonial South*, as needed.

- Pass out the activity. Then allow students time to read the menu and make their dinner selections. Next, have them make a list of the foods that would be served for a special-occasion dinner at their house. When they are finished, lead a discussion to compare the food items used during the colonial south to the special-occasion dinner of their family. How many dishes are familiar? Have the students eaten any of these regional specialties?

Extended Activity:

- Ask students to bring in some simple or ready-prepared foods that are southern in origin. Dessert choices may include ready-made pecan or sweet potato pies. Other choices include biscuits with jelly or honey and biscuits with ham (sandwiches).

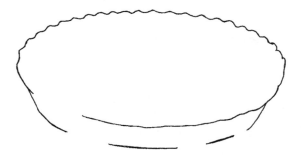

3-13 DINING IN THE COLONIAL SOUTH

There are many restaurants throughout the South that offer typical foods eaten during the colonial era. Below is a menu listing some of the specialties associated with the delicious food and great hospitality of the colonial south.

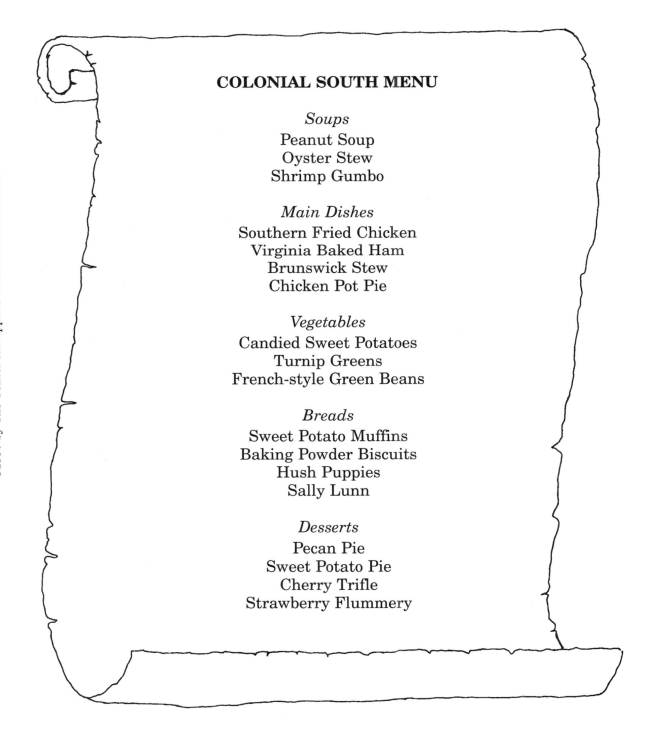

COLONIAL SOUTH MENU

Soups
Peanut Soup
Oyster Stew
Shrimp Gumbo

Main Dishes
Southern Fried Chicken
Virginia Baked Ham
Brunswick Stew
Chicken Pot Pie

Vegetables
Candied Sweet Potatoes
Turnip Greens
French-style Green Beans

Breads
Sweet Potato Muffins
Baking Powder Biscuits
Hush Puppies
Sally Lunn

Desserts
Pecan Pie
Sweet Potato Pie
Cherry Trifle
Strawberry Flummery

3-13 DINING IN THE COLONIAL SOUTH

Look over the southern colonial menu offerings. Then, in the spaces provided on the left, make your selections for a typical elegant colonial dinner.

Next, in the spaces provided on the right, list the items your family might have for a special occasion. Then compare the southern colonial dinner to your own. Are there any similarities? What are the differences?

Colonial South Menu (choose as many as you want)	*Special-Occasion Dinner* (choose as many as you want)
Soup	Soup
_____	_____
_____	_____
_____	_____
Main Dishes	Main Dishes
_____	_____
_____	_____
_____	_____
_____	_____
Vegetables	Vegetables
_____	_____
_____	_____
_____	_____
Breads	Breads
_____	_____
_____	_____
_____	_____
_____	_____
Desserts	Desserts
_____	_____
_____	_____
_____	_____
_____	_____

3-14 SWEET POTATO MUFFINS

For the Teacher

Equipment Needed:

- copies of Activity 3-14
- mixing bowls
- hand mixer
- spoon
- measuring spoons
- measuring cup
- paper muffin cups
- muffin tins

Supplies Needed:

- canned sweet potatoes
- egg
- milk
- vegetable oil
- flour
- white sugar
- brown sugar
- baking powder
- cinnamon
- all-spice
- salt
- chopped walnuts
- (*optional*) cinnamon sugar

Teacher Preparation:

- Reproduce Activity 3-14, *Sweet Potato Muffins*, as needed and organize equipment and supplies.
- Give a demonstration on making Sweet Potato Muffins as students follow along with the recipe. Follow up with a muffin tasting treat.
- **ALTERNATIVE**: Go over the recipe with students. Then ask for volunteers and make an out-of-class assignment for students to make muffins at home and bring them to school for a special Southern treat day. Encourage students to ask for adult assistance when baking the muffins.

Extended Activity:

- Contact the Consumer and Family Living teacher well in advance to coordinate a Southern colonial lunch or dessert lab activity while your classes are learning about the South.

3-14 SWEET POTATO MUFFINS

Sweet breads were popular during the colonial era in the South. They were especially desirable as a light snack served with tea between meals. Sweet potato and corn muffins represent two types of breads served in taverns or eateries in Colonial Williamsburg. Sweet potato muffins are made from flour and considered to be a finer, lighter bread. Corn muffins, on the other hand, use corn meal which is heavier and more substantial. This recipe makes 1 dozen muffins.

You need:

1	cup canned sweet potatoes, drained
1	egg
3/4	cup milk
1/2	cup vegetable oil
2	cups flour
1/2	cup brown sugar
1	cup white sugar
3	teaspoons baking powder
1	teaspoon cinnamon
1/2	teaspoon all-spice
	dash salt
2/3	cup chopped walnuts
	(*optional*) cinnamon sugar

What to do:

1. Preheat oven to 375°.
2. In a small mixing bowl, mash enough sweet potatoes with a fork to measure 1 cup.
3. In a medium-sized mixing bowl, beat egg. Then add sweet potatoes, milk, and vegetable oil. Blend thoroughly with a hand mixer.
4. Add flour, sugars, baking powder, cinnamon, all-spice, and salt to liquid mixture. Blend together until thoroughly mixed.
5. By hand, stir in walnuts.
6. Place paper muffin cups into muffin tins.
7. Fill each paper cup about three-fourths full with batter.
8. (*optional*) Sprinkle tops with cinnamon sugar.
9. Bake about 20 minutes or until an inserted toothpick comes out clean.
10. Cool. Then serve with margarine, butter, or cream cheese, if desired.

3-15 SOUTHERN PEANUT PIE

For the Teacher

Equipment Needed:

- copies of Activity 3-15
- 9" pie plate
- mixing bowl
- spoon
- measuring cup
- measuring spoons
- hand mixer
- cookie sheet

Supplies Needed:

- ready-made unbaked pie crust
- eggs
- sugar
- corn syrup
- margarine or butter
- salted peanuts

Teacher Preparation:

- Reproduce Activity 3-15, *Southern Peanut Pie*, as needed and organize equipment and supplies.
- Give a demonstration on making Southern Peanut Pie as students follow along with the recipe. Follow up with a peanut pie tasting treat.
- **ALTERNATIVE**: Go over the recipe with students. Then ask for volunteers and make an out-of-class assignment for students to make the pie at home and bring it to school for a special Southern treat day. Encourage students to ask for adult assistance when making the pie.

3-15 SOUTHERN PEANUT PIE

Pecans and peanuts are grown in the South, so cooks have found many delicious ways to use them in their recipes. Perhaps the most well-known southern dessert is Pecan Pie. However, pies and other sweets are made from peanuts as well. In this recipe, salted peanuts are combined with corn syrup and eggs to provide a variation to the traditional Southern Pecan Pie. This recipe serves 6 to 8.

You need:

1	ready-made unbaked pie crust
3	eggs
2/3	cup sugar
1	cup corn syrup
1/3	cup margarine or butter
1	cup salted peanuts
	(*optional*) whipped cream

What to do:

1. Preheat oven to 375°.
2. Line 9" pie pan with ready-made pie crust and flute edges.
3. In a mixing bowl, beat eggs.
4. Add sugar, corn syrup, and melted margarine. Then mix thoroughly.
5. Stir in peanuts.
6. Pour into pastry-lined pie shell.
7. Place pie in the middle of a cookie sheet and bake for 40–50 minutes or until golden brown.
8. Cool.
9. Serve with whipped cream, if desired.

Southern Pecan Pie: Substitute 1 cup pecan halves or broken pecans for the salted peanuts.

BIBLIOGRAPHY FOR THE SOUTHERN COLONIES

Art

Hoople, Cheryl. *The Heritage Sampler: A Book of Colonial Arts and Crafts.* New York: Dial Press, 1975.

Children's Fiction

Lester, Julius. *The Tales of Uncle Remus.* New York: Dial Books, 1987.

Children's Nonfiction

Kent, Deborah. *America the Beautiful: Maryland.* Chicago: Children's Press, 1990.

Kent, Deborah. *America the Beautiful: South Carolina.* Chicago: Children's Press, 1990.

Kent, Zachary. *America the Beautiful: Georgia.* Chicago: Children's Press, 1988.

McNair, Sylvia. *America the Beautiful: Alabama.* Chicago: Children's Press, 1989.

McNair, Sylvia. *America the Beautiful: Virginia.* Chicago: Children's Press, 1992.

Stein, Conrad. *America the Beautiful: North Carolina.* Chicago: Children's Press, 1990.

Stein, Conrad. *America the Beautiful: West Virginia.* Chicago: Children's Press, 1991.

Stone, Lynn. *America the Beautiful: Florida.* Chicago: Children's Press, 1987.

Cookbooks

Barchers, Suzanne and Patricia Marden. *Cooking Up U.S. History.* Englewood, CO: Teacher Ideas Press, 1991.

Parham, Vanessa Roberts. *The African-American Heritage Cookbook.* South Pasadena, CA: Sandcastle Publishing, 1993.

Music

Staff. *Academic American Encyclopedia, Volume 1.* Danbury, CT: Grolier, 1996.

Pastimes

Kalman, Bobbie. *Games from Long Ago.* New York: Crabtree Publishing, 1995.

Kalman, Bobbie, and David Schimpky. *Old-Time Toys.* New York: Crabtree Publishing, 1995.

Social Studies

Bass, Herbert. *People in Time and Place: Our Country*. Parsippany, NJ: Silver Burdett & Ginn, 1991.

Davidson, James West and John Batchelor. *The American Nation*. Englewood Cliffs, NJ: Prentice Hall, 1991.

Travel

Staff. *Mobile 1996 Travel Guide, Mid-Atlantic*. New York: Fodor's Travel Publications, 1996.

Staff. *Mobile 1996 Travel Guide, Southeast*. New York: Fodor's Travel Publications, 1996.

UNIT TWO

AN EXPANDING NATION

Section 4, The Midwest and Great Plains—The settling of America by Europeans is the story of people moving westward. During the late 1700s and early 1800s a flood of pioneers crossed the Appalachian Mountains into the region called **the Northwest Territory**. Today this area is often referred to as **the Midwest** and includes the states of Michigan, Ohio, Indiana, Illinois, Wisconsin, and Minnesota.

In 1803 the United States bought a large section of land from France that nearly doubled the size of America. This acquisition was called **The Louisiana Purchase** and consisted of the land west of the Mississippi River to the Rocky Mountains. A large portion of this territory has become known as **the Great Plains** and includes the states of Iowa, Missouri, Kansas, Nebraska, North Dakota, and South Dakota.

Although you will learn about all the states in the Midwest and Great Plains, known as "the Heartland," the focus of Section 4 is **Greenfield Village** in Dearborn, Michigan. The village portrays how farm families lived and worked during the 1800s. During the 19th century, the Firestone family operated a farm in Ohio. Its restored home and other buildings have been moved to Greenfield Village where the public is invited to visit.

Section 5, The Mississippi Valley—The pioneers who crossed the Appalachian Mountains from the southern colonies settled the land below the Ohio River. Today this region is called **the Mississippi Valley** or **South Central** and includes the states of Kentucky, Arkansas, Tennessee, Mississippi, and Louisiana. Generally the Mississippi Valley is considered to be a part of the South.

Steamboatin' on the mighty Mississippi River was an opulent lifestyle for the privileged during the 19th century. In Section 5 you will learn about life on the Mississippi. Also featured in this section is **New Orleans**, a unique city in America that developed from three distinct cultures—Creoles, Cajuns, and African-Americans.

SECTION 4

THE MIDWEST AND GREAT PLAINS

Below is an outline of the interdisciplinary activities included in this section. They are designed to bring a broad range of hands-on cultural lessons and activities into the social studies classroom. Pick and choose the ones that best fit into your program.

Social Studies

4-1   Getting to Know the Heartland
4-2   People of the Heartland
4-3   19th-Century Farm Life
4-4   Take a Trip to the Heartland

Mathematics

4-5   What Will It Cost?

Language Arts

4-6   Heartland Terms
4-7   Folktales and Literature

Physical Education

4-8   Pastimes and Games

Music

4-9   Sounds of the Heartland

Art

4-10   Quilting Bees
4-11   Pierced Paper

Consumer and Family Living

4-12   Basics of Heartland Cooking
4-13   A Midwest Work-Play Dinner
4-14   Cider Pie
4-15   Strawberry Shortcake

Bibliography for the Midwest and Great Plains

MAP OF THE MIDWEST AND GREAT PLAINS

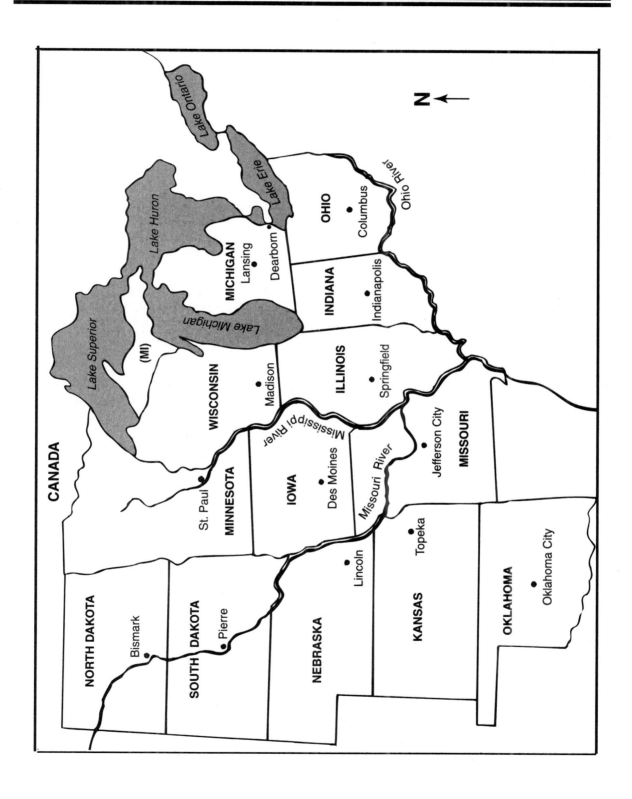

4-1 GETTING TO KNOW THE HEARTLAND

For the Teacher

Materials Needed:

- copies of Activity 4-1
- labeled map of Midwest and Great Plains (enlarged on opaque projector)
- copies of unlabeled maps of Midwest and Great Plains
- (colored) pencils

Teacher Preparation:

- Reproduce Activity 4-1, *Getting to Know the Heartland*, as needed. Also reproduce copies of unlabeled maps of the Midwest and the Great Plains as needed.
- Pass out the activity and maps to each student. Then allow time for students to locate and label the Midwest and Great Plains as outlined in the activity. When they are finished, review the geography with them.

Extended Activities:

- Reproduce additional copies of the maps and have students identify other features of the Midwest and Great Plains states, such as population distribution, land use, or climate. PC Globe® computer program can provide much of the information needed for this activity. Consult your school's media person for assistance, too.
- Reproduce the chart of *The Fifty States* (at back of book) as needed. Pass out the chart and have students make a list of the Midwest and Great Plains states, date they entered the Union, order of entry, capital, and largest city. *List states in order they entered the union.* Answers should appear as follows:

Midwest State	Date Entered Union	Order of Entry	Capital	Largest City
Ohio	1803	17	Columbus	Columbus
Indiana	1816	19	Indianapolis	Indianapolis
Illinois	1818	21	Springfield	Chicago
Michigan	1837	26	Lansing	Detroit
Wisconsin	1848	30	Madison	Milwaukee
Minnesota	1858	32	St. Paul	Minneapolis

Great Plains State	Date Entered Union	Order of Entry	Capital	Largest City
Missouri	1821	24	Jefferson City	St. Louis
Iowa	1846	29	Des Moines	Des Moines
Kansas	1861	34	Topeka	Wichita
Nebraska	1867	37	Lincoln	Omaha
North Dakota	1889	39	Bismarck	Fargo
South Dakota	1889	40	Pierre	Sioux Falls
Oklahoma	1907	46	Oklahoma City	Oklahoma City

4-1 GETTING TO KNOW THE HEARTLAND

Use the map provided to locate and label the following **Midwest** features:

State: Illinois
Capital: Springfield

State: Indiana
Capital: Indianapolis

State: Ohio
Capital: Columbus

State: Michigan
Capital: Lansing
19th-century settlement: Dearborn

State: Minnesota
Capital: St. Paul

State: Wisconsin
Capital: Madison

Bodies of water: Lake Erie, Lake Huron, Lake Michigan, Lake Superior, Lake Ontario, Ohio River

Neighboring country: Canada

4-1 GETTING TO KNOW THE HEARTLAND

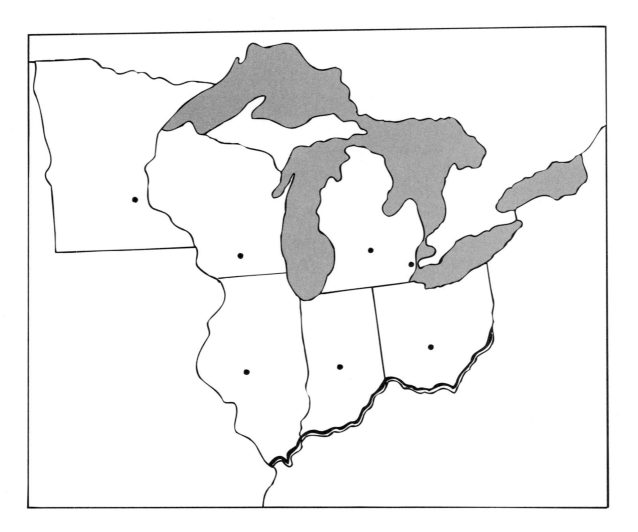

4-1 GETTING TO KNOW THE HEARTLAND (continued)

Use the map provided to locate and label the following **Great Plains** features:

State: Iowa
Capital: Des Moines

State: Kansas
Capital: Topeka

State: Missouri
Capital: Jefferson City

State: Nebraska
Capital: Lincoln

State: North Dakota
Capital: Bismarck

State: South Dakota
Capital: Pierre

State: Oklahoma
Capital: Oklahoma City

Bodies of water: Mississippi River, Missouri River

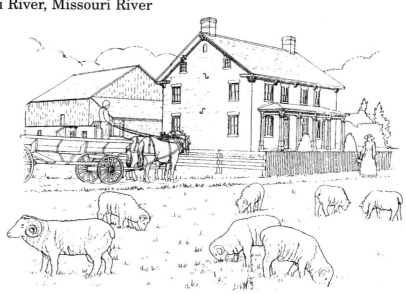

4-1 GETTING TO KNOW THE HEARTLAND

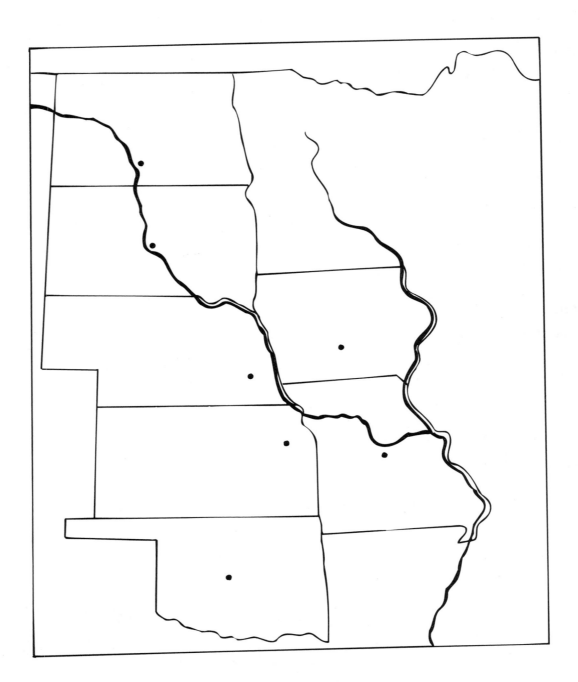

4-2 PEOPLE OF THE HEARTLAND

For the Teacher

Materials Needed:

- copies of Activity 4-2
- pencils
- research materials

Teacher Preparation:

- Reproduce Activity 4-2A and 4-2B, *People of the Heartland*, as needed.
- Pass out the activity and allow time for students to complete the word search puzzle. When they are finished, review the answers (given below) with them.

Answer Key:

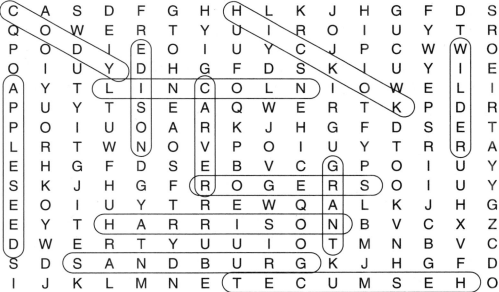

Extended Activities:

- Encourage students to pick one of the famous people in the puzzle (or another person from the heartland who has made a contribution to America) and assign research papers on his or her life and contributions. Use the outline provided in Activity 4-2B to develop the reports.
- Films have been made about most of the famous people in the puzzle. Select one and show it to your classes.

4-2A PEOPLE OF THE HEARTLAND

Listed below are some of the people who lived in or had some influence on the development of the Midwest and Great Plains. In the word search puzzle, locate and circle the names of these famous people. **Hint:** When locating the names, look for *the last name only*. You will find them across, diagonal, or down. After completing the puzzle, choose one of the famous persons and write a report of his or her life and accomplishments.

Abraham Lincoln   (1809–1865) 16th president of the United States

Ulysses S. Grant   (1822–1885) 18th president of the United States

Thomas Edison   (1847–1931) one of the world's greatest inventors

James (Wild Bill) Hickok   (1837–1876) frontiersman known for his shooting ability

Laura Ingalls Wilder   (1867–1957) wrote *Little House on the Prairie,* among others

William Henry Harrison   (1773–1841) 9th president of the United States

Carl Sandburg   (1878–1967) poet regarded as voice of the Midwest common man

Will Rogers   (1879–1935) humorist and entertainer

George Washington Carver   (1864–1943) botanist who developed products from peanuts and sweet potatoes

"Buffalo Bill" Cody   (1846–1917) guide, scout, and Pony Express rider

Tecumseh   (1768–1813) Shawnee Indian leader

Johnny Appleseed   (1774–1847) born John Chapman, American folk hero

©1997 by The Center for Applied Research in Education

```
C  A  S  D  F  G  H  H  L  K  J  H  G  F  D  S
Q  O  W  E  R  T  Y  U  I  R  O  I  U  Y  T  R
P  O  D  I  E  O  I  U  Y  C  J  P  C  W  W  O
O  I  U  Y  D  H  G  F  D  S  K  I  U  Y  I  E
A  Y  T  L  I  N  C  O  L  N  I  O  W  E  L  I
P  U  Y  T  S  E  A  Q  W  E  R  T  K  P  D  R
P  O  I  U  O  A  R  K  J  H  G  F  D  S  E  T
L  R  T  W  N  O  V  P  O  I  U  Y  T  R  R  A
E  H  G  F  D  S  E  B  V  C  G  P  O  I  U  Y
S  K  J  H  G  F  R  O  G  E  R  S  O  I  U  Y
E  O  I  U  Y  T  R  E  W  Q  A  L  K  J  H  G
E  Y  T  H  A  R  R  I  S  O  N  B  V  C  X  Z
D  W  E  R  T  Y  U  U  I  O  T  M  N  B  V  C
S  D  S  A  N  D  B  U  R  G  K  J  H  G  F  D
I  J  K  L  M  N  E  T  E  C  U  M  S  E  H  O
```

4-2B PEOPLE OF THE HEARTLAND

Use the outline below to research and write about one of the famous people of the Midwest and Great Plains listed in Activity 4-2A.

Name of famous person _____

Profession_____

Date of birth and death _____

Write a summary about his or her family and personal life.

_____
_____
_____
_____
_____
_____
_____
_____
_____

Summarize what this person contributed to make him or her famous.

_____
_____
_____
_____
_____
_____
_____
_____

4-3 19TH-CENTURY FARM LIFE

For the Teacher

Materials Needed:

- copies of Activity 4-3
- pencils

Teacher Preparation:

- Reproduce Activity 4-3, *19th-Century Farm Life*, as needed.
- Pass out the activity and allow time for students to complete the story. When they are finished, review the answers (given below) with them.

Answer Key:

(1) Appalachian	(14) land owners
(2) the Midwest	(15) businesses
(3) Native Americans	(16) log cabin
(4) fur trappers	(17) house raising
(5) pioneer	(18) barn raising
(6) towns	(19) quilting
(7) river	(20) apple
(8) hotel	(21) corn husking
(9) general store	(22) taffy pulling
(10) blacksmith	(23) benches
(11) horse stable	(24) reading (or writing)
(12) mill	(25) writing (or reading)
(13) doctor	(26) arithmetic

Extended Activity:

- There are many historic sites and landmarks in the Midwest and Great Plains worth visiting. The one featured in this section is **Greenfield Village** in Dearborn, Michigan. The village depicts farm life during the 1800s. Two other historic sites that demonstrate life during this era include **Connor Prairie** in Noblesville, Indiana, and **Living History Farms** in Des Moines, Iowa. Show a film or develop an exhibit on farm life in the heartland. Contact the Visitor Information Center in Detroit, Indianapolis, or Des Moines for specific orientation programs.

4-3 19TH-CENTURY FARM LIFE

Read the story carefully. Then fill in the blanks with words from the WORD BANK that best complete the sentences. *Hint*: Each dash in a blank represents space for one letter. Therefore, if there are five dashes in a blank, choose the best word available that has five letters.

WORD BANK

river	doctor	mill
hotel	Appalachian	the Midwest
fur trappers	house raising	log cabin
apple	benches	reading
arithmetic	writing	taffy pulling
general store	Native Americans	horse stable
blacksmith	pioneer	towns
businesses	land owners	barn raising
quilting	corn husking	

From the earliest days of European settlement in America, the story is one of people moving west. The first major movement west came when settlers crossed the (1) _____ Mountains and established farms and towns in the Northwest Territory. The Old Northwest Territory consisted of the present-day states of Ohio, Indiana, Illinois, Wisconsin, and part of Minnesota. Today this region is called (2) ___ _____.

The first people who inhabited the Midwest were the American Indians. Sometimes they are referred to as (3) _____ _____. They were followed by European (4) ___ _____ who hunted and sold animal furs for profit.

In the late 1700s, when trails were cleared across the Appalachian Mountains, pioneer families began to push westward into the Old Northwest Territory. A (5) _____ is a person or group who settles a new territory. At first life for the pioneers was difficult and many families struggled to survive. By the early 1800s farmers and businessmen began to prosper and (6) _____ were established. Towns usually developed near a (7) _____. The river presented a mode of transportation for people. It also provided a way for merchants and farmers to ship and receive goods.

4-3 19TH-CENTURY FARM LIFE *(continued)*

Each town had a Main Street where there were businesses and shops. There was usually

a (8) _ _ _ _ _, (9) _ _ _ _ _ _ _ _ _ _ _ _, (10) _ _ _ _ _ _ _ _ _ _, (11) _ _ _ _ _ _ _ _ _ _ _,

and a (12) _ _ _ _ (for grinding grain into flour). There was also a (13) _ _ _ _ _ _ nearby

to take care of the sick. On or near Main Street were the town's most beautiful homes.

They belonged to men who were large (14) _ _ _ _ _ _ _ _ _ _ or owned successful

(15) _ _ _ _ _ _ _ _ _.

Many farm families of the 1800s lived near the town on several acres of land called

homesteads. Most homes consisted of a one-room (16) _ _ _ _ _ _ _ _. The more

prosperous farmers built more elaborate farm houses. When new farm families arrived

to the area, it was a custom for neighbors to gather and build a home. This custom

was called a (17) _ _ _ _ _ _ _ _ _ _ _ _. As farmers prospered, they needed a barn.

Again families would join together to help erect the building. This custom was called

(18) _ _ _ _ _ _ _ _ _ _ _.

Other work-play parties were also practiced. These group gatherings were called bees.

There were (19) _ _ _ _ _ _ _ _ bees, (20) _ _ _ _ _ bees, (21) _ _ _ _ _ _ _ _ _ _ _ bees,

and (22) _ _ _ _ _ _ _ _ _ _ _ _ bees. After the work was done the families ate, danced,

and played games.

Schools in pioneer towns were usually one-room log cabins. Many children did not attend

because there was too much work to do. Boys tended crops and hunted game for food.

Girls cooked, made clothing, and cared for younger children. Those who attended school

began an hour after the sun rose and quit an hour before the sun set. The students sat on

wooden (23) _ _ _ _ _ _ _ without backs. Basically, teachers were responsible for teaching

students the basics of (24) _ _ _ _ _ _ _, (25) _ _ _ _ _ _ _, and (26) _ _ _ _ _ _ _ _ _ _.

4-4 TAKE A TRIP TO THE HEARTLAND

For the Teacher

Materials Needed:

- copies of Activity 4-4
- travel agency pamphlets
- travel books (such as *Mobil Travel Guide*)

Note:

There is some variance on which states are considered **the Midwest.** This version includes the states of Illinois, Indiana, Michigan, Minnesota, Ohio, and Wisconsin. Travel books also vary on what states are considered part of **the Great Plains.** This version includes the states of Iowa, Kansas, Missouri, Nebraska, North Dakota, and South Dakota.

Teacher Preparation:

- Reproduce Activity 4-4, *Take a Trip to the Heartland*, as needed and organize reference materials.
- Divide classes into small groups and assign specific states or regions of the Midwest or Great Plains for students to visit. Instruct classes to center their trips around historical places and events when possible.
- Pass out travel materials and the journal activity. Then allow time for students to complete the activity. Encourage the inclusion of photographs or illustrations, if possible. When students are finished, allow time for groups to share their journals with the rest of the class.

Extended Activities:

- Show classes a travel video on one or more states from either the Midwest or Great Plains region. Sources for travelogue tapes include educational channel television, video stores, or libraries.
- Encourage students to learn more about the economy of the states they are visiting. What products or services does the state make or provide? What are the major types of jobs in the state? Information on state economy can be found in encyclopedias.

4-4 TAKE A TRIP TO THE HEARTLAND

DESTINATION _____

For each day, describe the location, place visited, and special activity (such as art, music, food, or holiday).

DAILY ITINERARY

Day 1 _____
_____
_____

Day 2 _____
_____
_____

Day 3 _____
_____
_____

Day 4 _____
_____
_____

Day 5 _____
_____
_____

Day 6 _____
_____
_____

Day 7 _____
_____
_____

4-5 WHAT WILL IT COST?

For the Teacher

Materials Needed:

- copies of Activity 4-5
- travel books
- pencils or pens

Teacher Preparation:

- Reproduce Activity 4-5, *What Will It Cost?*, as needed.
- Pass out the activity and allow time for students to solve the problems. When they are finished, review the answers (given below) with them.

Answer Key:

1. $31; $6; $37
2. $23.80; $3.57; $27.37
3. $16
4. $6
5. $28; $1.40; $29.40
6. $37; $27.37; $16; $6; $29.40; $115.77

Extended Activity:

- Have students estimate the costs for one day of *their* destination for a family of four (2 adults and 2 students). Approximate hotel and dining costs can be found in most travel books. Other expenses can be estimated. Although Activity 4-5 can be used as a guide, encourage students to make other selections on how the family will spend the day.

4-5 WHAT WILL IT COST?

A family of four (2 adults and 2 students) are visiting the Midwest. They decide to visit *Greenfield Village* in Dearborn, Michigan, a 19th-century town. Solve the problems to see how much money they will spend for the day.

1. Admission charge to *Greenfield Village* is $9 for adults and $6.50 for students. In addition, a guided tour of the Firestone family farm house is $1.50 per person. The family needs 2 adult and 2 student admissions as well as 4 tickets for the guided tour.

   What is the cost for the admission tickets? $_____

   What is the cost of the guided tour tickets? $_____

   What is the total cost for tickets? $_____

2. The family has lunch at the village. The lunches are $6.95 for adults and $4.95 for students. The family needs 2 adult and 2 student meals.

   What is the cost of the lunches? $_____

   Add a 15% tip. $_____

   What is the total cost for lunch? $_____

3. The family elects to attend a special event of the village. It includes a hayride to a site nearby where they listen to local legends as they sit around a campfire. Cost is $4 per person. They need 4 tickets.

   What is the cost of the hayride and storytelling performance? $_____

4. For a late afternoon treat the family visits the Village Bakery for dessert. Costs are as follows: 2 pieces of apple pie for $1.50 each, 1 cherry cobbler for $1.25, and 1 large double fudge brownie for $1.75.

   What is the total cost for desserts? $_____

5. The family ends their day at the town Museum Shop where they purchase the following items: a jar of homemade apple butter for $4, a set of hand-dipped candles for $6, 2 pottery mugs at $5 each, and a pioneer game called "Nine Pins" for $8.

   What is the cost for all items? $_____

   Add a 5% sales tax. $_____

   What is the total cost for museum items? $_____

6. Add all the expenses to see how much money the family has spent for the day.

   Total cost for #1. $_____

   Total cost for #2. $_____

   Total cost for #3. $_____

   Total cost for #4. $_____

   Total cost for #5. $_____

   Total cost for the day. $_____

©1997 by The Center for Applied Research in Education

4-6 HEARTLAND TERMS

For the Teacher

Materials Needed:

- copies of Activity 4-6
- copies of *Glossary of Terms* (at back of book)

Teacher Preparation:

- Reproduce Activity 4-6, *Heartland Terms*, as needed. Also reproduce copies of the *Glossary* as needed.
- Pass out the activity and allow time for students to complete the activity. When they are finished, review the terms (answers given below) with them.

Answer Key:

b.	Midwest	g.	covered wagon
i.	Great Plains	q.	trapper
e.	Great Lakes	r.	frontiersman
j.	Mississippi River	h.	homestead
a.	Ohio River	p.	flatboat
c.	Louisiana Purchase	d.	sod houses
k.	pioneer	l.	pass
m.	log cabin	f.	fiddle
o.	territory	n.	square dance

Extended Activity:

- Use some of the terms in the activity as topics for further research. Appropriate titles include The Pioneers of the Midwest, The Pioneers of the Great Plains, Log Cabins of the Midwest, Sod Houses of the Plains, Travel Routes West, and The Louisiana Purchase.

4-6 HEARTLAND TERMS

Expand your vocabulary by learning some terms associated with the Midwest and Great Plains. Match the correct definitions to the words.

_____Midwest

_____Great Plains

_____Great Lakes

_____Mississippi River

_____Ohio River

_____Louisiana Purchase

_____pioneer

_____log cabin

_____territory

_____covered wagon

_____trapper

_____frontiersman

_____homestead

_____flatboat

_____sod houses

_____pass

_____fiddle

_____square dance

a. river that flows from Pennsylvania to Mississippi River and a major route followed by many pioneers

b. Upper Mississippi valley region that includes states around the Great Lakes

c. large section of land purchased in 1803 that extends from Mississippi River to Rocky Mountains

d. homes built by pioneers of the Plains made from the thick, heavy soil of the region

e. chain of five large lakes (Superior, Michigan, Huron, Erie, and Ontario)

f. a musical instrument (a type of violin) often played by pioneers

g. a wagon with a canvas top often used by pioneers for traveling

h. the home and adjoining land occupied by a family

i. a region of the U.S. east of the Rocky Mountains and west of the Mississippi River noted for being flat

j. this mighty river flows north and south from Minnesota to the Gulf of Mexico

k. a person or group that are the first to settle a new territory

l. a narrow valley between mountains

m. a home made from logs and the most common type of dwelling built by the pioneers of the Midwest

n. a type of dance for four couples who form a hollow square

o. a specific geographical region or area

p. a raft type of boat with a flat bottom that can travel through shallow water

q. a person who traps animals usually for the purpose of selling their fur

r. a person who lived or worked on frontier land

4-7 FOLKTALES AND LITERATURE

For the Teacher

Materials Needed:

- copies of Activity 4-7
- practice paper and pencils
- drawing paper and pens
- (*optional*) black markers and/or colored pencils

Teacher Preparation:

- Reproduce Activity 4-7, *Folktales and Literature*, as needed and organize materials.
- Pass out the activity and allow students time to read the story. When they are finished, instruct them to create their own folktale. They can develop a Johnny Appleseed adventure story or create a pioneer legend of their own.
- Using drawing paper and pens, have students rewrite their stories in their best printing or writing.
- (*optional*) Encourage students to illustrate their stories with markers and/or colored pencils.

Extended Activity:

- Set aside time for reading folktales or literature that relate to the Midwest, Great Plains, or pioneer era. Contact the media person in your building or community for assistance in gathering appropriate titles. Whenever possible, take classes to the library for this activity. There are a number of books available that tell stories about the Midwest and Great Plains. A brief list follows that will help you get started. **Note**: Remember, this is merely a list of some options. Regional differences vary, so use whatever is available in your area.

FOLKTALES

American Tall Tales by Mary Pope Osborne (New York: Random House, 1991). This book is about some of America's favorite heroes. From Indiana, Ohio, and Illinois there is Johnny Appleseed, the barefoot, seed-sowing wanderer who planted apple seeds along the trail for the pioneers who followed.

POEMS

The Old Swimmin' Hole by James Whitcomb Riley (various editions available)
Rhymes of Childhood by James Whitcomb Riley (various editions available)
Poems Here at Home by James Whitcomb Riley (various editions available)

Riley, known as the "Hoosier poet," wrote about the joys of Indiana in his poems. Some of his best are the three listed above.

CHILDREN'S LITERATURE

Little House on the Prairie by Laura Ingalls Wilder (various editions available). Although *Little House on the Prairie* is the most popular, Laura Ingalls wrote a series of books about her life during the pioneer era. She was born in a log cabin in Wisconsin and traveled with her family by covered wagon through Kansas, Minnesota, and the Dakota Territory. The wonderful stories she tells have become American classics. Some of her other titles include *Little House in the Big Woods; Farmer Boy; On the Banks of Plum Creek; By the Shores of Silver Lake; The Long Winter; Little Town on the Prairie;* and *These Happy Golden Years.*

Caddie Woodlawn by Ryrie Brink (Newbery Medal Award Book) (various editions available). This is a story about an eleven-year-old tomboy growing up on the Wisconsin frontier during the mid 1800s.

THE ORPHAN TRAIN QUARTET: *A Family Apart; Caught in the Act; In the Face of Danger;* and *A Place to Belong* by Joan Lowery Nixon (Bantam Doubleday Dell, 1989). The Children's Aid Society sent over 100,000 orphan children from the slums of New York (by train) to the Great Plains in search of new families. Although the characters are fictitious, the books were inspired by the true events that occurred between 1854 and 1929 from these trips.

CLASSICAL LITERATURE

The Adventures of Tom Sawyer by Mark Twain (various editions available)

Adventures of Huckleberry Finn by Mark Twain (various editions available)

Samuel Clemens, whose pen name was Mark Twain, spent his childhood in Hannibal, Missouri. He is one of the country's best-loved writers. Tom Sawyer and Huck Finn represent some of his most lovable characters. **Note:** These books are also listed in Section 5, Mississippi Valley, since they deal with life along the Mississippi River.

CLASSICAL LITERATURE *(suggested for older students)*

Friendly Persuasion by Jessamyn West (various editions available). This story describes Quaker life in the mid 1800s and emphasizes the ideals of brotherhood.

A Tour of the Prairies by Washington Irving (various editions available) An American author who specialized in tales of American folk life, Irving wrote about the prairies after a tour of Oklahoma in the 1830s.

O Pioneers! and *My Antonia* by Willa Sibert Cather (various editions available). Cather wrote many books portraying pioneer life on the Nebraska frontier. The ones listed are two well-known titles.

Old Jules by Mari Sandoz (Lincoln: University of Nebraska Press, 1985)

Crazy Horse by Mari Sandoz (Lincoln: University of Nebraska Press, 1992)

Cheyenne Autumn by Mari Sandoz (Lincoln: University of Nebraska Press, 1992)

Sandoz wrote many fictional and nonfictional accounts of pioneer life on the Great Plains. Her father was a friend of the Sioux and Cheyenne Indians and became the subject of *Old Jules.*

4-7 FOLKTALES AND LITERATURE

The following is an adaptation of one of the *American Tall Tales* by Mary Pope Osborne.

JOHNNY APPLESEED

There's a ghost that lives in Indiana and Ohio. He moves through the apple orchards he planted long ago. Some farmers of the region have heard him singing softly above the rustling trees and call him Johnny Appleseed. This is his story.

One morning long ago, two brothers sat on a bank along the Ohio River near Pittsburgh. Their names were John and Nathaniel Chapman. They had just journeyed from a farm in Massachusetts to live in the hills of Pennsylvania. As they sat watching pioneer families moving west on flatboats, John told his brother that he wanted to become an apple missionary.

"A what?" asked Nathaniel.

"I want to spread apples throughout the Ohio valley," explained John, "to help the brave pioneers start a new life. I will call myself the apple missionary."

Nathaniel wanted John to stay near him but he knew nothing would keep his brother from trying to make life better for others. Early the next morning John gathered and dried many apple seeds. Then he put them in deerskin sacks and loaded them into a canoe.

As John paddled his canoe down the Ohio River, he called to settlers along the way. "Apple seeds for apple orchards," he called, and settlers eagerly accepted them. But John didn't just give his seeds to the pioneers. He also showed them how to plant the seeds and gave advice on raising the trees.

Soon John abandoned his canoe. He slung one of his deerskin sacks over his shoulder and headed for the thick woods. When he came upon a clearing, John dug into the earth and planted some apple seeds. Soon John made friends with the animals of the forest. He traveled, planted apple seeds, talked to the animals, and ate nuts and berries.

For forty years John Chapman lived in the frontier lands around the Ohio River. As he traveled through the region, he planted apple trees and made friends with many people.

He made friends with the Indians of the Old Northwest Territory. He met the old fur traders along the trails. He met settlers from New England and the Middle Atlantic as they settled or passed through on their way further west.

Everyone who traveled the frontier lands knew about John Chapman and his mission to plant apple orchards for everyone in the territory. In fact, most of the people never knew his last name. He was simply called "Johnny Appleseed."

4-8 PASTIMES AND GAMES

For the Teacher

Materials Needed:

- copies of Activity 4-8
- items mentioned in "Teacher Preparation"

Teacher Preparation:

- Reproduce Activity 4-8, *Pastimes and Games*, as needed.

- Pass out the activity and go over the pastimes outlined. If possible, *allow students to help make choices on which activities will be selected. Then set aside some time for participation.*

- If one or both of the apple activities are selected, ask for volunteers to bring in materials for the games. **Warning**: *Bobbing for Apples* is lots of fun, but messy. It is best suited for the outside on a warm day.

- For those interested in competitive educational activities, *spelling bees* or *geography bees* are ideal activities.

- If participating in sports is possible, contact the Physical Education person in your building well in advance and organize games of *badminton.*

- If students show interest in playing games of *marbles, checkers, Nine Pins,* or *horse shoes,* ask for volunteers to bring in these activities to share with the class. Inexpensive plastic games of *bowling* can be substituted for Nine Pins and rubber-based horse shoe games are recommended in place of the heavier, metal versions. They are safer and portable.

- *Tug of War* activities are suggested for warm days when students can go outside.

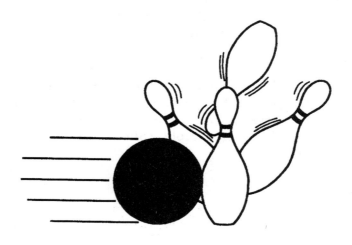

4-8 PASTIMES AND GAMES

PASTIMES

Work-play party functions played a major role in the lives of 19th-century farm communities. Whenever there was a large task that needed to be done, neighbors joined together to accomplish the task at hand. These parties were called *bees*. There were corn husking bees, apple bees, quilting bees, and canning bees. When the work was finished, the people joined for feasting, dancing, and playing games.

APPLE BEES

In the autumn at apple harvest, settlers gathered to prepare the fruit for the long winter ahead. They prepared dried apples, apple butter, apple cider, and canned apples. As you can imagine, games played at these work-party activities involved apples.

One game was called *Snap Apple*. To play this game, hang an apple from the ceiling with a string. By turn, participants try to take a bite out of the apple without using their hands.

BOBBING FOR APPLES

Bobbing for apples was popular as well. To play this game, float several apples in a tub of water. Taking turns, players put their hands behind their back and remove the apple from the water with their teeth. Since the apples bounce and bob out of reach easily, this activity is harder than it sounds. Nevertheless, it is a lot of fun and creates much excitement for people of all ages.

LEARNING BEES

Besides working bees, there were also learning bees. Two types were *spelling bees* and *geography bees*. Children of the heartland often engaged in spelling bees. In fact, spelling bees are still used in many schools today. Students take turns spelling words; the winner is the person who can spell the most words correctly. Geography bees are played in the same manner using social studies questions. Naming state capitals or largest cities would make an ideal geography bee activity.

4-8 PASTIMES AND GAMES (continued)

SPORTS

During the 1800s an early version of the outdoor sport of *Badminton* was played. It was called *battledore and shuttlecock*. The battledore was the racket and the shuttlecock was the birdie. The goal of the game was to divide into teams and keep the shuttlecock in the air for as long as possible.

GAMES

Like the early colonists, children of the Midwest and Great Plains enjoyed playing games of *marbles, checkers*, or *Nine Pins*. Two other types of games might have included *horse shoes* and *tug of war*.

Horse shoes has been a popular game in America for a long time. Inexpensive rubber horse shoe games are available that are safer and more portable than the original iron versions.

Tug of war is played by selecting two teams at the ends of a long rope. The winner is the team that pulls the other beyond a specified point.

4-9 SOUNDS OF THE HEARTLAND

For the Teacher

Materials Needed:

- CD, cassette, or film
- audio-visual equipment

Teacher Preparation:

- Social events for pioneer families centered around church socials and community dances. Dancing was a favorite pastime among most young people and grownups. At holiday celebrations, housewarmings, or weddings, the pioneers dressed in their best clothes and enjoyed hours of dancing. A favorite kind was *square dancing*. A local fiddler played the tunes while a caller led the dancers through the steps. In fact, many communities today still enjoy square dancing. Encourage your students to learn some square dance steps. For opportunities to listen to square dance music, check with the local library, record store, or your school's music teacher for assistance.

- Since religion and the church was the center of many pioneer lives, *hymns* were a popular type of music of the Midwest and Great Plains. Favorite songs were passed down from one generation to another. American hymns are still an important part of most church services across the country. For an opportunity to listen to hymns, check your local library or music store. Also, consider the following options:

America's 25 Favorite Hymns
With voices and orchestra arranged and conducted by Don Marsh (Brentwood Music, Inc., Brentwood, TN, 1994). A celebration of some of the greatest songs of the Church with 25 timeless hymns including "How Great Thou Art" and "Amazing Grace."

America's 25 Favorite Hymns, Volume 2
(Brentwood Music, Inc., Brentwood, TN, 1994).

- For an opportunity to view a musical film production relating to the Midwest and Great Plains, consider the following options. (It is always advised to preview a film and obtain parental consent before showing it to students.)

Oklahoma, a musical by Rogers and Hammerstein
This American classic tells the story of young love in middle America. It stars Shirley Jones and Gordon MacRae. Musical titles include "O What a Beautiful Morning," "Oklahoma," and "People Will Say We're In Love."

Calamity Jane, a musical film production
Saddle up with Calamity Jane for a romp through the rootin' tootin' musical west of the Dakotas where she joins Wild Bill Hickok for love and romance. It stars Doris Day as Calamity Jane and Howard Keel as Wild Bill Hickok.

4-10 QUILTING BEES

For the Teacher

Materials Needed:

- copies of Activity 4-10
- 1/4" graph paper and pencils
- rulers
- 5" × 5" white paper
- 18" × 24" paper (background for 12 paper quilts)
- black markers
- (*optional*) colored markers and/or pencils
- glue

Teacher Preparation:

- Reproduce Activity 4-10, *Quilting Bees*, as needed and organize materials. Although it is not necessary to make the quilt plans on graph paper, it is much easier for students to plan the designs accurately. The suggested size for the paper quilt squares is 5" × 5" because it is an easy size to make and apply to an 18" × 24" background paper quilt.

- Pass out the activity and go over the information with your students.

- Distribute the materials and allow time for students to create some paper quilt patterns.

- When they are finished, glue 12 patches to 18" × 24" sheets of paper. There will be 3 patches across and 4 down. Display the quilts around the room.

- **ALTERNATIVE:** Use colored papers instead of markers to create cut-paper pattern designs. Although cut-paper patterns create a little more mess than the marker version, it looks more like a "real" quilt than the markers.

Extended Activity:

- For a more advanced project, contact the Consumer and Family Living teacher well in advance for a cooperative *fabric quilt* lesson while your students are learning about the Midwest and Great Plains.

Photo 4-1 *Quilted hot pad, collection of the author.*
The project shown in this photo is an example of a machine-made quilted pot holder suitable for beginning sewing classes.

4-10 QUILTING BEES

Quilting bees were popular during colonial and frontier times in America. Women spent many evenings cutting small scraps of fabric into squares, triangles, and rectangles to make attractive and interesting patterns for a quilt. Then mothers, aunts, grandmothers, and young ladies would gather to visit, lunch, and work for hours sewing patches to a fabric background.

Make a paper quilt the easy way by following the steps below. How many different designs can you make from a simple square or triangle? Maybe you will want to be a little more adventuresome and create a drawing instead of a design. Some common colonial and frontier drawings used hearts, flowers, houses, or pets as subject matter for their quilts.

Steps to Making Paper Quilts

1. On scrap paper develop several different quilt patterns from a square, a triangle, or a circle. Look at the illustrations to get some ideas. Then see how many you can create.

2. Choose two or three of the designs you like best and lightly draw them on a 5" x 5" piece of white drawing paper. Using a ruler will help keep the lines straight and give the appearance of a real quilt design.

3. Outline the design in black marker.

4. Use black and colored markers or pencils to color in part of the design.

    Hint: Reversing the design as shown in the illustration below gives an entirely different look to the same pattern.

4-10 QUILTING BEES (continued)

After the quilting patterns are complete, attach 12 of them to a sheet of 18" x 24" paper. The quilt will have three patterns across and four patterns down. Plan the quilt carefully so the overall effect will be attractive. Look at the sample below to see how the patterns should appear.

4-11 PIERCED PAPER

For the Teacher

Materials Needed:

- copies of Activity 4-11
- assorted sizes of pins and needles
- 6" × 6" white drawing paper (for pierced paper hanging baskets)
- 9" × 12" white drawing paper (for pierced paper flat drawings)
- cardboard (to put beneath projects)
- scissors
- glue
- ribbon or yarn to hang baskets
- (*optional*) black construction paper as backing for flat pierced drawings

Teacher Preparation:

- Reproduce Activity 4-11, *Pierced Paper*, as needed and organize materials.
- Pass out the activity and go over the information with your students. If possible, allow them to choose whether they would like to make pierced paper hanging baskets or pierced paper flat drawings.
- Distribute the materials and allow time for students to draw and pierce their projects.
- *Baskets*: Glue ribbon to inside of basket and fill with dried flowers.
- *Flat drawings*: Glue drawing to a black construction paper background so the pierced shapes will stand out.
- When they are finished, display some of the projects around the room.

4-11 PIERCED PAPER

Pierced paper crafting was a popular art form during the colonial and frontier era in America. Pierced paper crafting refers to designs created with various pin points. At first the designs served as stencils for transferring embroidery patterns. As designs grew more complex, they became works of art in themselves. Sometimes the pierced designs were painted lightly with watercolor paints. However, the backgrounds *always* remained white. Create your own pierced paper craft by following the easy steps outlined below.

Steps to Making Pierced Paper Baskets

1. On 6" × 6" drawing paper develop two or three basic design shapes. The basic design for the basket can be in a heart, square, rectangle, half-moon, or round shape.

2. Pick the design you like best and lightly draw a pattern inside the basic shape using dots only.

3. Pierce the paper dots with various sizes of pins and needles where you have planned your pattern.

4. Cut out a second basic shape exactly the same size as the first one. This will be the back of the basket.

5. Turn the pierced paper over *so that any pencil marks will be on the inside of the basket.*

6. Gently glue the front of the basket to the back along the edges only.

7. Gently glue a ribbon to the inside of the basket for a handle.

8. (*optional*) Fill the basket with dried flowers or candy and hang.

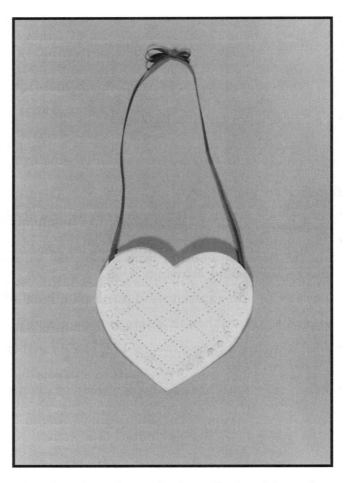

Photo 4-2 *Pierced paper basket, collection of the author.* This pierced paper hanging basket was done by a student while classes were learning about colonial America. First, the basic heart shape was cut out. Then a dot pattern was planned and pierced with various needles. After the piercing was complete, a second basic heart shape was cut out for the backing. The student gently glued the front shape of the heart to the back, using the glue cautiously and only along the very edges. Finally, the student glued a bright red ribbon for a handle and filled the basket with dried fall flowers.

4-11 PIERCED PAPER *(continued)*

Not all students wanted to make pierced paper baskets. Some of them developed **flat pierced paper drawings** on white construction paper. First, they *lightly* sketched nature drawings using potted plants as subject matter. Next, they pierced holes in various sizes on top of the sketched drawing using several sizes of pins and needle points. Notice how carefully and evenly this student pierced the paper. When the piercing was complete, *the paper was turned over so no pencil marks would show*. Then the student carefully glued the pierced drawing to a black construction paper background. The black paper allowed the pierced holes to stand out more.

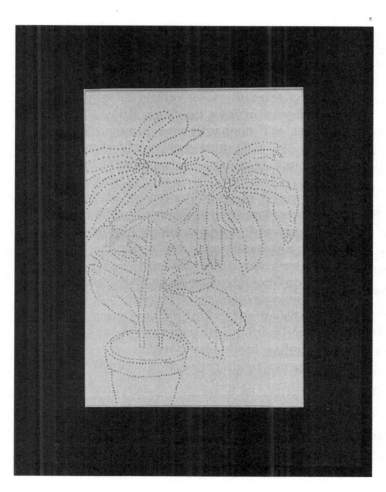

Photo 4-3 *Pierced paper drawing, collection of the author.*

4-12 BASICS OF HEARTLAND COOKING

For the Teacher

Materials Needed:

- copies of Activity 4-12
- pencils

Teacher Preparation:

- Reproduce Activity 4-12, *Basics of Heartland Cooking*, as needed.
- Pass out the activity and allow time for students to read the information and complete the worksheet. (Answers are given below.) When they are finished, review the food basics of the Midwest and Great Plains.

Answer Key:

Meats: beef; pork; chicken

Beef dishes: country-fried steaks; beef pot roasts

Pork dishes: pork roasts; homemade sausage patties

Chicken dishes: chicken and homemade noodles; fried chicken

Seafood: perch; cod; haddock; catfish

Vegetables: corn; potatoes; tomatoes; green beans; cabbage; squash

Corn dishes: corn-on-the-cob; corn pudding; corn, with onions and peppers; corn chowder soup

Potato dishes: mashed potatoes with gravy; fried potatoes

Fruits: apples; cherries; blueberries; strawberries

Fall fruit: persimmon

Preparation: persimmon pudding

Breads: wheat bread; honey-wheat dinner rolls

Quick breads: coffee cakes; cinnamon buns

Types of dessert: pies; cobblers

Fruits used: apples; cherries; blueberries

Two other desserts: strawberry shortcake; homemade ice cream

Extended Activity:

- Encourage students to collectively develop a Midwest and Great Plains cookbook. Divide classes into groups and assign specific topics to each group. Appropriate topics include Soups, Breads, Vegetables, Seafood, Meats, and Desserts. After students have collected and submitted their recipes, duplicate them and allow each person to organize a cookbook of his or her own.

4-12 BASICS OF HEARTLAND COOKING

The large area of the Midwest and Great Plains extends from Ohio to the Rocky Mountains and from Canada to Oklahoma. Like any region, this area is quite diverse. Nevertheless, the foods of the Midwest and Great Plains depend in large part to the crops and livestock grown and raised on the farms of the areas. From the crops and meats, the Midwest and Great Plains cooks developed hearty foods, simply prepared.

BASIC FOODS

Meats: Many cattle farms are found in the Midwest and Great Plains so *beef* and *pork* are an important part of meal planning. The beef of Kansas and Nebraska produce many country-fried steaks and beef pot roasts. The pork of Iowa turn into hundreds of succulent pork roasts and homemade sausage patties. In addition, many small farmers raise *chickens*. Midwest cooks have made chicken with homemade noodles and fried chicken two household traditions.

Seafood: The lakes and rivers of the region abound with fish. Pan-fried fish is a favorite type of preparation, although baked and broiled methods are used as well. *Perch, cod, haddock*, and *catfish* are all eaten.

Vegetables: *Corn* is king in the midwest. From this plentiful vegetable comes *corn-on-the-cob* covered with butter, *corn pudding, corn with onions and peppers,* and *corn chowder soup*. Almost as popular are *potatoes*. Favorite family dinners always included a dish of creamed *mashed potatoes with gravy. Fried potatoes* are a close second for preparing this vegetable. In addition to corn and potatoes, other common vegetables include *tomatoes, green beans, cabbage*, and *squash*.

Fruits: The most common fruit in the Midwest are *apples*. However *cherries, blueberries*, and *strawberries* are popular as well. *Apple pies* have become the most symbolic of American cooking as the saying emerged "as American as apple pie." Regionally, *persimmons* are a well-known fall fruit. This distinctly midwestern fruit is prepared into a persimmon pudding.

Breads: The Midwest is wheat country so tables are plentiful with homemade loaves of *wheat bread* and *honey-wheat dinner rolls*. Quick breads, such as *coffee cakes* and *cinnamon buns*, are also popular.

Desserts: Hearty baked goods with locally grown products are a trademark of midwest kitchens. *Pies* and *cobblers* represent the most common *types* of dessert using *apples, cherries*, and *blueberries* as the fruit bases. In addition, *strawberry shortcake* has become a midwest tradition, especially during the early summer months. Perhaps the most loved dessert of all, however, is *homemade ice cream*. Ice cream socials have become the theme for many social events in the midwest.

Name _____ **Date** _____ **Period** _____

4-12 BASICS OF HEARTLAND COOKING

Use the boxes below to outline some of the food basics of America's heartland.

Types of meats: _____	
_____	
_____	

Favorite dishes from beef: _____ _____
Favorite dishes from pork: _____ _____
Favorite dishes from chicken: _____ _____
Favorite dishes from seafood: _____ _____
_____ _____

Favorite vegetables: _____ _____
(Name six) _____ _____
_____ _____

Favorite corn dishes: _____ _____
(Name four) _____ _____

Favorite potato dishes: _____
(Name two) _____

Favorite fruits: _____ _____
(Name four _____ _____

A favorite fall fruit: _____
How is it prepared? _____

Favorite breads: _____ _____
Favorite quick breads: _____ _____

Favorite types of dessert: _____ _____

Favorite fruits used: _____ _____
(Name three) _____

Two other midwest _____
dessert favorites: _____

4-13 A MIDWEST WORK-PLAY DINNER

For the Teacher

Hint: It is helpful to complete Activity 4-12, *Basics of Heartland Cooking*, before participating in this one.

Materials Needed:

- copies of Activity 4-13
- pencils or pens

Teacher Preparation:

- Reproduce Activity 4-13, *A Midwest Work-Play Dinner*, as needed.
- Pass out the activity. Then allow students time to read the menu and make their dinner selections. When they are finished, lead a discussion to compare and contrast a typical heartland work-play dinner with a special-occasion dinner in their family.

Extended Activity:

- Ask students to bring in some simple ready-prepared food items popular in the Midwest and Great Plains. Appropriate dessert choices include ready-made apple, cherry, or blueberry pies or cobblers. Other options include popcorn and apple cider or ice cream topped with strawberries. In addition, hot cups of sassafras tea make a good choice. Many supermarkets carry bottled, instant sassafras concentrates for easy preparation. If students like the taste of root beer, they'll like sassafras.

4-13 A MIDWEST WORK-PLAY DINNER

Work-play dinners were a common practice throughout America's heartland during the 18th and 19th centuries. Families made the tasks of husking corn, raising barns, harvesting apples, or butchering meats more enjoyable by joining together to complete the work at hand. After the work was finished, they joined together for large dinners, games, and music. The dinners were famous for serving hearty foods, simply prepared. The women spent days preparing for the work-play dinners and the events were a major part of the social events of the era.

The menu below represents a typical **Midwest Work-Play Dinner**. Later these meals were served to "threshing" crews who harvested the grain at harvest time.

A MIDWEST WORK-PLAY DINNER

Meats
Chicken and Homemade Noodles
Pan-fried Chicken
Country-fried Steak
Succulent Roast of Pork
Homemade Sausage Patties

Vegetables
Creamed and buttered mashed potatoes
Country Brown Gravy
Buttered Green Beans
Creamed Corn
Buttered Peas

Salads
Sliced Cucumbers and Onions in Vinegar
Sliced Tomatoes
Cabbage Slaw
Pickled Peppers

Breads
Whole Wheat or White Dinner Rolls
Homemade Strawberry Jam

Desserts
Apple Cobbler or Pie
Cherry Pie
Blueberry Pie

Beverages
Lemonade   Iced Tea   Coffee

Name _____ **Date** _____ **Period** _____

4-13 A MIDWEST WORK-PLAY DINNER

After you have looked over the midwest dinner menu, use the outline below to make your own dinner selections. Since the dinners were served family style, guests could make as many foods choices as they wanted. You may do the same. After you have completed your midwest dinner selections, outline in the spaces a special-occasion dinner in your family. Compare the midwest dinner with your own special meal. Are there any similarities? What are the differences?

A Midwest Work-Play Dinner

Meats _____

_____

Vegetables _____

_____

Salads _____

_____

Bread(s) _____

Desserts _____

_____

Beverage(s) _____

A Special-Occasion Dinner (your family might serve)

Meat _____

_____

Vegetables _____

_____

Salads _____

_____

Bread(s) _____

_____

Desserts _____

_____

Beverage(s) _____

4-14 CIDER PIE

For the Teacher

Equipment Needed:

- copies of Activity 4-14
- 8" pie plate
- spoon
- mixing bowl
- hand mixer
- measuring cup
- measuring spoons

Supplies Needed:

- ready-made unbaked pie crust
- frozen apple juice
- eggs
- brown sugar
- margarine
- all-spice
- (*optional*) whipped cream or ice cream

Teacher Preparation:

- Reproduce Activity 4-14, *Cider Pie*, as needed and organize equipment and supplies.
- Give a demonstration on making the pie as students follow along with the recipe. Follow up with a cider pie tasting treat.
- **ALTERNATIVE:** Go over the recipe with students. Then make an outside-the-classroom assignment for students to make the pie at home and bring it to school for a special pioneer treat day. Cider pie is especially delicious served with whipped cream or ice cream. Encourage students to ask for adult supervision when making the pie.

Extended Activity:

- Contact the Consumer and Family Living teacher well in advance to coordinate a Midwest and Great Plains lunch or dessert lab activity while your classes are learning about America's heartland.

4-14 CIDER PIE

Johnny Appleseed has often been credited for introducing apples to the midwest. In truth, the folk hero only visited a small part of the frontier. Born John Chapman, he spent 40 years traveling through Ohio and Indiana making sure the pioneers who followed had apple trees. The heartland pioneers prepared many recipes using apples. They often made apple cider with less-than-perfect fruit. Sometimes they boiled the cider down until it was very thick. From the thick juice they made Cider Pie. The ingenuity of these brave pioneers seems admirable in our modern age of supermarkets and conveniences. In this recipe, frozen apple juice concentrate has been substituted for boiled-down cider. This pie serves 6 to 8.

You need:

1	ready-made unbaked pie crust for an 8" pie
3	eggs
1	6-ounce can frozen apple juice concentrate, thawed
1/2	cup brown sugar, packed
2	tablespoons margarine, melted
1/4	teaspoon all-spice
	(*optional*) whipped cream or ice cream

What to do:

1. Heat oven to 425°.
2. Bake (unpricked) pie shell for 4 minutes.
3. Remove from oven and reduce temperature to 350°.
4. In a mixing bowl, beat eggs. Then add apple juice concentrate, brown sugar, margarine, and all-spice.
5. Pour mixture into pie shell.
6. Bake at 350° for 25–30 minutes or until inserted knife comes out clean.
7. Cool pie completely.
8. (*optional*) Serve with whipped cream or ice cream, if desired.

4-15 STRAWBERRY SHORTCAKE

For the Teacher:

Equipment Needed:

- copies of Activity 4-15
- mixing bowls
- measuring cup
- measuring spoons
- spoon
- cookie sheet

Supplies Needed:

- all-purpose baking mix (such as Bisquick®)
- milk
- sugar
- margarine
- strawberries
- (*optional*) whipped cream or ice cream

Teacher Preparation:

- Reproduce Activity 4-15, *Strawberry Shortcake*, as needed and organize equipment and supplies.

- Give a demonstration on making strawberry shortcake as students follow along with the recipe. Follow up with a shortcake tasting treat.

- **ALTERNATIVE:** Go over the recipe with students. Then make an outside-the-classroom assignment for students to make it at home and bring it to school for a special strawberry shortcake treat day. Both whipped cream and ice cream are delicious served with the shortcakes. Use whatever is easier or sounds more appetizing. Encourage students to ask for adult supervision when making the shortcakes.

4-15 STRAWBERRY SHORTCAKE

For many years it has been a Midwest tradition to serve Strawberry Shortcakes at church and social functions in the early summer months when strawberries were available. In modern times strawberries are available throughout the spring and fall seasons as well, so the shortcakes can be enjoyed almost the year around. This special-treat dessert is delicious served with either whipped cream or ice cream. This recipe (from the Bisquick® box) makes 8 shortcakes.

You need:

2-1/3	cups all-purpose baking mix (Bisquick®)
1/2	cup milk
3	tablespoons sugar
3	tablespoons margarine, melted
1	quart strawberries, washed, sliced and sweetened to taste.

(*optional*) 1 quart vanilla ice cream or 1 large container of whipped topping

What to do:

1. Preheat oven to 400°.
2. In a mixing bowl, combine milk, sugar, and melted margarine.
3. Add all-purpose baking mix to milk mixture.
4. Stir until blended.
5. Drop by spoonfuls onto ungreased cookie sheet.
6. Bake 10–12 minutes or until golden brown. Cool.
7. To assemble strawberry shortcakes, split cakes into halves. Fill and top with strawberries and ice cream or whipped cream.

BIBLIOGRAPHY FOR THE MIDWEST AND GREAT PLAINS

Art

Hoople, Cheryl. *The Heritage Sampler: A Book of Colonial Arts and Crafts*. New York: Dial Press, 1975.

Children's Fiction

Osborne, Mary Pope. *American Tall Tales*. New York: Random House, 1991.

Children's Nonfiction

Hargrove, Jim. *America the Beautiful: Nebraska*. Chicago: Children's Press, 1989.

Heinrichs, Ann. *America the Beautiful: Oklahoma*. Chicago: Children's Press, 1989.

Herguth, Margaret S. *America the Beautiful: North Dakota*. Chicago: Children's Press, 1990.

Kent, Deborah. *America the Beautiful: Iowa*. Chicago: Children's Press, 1991.

Kent, Deborah. *America the Beautiful: Ohio*. Chicago: Children's Press, 1989.

Kent, Zachary. *America the Beautiful: Kansas*. Chicago: Children's Press, 1991.

Lepthien, Emilie U. *America the Beautiful: South Dakota*. Chicago: Children's Press, 1991.

Sanford, William R. and Carl R. Green. *America the Beautiful: Missouri*. Chicago: Children's Press, 1990.

Stein, R. Conrad. *America the Beautiful: Illinois*. Chicago: Children's Press, 1987.

Stein, R. Conrad. *America the Beautiful: Indiana*. Chicago: Children's Press, 1990.

Stein, R. Conrad. *America the Beautiful: Michigan*. Chicago: Children's Press, 1987.

Stein, R. Conrad. *America the Beautiful: Minnesota*. Chicago: Children's Press, 1992.

Stein, R. Conrad. *America the Beautiful: Wisconsin*. Chicago: Children's Press, 1987.

Cookbooks

Editors. *Better Homes and Gardens Heritage of America Cookbook*. Des Moines: Better Homes and Gardens Books, 1993.

Pastimes

Kalman, Bobbie. *Games from Long Ago*. New York: Crabtree Publishing, 1995.

Kalman, Bobbie and David Schimpky. *Old-Time Toys*. New York: Crabtree Publishing, 1995.

Warner, John F. *Colonial American Home Life*. New York: Franklin Watts, 1993.

Travel

Staff. *Mobil 1995 Travel Guide, Great Lakes.* New York: Fodor's Travel Publications, 1995.

Staff. *Mobil 1995 Travel Guide, Northwest and Great Plains.* New York: Fodor's Travel Publications, 1995.

THE MISSISSIPPI VALLEY

Below is an outline of the interdisciplinary activities included in this section. They are designed to bring a broad range of cultural lessons and hands-on activities into the social studies classroom. Pick and choose the ones that best fit into your program.

MAP OF THE MISSISSIPPI VALLEY

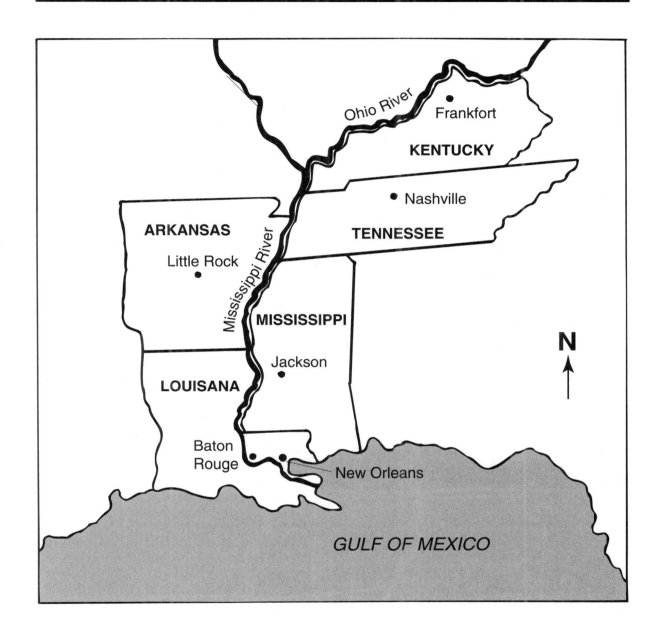

5-1 GETTING TO KNOW THE MISSISSIPPI VALLEY

For the Teacher

Materials Needed:

- copies of Activity 5-1
- labeled map of Mississippi Valley (enlarged on opaque projector)
- copies of unlabeled map of Mississippi Valley
- (colored) pencils

Teacher Preparation:

- Reproduce Activity 5-1, *Getting to Know the Mississippi Valley*, as needed. Also reproduce copies of the unlabeled map of the Mississippi Valley as needed.

- Pass out the activity and map to each student. Then allow time for students to locate and label the Mississippi Valley as outlined in the activity. When they are finished, review the geography with them.

Extended Activities:

- Reproduce additional copies of the unlabeled map and have students identify other features of the Mississippi Valley states, such as early settlements, population distribution, land use, or climate. PC Globe® computer program can provide much of the information needed for this activity. Consult your school's media person for assistance, too.

- Reproduce the chart of *The Fifty States* (at back of book) as needed. Pass out the chart and have students make a list of the Mississippi Valley states, date they entered the Union, order of entry, capital, and largest city. *List states in order they entered the Union.* Answers should appear as follows:

State	Date Entered Union	Order of Entry	Capital	Largest City
Kentucky	1792	15	Frankfort	Louisville
Tennessee	1796	16	Nashville	Memphis
Louisiana	1812	18	Baton Rouge	New Orleans
Mississippi	1817	20	Jackson	Jackson
Arkansas	1836	25	Little Rock	Little Rock

Name _____ Date _____ Period _____

5-1 GETTING TO KNOW THE MISSISSIPPI VALLEY

Use the map provided to locate and label the following features:

State: Arkansas
Capital: Little Rock

State: Kentucky
Capital: Frankfort
River: Ohio River

State: Louisiana
Capital: Baton Rouge
Early settlement: New Orleans

State: Mississippi
Capital: Jackson

State: Tennessee
Capital: Nashville

Bodies of water: Mississippi River, Gulf of Mexico

5-1 GETTING TO KNOW THE MISSISSIPPI VALLEY

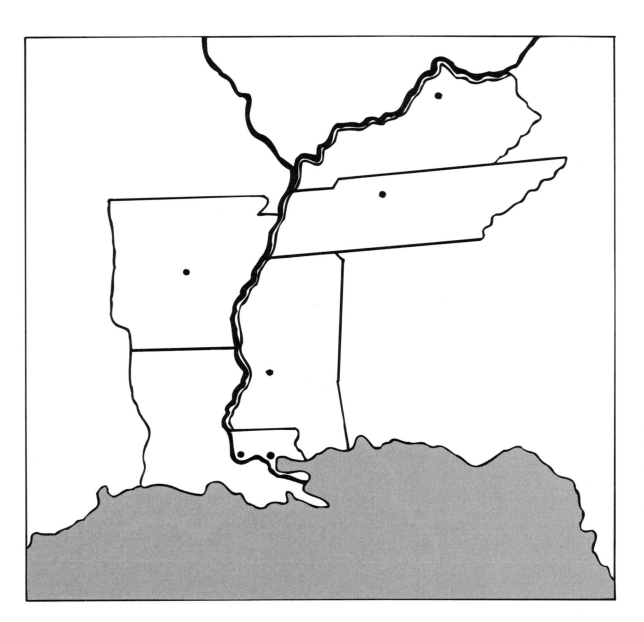

5-2 PEOPLE OF THE MISSISSIPPI VALLEY

For the Teacher

Materials Needed:

- copies of Activity 5-2
- pencils
- research materials

Teacher Preparation:

- Reproduce Activity 5-2A and 5-2B, *People of the Mississippi Valley,* as needed.
- Pass out the activity and allow enough time for students to complete the word search puzzle. When they are finished, review the answers (given below) with them.

Answer Key:

```
A  D  S  E  Q  U  O  Y  A  H  I  L  Y  T  R  E
I  O  T  P  O  I  U  Y  T  R  E  A  Q  B  H  I
I  O  J  O  H  N  S  O  N  I  E  S  U  Y  T  R
O  P  A  I  D  I  O  P  E  R  E  A  I  O  D  S
N  B  C  U  Y  D  P  O  B  E  W  L  M  N  B  V
B  V  K  E  W  Q  R  T  O  E  W  L  N  B  V  C
P  O  S  U  Y  T  C  R  O  C  K  E  T  T  N  B
I  O  O  U  L  D  S  A  N  I  U  Y  T  A  N  M
I  U  N  L  I  N  B  V  E  Z  X  C  V  Y  B  G
P  O  I  U  N  Q  W  E  R  T  Y  U  I  L  V  C
Z  X  C  V  C  I  U  C  P  O  I  U  Y  O  E  W
Q  W  E  R  O  E  H  N  L  Q  W  E  R  R  I  O
V  F  F  I  L  S  O  N  E  A  P  O  I  U  Y  T
A  S  D  F  N  Q  W  E  R  T  R  I  O  Y  N  P
I  D  E  S  O  T  O  I  O  P  E  K  Q  W  E  R
M  N  B  V  C  X  Z  A  S  D  F  G  H  J  K  L
```

Extended Activities:

- Allow students to pick one of the famous people in the puzzle (or another person from the Mississippi Valley who has made a contribution to America) and assign research papers on his or her life and contributions. Use the outline provided in Activity 5-2B to develop the reports.
- Films have been made about some of the famous people in the puzzle. Select one and show it to your classes.

5-2A PEOPLE OF THE MISSISSIPPI VALLEY

The story of America is a story of people moving westward. Leading the way in the wilderness that is the present-day states of Kentucky and Tennessee were Indians, trappers, and pioneer farmers. Some of the people who settled in the lower Mississippi Valley included Creoles (descendants of French and Spanish colonists), Cajuns (descendants of Acadians from Nova Scotia), white settlers of European descent, and Africans.

Boone

Listed below are some people who lived in or had some influence on the development of the Mississippi Valley region. In the word search puzzle, locate and circle the names of these famous people. **Hint:** When locating the names, look for *the last name only*. You will find them across, diagonal, or down. After completing the puzzle, choose one of the famous persons and write a report on his or her life and accomplishments.

Daniel Boone   (1734–1820) frontiersman, explorer

George Rogers Clark   (1752–1818) explorer; helped secure regional territory

John Filson   (1747–1788) wrote a book that made Daniel Boone famous

Abraham Lincoln   (1809–1865) 16th president of the United States

Mary Todd   (1818–1882) later became wife of President Lincoln

Zachary Taylor   (1784–1850) 12th president of the United States

Davy Crockett   (1786–1836) frontiersman, scout, Tennessee legislator

Sequoyah   (1760–1843) Cherokee Indian who invented Cherokee alphabet

Andrew Jackson   (1767–1845) 7th president of the United States

Andrew Johnson   (1808–1875) 17th president of the United States

Robert Cavelier LaSalle   (1643–1687) French explorer; claimed Louisiana for France

Hernando DeSoto   (1500–1542) Spanish explorer; discovered Mississippi River

Crockett

©1997 by The Center for Applied Research in Education

```
A  D  S  E  Q  U  O  Y  A  H  I  L  Y  T  R  E
I  O  T  P  O  I  U  Y  T  R  E  A  Q  B  H  I
I  O  J  O  H  N  S  O  N  I  E  S  U  Y  T  R
O  P  A  I  D  I  O  P  E  R  E  A  I  O  D  S
N  B  C  U  Y  D  P  O  B  E  W  L  M  N  B  V
B  V  K  E  W  Q  R  T  O  E  W  L  N  B  V  C
P  O  S  U  Y  T  C  R  O  C  K  E  T  T  N  B
I  O  O  U  L  D  S  A  N  I  U  Y  T  A  N  M
I  U  N  L  I  N  B  V  E  Z  X  C  V  Y  B  G
P  O  I  U  N  Q  W  E  R  T  Y  U  I  L  V  C
Z  X  C  V  C  I  U  C  P  O  I  U  Y  O  E  W
Q  W  E  R  O  E  H  N  L  Q  W  E  R  R  I  O
V  F  F  I  L  S  O  N  E  A  P  O  I  U  Y  T
A  S  D  F  N  Q  W  E  R  T  R  I  O  Y  N  P
I  D  E  S  O  T  O  I  O  P  E  K  Q  W  E  R
M  N  B  V  C  X  Z  A  S  D  F  G  H  J  K  L
```

5-2B PEOPLE OF THE MISSISSIPPI VALLEY

Use the outline below to research and write about one of the famous people of the Mississippi Valley listed in Activity 5-2A.

Name of famous person _____

Profession _____

Write a summary about his or her family and personal life.

_____
_____
_____
_____
_____
_____
_____
_____
_____

Summarize what this person contributed to make him or her famous.

_____
_____
_____
_____
_____
_____
_____
_____
_____

Boone

Crockett

5-3 LIFE ON THE MISSISSIPPI

For the Teacher

Materials Needed:

- copies of Activity 5-3
- pencils

Teacher Preparation:

- Reproduce Activity 5-3, *Life on the Mississippi,* as needed.
- Pass out the activity and allow time for students to complete the story. When they are finished, review the answers (given below) with them.

Answer Key:

(1) cotton

(2) steamboats

(3) sofas

(4) chairs

(5) chandeliers

(6) stained glass

(7) cargo ships

(8) ferries

(9) flatboats

(10) log rafts

(11) comedies (or musicals)

(12) musicals (or comedies)

(13) melodramas

(14) dramas

(15) games

(16) books

(17) music

(18) fried chicken

(19) pecan pie

(20) France

(21) Italy

(22) England

Extended Activity:

- Steamboatin' River Cruises have gained wide acceptance in America, both as a different way to see the Mississippi valley from the river and as an opulent lifestyle. Develop an exhibit on this uniquely American tradition. Contact The Delta Queen Steamboat Co., 30 Robin Street Wharf, New Orleans, Louisiana 70130-1890 or your local travel agent for orientation and bulletin board materials.

5-3 LIFE ON THE MISSISSIPPI

Read the story carefully. Then fill in the blanks with words from the WORD BANK that best complete the sentences. **Hint:** Each dash in a blank represents one letter. Therefore, if there are five dashes in a blank, choose the best word available that has five letters.

©1997 by The Center for Applied Research in Education

WORD BANK

England	cotton	Italy
steamboats	France	pecan pie
log rafts	chairs	sofas
fried chicken	music	books
comedies	chandeliers	games
dramas	melodramas	musicals
stained glass	ferries	flatboats
cargo ships		

On the Mississippi River and its tributaries, the 1800s was known as "The Golden Days of Steamboating." Like the veins of a leaf, this river traces the historic pathway of American discovery. It was along this river system that 19th-century Americans flowed, pushing back the frontier and building the foundation of the nation that would follow.

Influenced by settlers and the rise of great (1) _ _ _ _ _ _ plantations, steamboat travel became a popular and luxurious way to travel. (2) _ _ _ _ _ _ _ _ _ _ are defined as steam-powered paddle wheelers. As the popularity of steamboats grew, they became more and more elaborate. In fact, the steamboat paddle wheelers along the Mississippi were hailed as a triumph in boat architecture.

5-3 LIFE ON THE MISSISSIPPI *(continued)*

Passengers on steamboats were thrilled by the luxurious accommodations.
Rooms were filled with jewel-toned carpets, parquet floors, and fine furniture. For
lounging comfort, expensive (3) _ _ _ _ _ and (4) _ _ _ _ _ _ were imported from Europe.
Gold-trimmed lighting fixtures called (5) _ _ _ _ _ _ _ _ _ _ hung from ceilings.
Main areas were fronted with rosewood and walnut and decorated with brilliant
(6) _ _ _ _ _ _ _ _ _ _ _ _ windows.

Equally as thrilling as the elaborate accommodations was observing America from the
river. What an awesome sight it must have been to see the variety of river traffic!
Besides the luxury steamboat paddle wheelers, there were other modes of transportation on the Mississippi River. They included (7) _ _ _ _ _ _ _ _ _ _, (8) _ _ _ _ _ _ _,
(9) _ _ _ _ _ _ _ _ _, and (10)_ _ _ _ _ _ _ _.

While traveling in comfort on paddle wheelers, guests were entertained in style. At
nightfall passengers dressed in elegant attire and attended moonlight dances. Other
evenings, guests were captivated by troupes of actors who gave performances in
(11) _ _ _ _ _ _ _, (12) _ _ _ _ _ _ _ _, (13)_ _ _ _ _ _ _ _ _ _, or (14) _ _ _ _ _ _. During
the day time, passengers relaxed on deck by playing (15) _ _ _ _ _, reading (16) _ _ _ _ _
(such as *Life on the Mississippi* by Mark Twain), or listening to (17) _ _ _ _ _ on a
strumming banjo.

Dining onboard a paddle wheeler was elaborate as well. There was so much food to
choose from and it was all so tempting. There were traditional southern favorites such
as (18) _ _ _ _ _ _ _ _ _ _ _ _ or (19) _ _ _ _ _ _ _ _. There were also moonlight buffets
that featured food from other countries. Special favorites included food specialties from
(20) _ _ _ _ _ _, (21) _ _ _ _ _, or (22) _ _ _ _ _ _ _.

Today steamboating vacations on the Mississippi River and its tributaries are once
again popular. Travelers looking for the opulence of a bygone era in America may choose
from one of many paddle-wheel adventures. The Delta Queen Steamboat Company offers
many "Discover Mark Twain's America" adventures along the Mississippi. Although
cruises may begin or end as far upper midwest as Minnesota, the lower part of the river,
called the Mississippi Valley, remains a popular destination.

5-4 TAKE A TRIP TO THE MISSISSIPPI VALLEY

For the Teacher

Materials Needed:

- copies of Activity 5-4
- travel agency pamphlets
- travel books (such as *Mobil Travel Guides*)

Note: There is some variance on which states are considered the Mississippi Valley. This version includes the states of Arkansas, Kentucky, Louisiana, Mississippi, and Tennessee.

Teacher Preparation:

- Reproduce Activity 5-4, *Take a Trip to the Mississippi Valley*, as needed and organize reference materials.

- Divide classes into small groups and assign specific states or regions of the Mississippi Valley for students to visit. Instruct classes to center their trips around historical places and events when possible.

- Pass out travel materials and the journal activity. Then allow time for students to complete the activity. Encourage the inclusion of photographs or illustrations, if possible. When students are finished, allow time for groups to share their journals with the rest of the class.

Extended Activities:

- Show classes a travel video on one or more states from the Mississippi Valley. Sources for travelogue tapes include educational channel television, video stores, or libraries.

- Encourage students to learn more about the economy of the states they are visiting. What products or services does the state make or provide? What are the major types of jobs in the state? Information on a state's economy can be found in encyclopedias.

5-4 TAKE A TRIP TO THE MISSISSIPPI VALLEY

DESTINATION _____

For each day, describe the location, place visited, and special activity (such as art, music, food, or holiday).

DAILY ITINERARY

Day 1 _____

_____

_____

Day 2 _____

_____

_____

Day 3 _____

_____

_____

Day 4 _____

_____

_____

Day 5 _____

_____

_____

Day 6 _____

_____

_____

Day 7 _____

_____

_____

5-5 WHAT WILL IT COST?

For the Teacher

Materials Needed:

- copies of Activity 5-5
- travel books
- pencils or pens

Teacher Preparation:

- Reproduce Activity 5-5, *What Will It Cost?,* as needed.
- Pass out the activity and allow time for students to solve the problems. When they are finished, review the answers (given below) with them.

Answer Key:

1. $7.50
2. $54.50
3. $3.00
4. $43.40; $6.51; $49.91
5. $32.00
6. $16.00
7. $7.50; $54.50; $3.00; $49.91; $32.00; $16.00; $162.91

Extended Activity:

- Have students estimate the costs for one day of *their* destination for a family of four (2 adults and 2 students). Approximate hotel and dining costs can be found in most travel books. Other expenses can be estimated. Although Activity 5-5 can be used as a guide, encourage students to make other selections on how the family will spend the day.

Name _____   Date _____   Period _____

5-5 WHAT WILL IT COST?

A family of four (2 adults and 2 students) are visiting the Mississippi Valley states. One of their stops is New Orleans, Louisiana. Listed below are some places they visit. Solve the problems to see how much money they will spend for the day.

1. The family begins the day in the French Market at Cafe du Monde for the famous beignets (donuts) and cafe au lait (half coffee/half milk). Breakfast costs are as follows: 4 beignets at $ .75 each, 2 cafe au lait at $1 each, and 2 hot chocolates at $1.25 each.

   What is the total cost for breakfast? $_____

2. After breakfast the family takes a river cruise on the steamboat *Natchez*. Cost for the cruise is $14.75 for adults and $12.50 for students. The family needs 2 adult and 2 student tickets.

   What is the total cost of the cruise? $_____

3. Next the family takes the St. Charles Avenue Streetcar to the Garden District. Cost is $.75 per person (one way).

   What is the total cost for 4 persons (one way)? $_____

4. The family eats lunch in the Garden District at the famous Commander's Palace. Lunch costs are as follows: $10, $12.50, $8.95, and $11.95.

   What is the cost for 4 lunches? $_____

   Add a 15% tip. $_____

   What is the total cost for lunches? $_____

5. After lunch the family visits the Audubon Park and Zoological Garden. Admission charge is $8 for adults and $4 for students. The family needs 2 adult and 2 student tickets. In addition, there is a $2 per person charge for a special animal exhibit.

   What is the total cost for all admissions? $_____

6. In the evening the family visits Preservation Hall for a New Orleans Jazz concert. Admission is $4 per person.

   What is the total price for 4 admissions? $_____

7. Add all the expenses to see how much money the family has spent.

   Total cost for #1. $_____

   Total cost for #2. $_____

   Total cost for #3. $_____

   Total cost for #4. $_____

   Total cost for #5. $_____

   Total cost for #6. $_____

   Total cost for the day. $_____

©1997 by The Center for Applied Research in Education

5-6 MISSISSIPPI VALLEY TERMS

For the Teacher

Materials Needed:

- copies of Activity 5-6
- copies of *Glossary of Terms* (at back of book)

Teacher Preparation:

- Reproduce Activity 5-6, *Mississippi Valley Terms*, as needed. Also reproduce copies of the *Glossary* as needed.
- Pass out the activity and allow time for students to complete the matching definitions. When they are finished, review the terms (answers given below) with them.

Answer Key:

h.	steamboat	a.	antebellum
m.	paddle wheeler	n.	cotton
q.	flatboat	g.	plantation
b.	bayou	r.	magnolia
i.	jazz	c.	Creole
o.	swamp	d.	Cajun
k.	banjo	f.	calliope
e.	Mississippi River	j.	hurricane
l.	silt	p.	slave

Extended Activity:

- Use some of the terms in the activity as topics for further research. Appropriate titles include The Life of Daniel Boone, the Cumberland Gap, Steamboatin' on the Mississippi, Antebellum Homes of Mississippi and Louisiana, the Creoles of Louisiana, The Cajuns of Louisiana, Life on the Bayou, and Hurricanes.

5-6 MISSISSIPPI VALLEY TERMS

Expand your vocabulary by learning some terms often associated with the Mississippi Valley region. Match the correct definitions to the words.

_____steamboat

_____paddle wheeler

_____flatboat

_____bayou

_____jazz

_____swamp

_____banjo

_____Mississippi River

_____silt

_____antebellum

_____cotton

_____plantation

_____magnolia

_____Creole

_____Cajun

_____calliope

_____hurricane

_____slave

a. (plantations) existing before the Civil War

b. secondary waterway or any marshy body of water

c. a descendant of Spanish and French settlers (mostly in Louisiana)

d. Acadia descendant from Nova Scotia

e. this mighty river flows north and south from Minnesota to the Gulf of Mexico

f. keyboard instrument resembling an organ with whistles; popular form of music on river boats

g. a large estate worked by resident labor

h. boats that are driven by steam power

i. a style of music developed in America from rag-time and blues

j. a tropical cyclone with high winds accompanied by rain, thunder, and lightning

k. a stringed musical instrument probably from Africa

l. a deposit of muddy water (as by a river)

m. a steamboat propelled by a large wheel that has paddles

n. a plant producing a major crop of the old South

o. wet spongy land partially covered with water

p. a person held in servitude or bondage

q. a boat with a flat bottom used for transporting goods especially in shallow water

r. beautiful white flower and the state flower of Louisiana

5-7 FOLKTALES AND LITERATURE

For the Teacher

Materials Needed:

- copies of Activity 5-7
- practice paper and pencils
- drawing paper and pens
- (*optional*) black markers and/or colored pencils

Teacher Preparation:

- Reproduce Activity 5-7, *Folktales and Literature*, as needed and organize materials.

- Pass out the activity and allow students time to read the story. When they are finished, instruct them to create their own folktale. They can develop a Mike Fink adventure story or create a riverboat person of their own.

- Using drawing paper and pens, have students rewrite their stories in their best printing or writing.

- (*optional*) Encourage students to illustrate their stories with markers and/or colored pencils.

Extended Activity:

- Set aside time for reading folktales or literature that relate to Mississippi Valley states, especially those of historical value. Contact the media person in your building or community for assistance in gathering appropriate titles. When possible, take classes to the library for this activity. There are a number of books available that tell stories about the Mississippi region. A brief list follows that will help get you started. **Note:** Remember, this is merely a list of some options. Regional differences may vary, so use whatever is available in your area.

FOLKTALES

Mike Fink by Carol Beach York (Mahwah, NJ: Troll Associates, 1980). In the early days of our country legends grew around the adventures of riverboat men. One particular riverboat folk hero is Mike Fink, who became a symbol of all those who worked on the Mississippi and Ohio rivers.

American Tall Tales by Mary Pope Osborne (New York: Random House, 1991). This book is about some of America's favorite heroes. From the Mississippi Valley states there is Davy Crockett, backwoodsman of Tennessee and Kentucky. There is also Sally Ann Thunder Ann Whirlwind, Davy Crockett's fictional wife.

Daniel Boone by Laurie Lawlor (Morton Grove, IL: A. Whitman, 1989) and *WE THE PEOPLE: Daniel Boone* by Dan Zadra (Mankato, MN: Creative Education, 1988). There are several books on the market about the adventures of Daniel Boone. Start with these two.

CLASSIC LITERATURE

Life on the Mississippi by Mark Twain (various editions are available)

The Adventures of Tom Sawyer by Mark Twain (various editions are available)

Adventures of Huckleberry Finn by Mark Twain (various editions are available)

Samuel Clemens, whose pen name was Mark Twain, is one of the country's best-loved writers. Twain loved the Mississippi River and wrote about it extensively. Even though his Tom Sawyer and Huck Finn characters are set in Missouri (also listed in Section 4, The Midwest and Great Plains), they represent life along the Mississippi River.

The Trail of the Lonesome Pine by John Williams Fox, Jr. (Lexington: University Press of Kentucky, 1984)

The Little Shepherd of Kingdom Come by John Williams Fox, Jr. (Lexington: University Press of Kentucky, 1987)

Fox writes about the mountain people as well as the aristocrats of Kentucky Blue Grass country. Both of these books have been made into films.

The Glass Menagerie by Tennessee Williams (various editions are available; suggested for older students). Williams is generally regarded as one of the foremost dramatists of the 20th century. Much of his work is set in the American South. *The Glass Menagerie* first appeared as a play and has been made into a film.

The Reivers by William Faulkner (various editions are available; suggested for older students)

A Fable by William Faulkner (various editions are available)

Faulkner is considered the greatest American novelist of the 20th century. Much of his writing revolves around imaginary Yoknapatawpha County. His stories are about all types of people from Mississippi—blacks, whites, and Indians.

Roots: The Saga of an American Family by Alex Haley (various editions available; for older students). This best-selling book was made into a popular television mini-series. It traces the events of a black family—from Africa to the slavery days in America's South and finally to freedom.

5-7 FOLKTALES AND LITERATURE

The following story is an adaptation from *Mike Fink* by Carol Beach York.

MIKE FINK

Mike Fink was a scout who grew up in Pennsylvania. He didn't have much schooling, so sometimes people thought he acted funny. However, he could jump higher, shoot straighter, and scout better than anyone else in Pennsylvania. But Mike wanted to leave Pennsylvania and become a riverboat man on the Mighty Mississippi. This story is about how it happened.

The United States was pretty new and it was beginning to grow and spread out. The rivers were the roads for America and the biggest of all was the Mississippi. If people wanted flour or sugar or nails or gunpowder, they all came to them on river boats. Wheat, corn, molasses, and cider were all carried on the river boat from town to town.

One day Mike Fink was talkin' to some riverboat men who were loadin' cargo for a trip down the Mississippi. They were strong, bold men who didn't take second place to anyone!

One of the riverboat men said to Mike, "Scoutin' may be hard work but river boatin' is harder." Mike couldn't believe his ears and told the riverboat man, "I can wrestle ten bears at one time or fight fifty men in one afternoon. I'm as tough as nails and as hard as an iron skillet. So river boatin' looks easy to me."

"Come get on board then," the riverboat man said, "and we'll see." As it turned out Mike Fink was born for river boatin'.

After Mike joined up on the riverboat, he soon found out how hard it was. Goin' downstream was bad enough. There were floatin' trees, sandbars, and storms to contend with. But at least the boat was goin' with the flow of the river. It was comin' back up the Mississippi that was really hard work. The river flow was against them. Therefore, the riverboat men had to row in deep water. When the water was shallow, the men drove the ends of long poles into the river bottom and pushed. Goin' upstream was slow, hard work.

Mike Fink soon realized it took tough men to be a riverboat man. But Mike was one of the toughest and he loved river boatin'. In fact, he took to river boatin' so fast that it wasn't very long before he built his own boat. He named his boat *Lightfoot*.

"I'm a rip roarin' riverboat man," he would shout as he journeyed up and down the Mississippi. "I'm half wild horse and half crazy alligator and I'm ready for anything."

5-8 PASTIMES AND GAMES

For the Teacher

Materials Needed:

- copies of Activity 5-8
- items mentioned in "Teacher Preparation"

Teacher Preparation:

- Reproduce Activity 5-8, *Pastimes and Games*, as needed.

- Pass out the activity and go over the pastimes outlined. If possible, *allow students to help make choices on which activities will be selected. Then set aside some time for participation.*

- If there is interest in creating a *Mardi Gras* atmosphere in the classroom, you will need the following materials: balloons, string, and crepe paper. For Mardi Gras banners, drawing paper (or lightweight cardboard), preferably in Mardi Gras colors of yellow, green, and purple. Involve the classes in making decorations or ask for volunteers for an outside-the-classroom assignment.

- If there is interest in creating the sounds of Mardi Gras, ask for volunteers to bring in some *jazz* CDs. Many musicians play jazz music, but two classic performers include Louie Armstrong and Duke Ellington.

- If making Mardi Gras *masks* is selected, refer to Activity 5-10 for easy-to-make instructions. Masks may serve as part of the decorations and make an ideal project for awarding prizes to funniest or most creative submissions.

- If indulging in New Orleans *carnival-style foods*, ask for volunteers to bring in ready-made choices or refer to activities 5-13 and 5-14 for an outside-the-classroom assignment to make at home and then bring to school to share with others.

- If Mardi Gras-style *games* are selected, you will need the following materials: balloons, string (for *Balloon Soccer*) and pencils, paper (for *Mardi Gras Words* or *Carnival Pyramid*).

- **PRIZES:** Everyone loves a prize! Award one or more to winners of the games. Prizes need not be expensive or elaborate. Some ideas include small chocolate candies, small pecan logs, petit fours, or French doughnuts.

5-8 PASTIMES AND GAMES

©1997 by The Center for Applied Research in Education

PASTIMES

One of the most elaborate annual pastimes in America is *Mardi Gras* in New Orleans. Mardi Gras is a winter carnival held just before the beginning of Lent. Although religious in origin, the festival has become an American excuse for throwing a party at the end of winter. Outlined below are some ideas for creating a Mardi Gras in your own classroom. Choose one or all and enjoy the spirit of one of America's favorite end-of-winter celebrations.

DECORATIONS

Whether you want to celebrate Mardi Gras in a small or large manner, decorations will create a festive atmosphere. Appropriate, inexpensive, and easy-to-do decorations are floating balloons and twisted crepe paper streamers in carnival colors of yellow, green, and purple. An idea that takes a little more thought involves making large letter banners with **HAPPY MARDI GRAS** greetings across the room.

DIXIELAND AND JAZZ

To capture the sound of Mardi Gras, bring in CDs of jazz music. Two artists synonymous with New Orleans are Pete Fountain and Louie Armstrong. There are, however, many other musicians who play jazz. Can you name one? Perhaps you or someone you know has a Jazz or Dixieland collection and would be willing to share some with your class.

MARDI GRAS MASKS

One of the oldest traditions of Mardi Gras is to dress in a costume for one of the many parades or dances that occur during the week of the carnival. Make your own Mardi Gras mask by following the easy-to-make directions in Activity 5-10, *Mardi Gras Masks*. When masks are complete ask your school's Art teacher to judge the best and funniest submissions. Display them around the room along with other Mardi Gras decorations.

MARDI GRAS ENTERTAINMENT

Grand parades and strolling entertainers represent two other Mardi Gras traditions. Although it is not feasible to participate in an elaborate float parade, you can adapt a carnival atmosphere in your classroom by inviting a friend or parent to dress as a clown or mime and perform a skit or pantomime for the class.

MARDI GRAS FOOD

Special feasts are prepared and eaten during carnival time. For your Mardi Gras, choose some ready-made or simple-to-prepare New Orleans-style foods. Appropriate choices include Pecan Logs, Pralines, or Pecan Pies. With a little extra effort, you can make Pecan Pralines or Praline Sundaes. See activities 5-13 and 5-14 for recipes.

MARDI GRAS GAMES

Create your own Mardi Gras party games by selecting one or more of the ones listed below.

BALLOON SOCCER

Use these party props in a soccer game for guaranteed laughs. Divide into groups of four to six students each. To play, clear an area of the room and have one group at a time participate while the others watch. Attach an inflated balloon to an ankle of each group member with a piece of string. Then guard your own balloon while trying to pop others.

MARDI GRAS WORDS

Your teacher will give you a sheet of paper with the words MARDI GRAS CARNIVAL written on it. See how many words you can make from them. Prizes will be awarded to the most words and the longest word. Some example words include: gain, drag, and maid.

CARNIVAL PYRAMID

Divide into pairs or small groups. Have a person in each group write the words MARDI GRAS CARNIVAL on a piece of paper. Then each group will try to build a word pyramid from the MARDI GRAS CARNIVAL words. Below is an example of how to build a word pyramid. Prizes may be awarded to the teams with the most word pyramids. **Note:** Two succeeding words *may not* begin with the same letter and no word may be used twice.

A

IS

CAN

NAIL

GRAIN

RASCAL

GRANDMA

DIAGRAMS

CARNIVALS

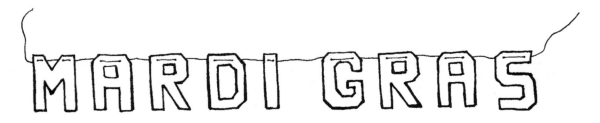

©1997 by The Center for Applied Research in Education

5-9 SOUNDS OF THE MISSISSIPPI VALLEY

For the Teacher

Materials Needed:

• CD, cassette, or film

• audio-visual equipment

Teacher Preparation:

• **Jazz** is a type of music developed by African-Americans around the early 1900s. The earliest documented jazz style emerged in New Orleans, Louisiana. In this style, the trumpet carried the melody and the clarinet played counter melodies. Leaders in jazz include Louie Armstrong, Duke Ellington, and Ella Fitzgerald. For opportunities to listen to music from or relating to the Mississippi Valley, consider the following options:

CD or cassette

Louis "Satchmo" Armstrong (1900–1971) was one of the most influential musicians in the history of jazz. Some specific recording titles include *Stardust, The Essence of Louis Armstrong,* and *Essential Louis Armstrong.*

Duke Ellington (1899–1974) was also one of the most respected musicians in the history of jazz. He was responsible for bringing jazz into concert halls. A few specific titles include *Duke Ellington and His Orchestra, Early Ellington,* and *Jazz Tribute.*

Ella Fitzgerald (1918–1996) was an American female jazz singer admired for her musicianship. Some specific recording titles include *Ella Fitzgerald, Ella Sings the Duke Ellington Song Book,* and *Jazz Masters.*

• For an opportunity to view a musical film production relating to life along the Mississippi River, consider the following option:

Show Boat, a musical by Kern and Hammerstein. This classical operetta tells the tale of life and love on a Mississippi riverboat troupe. With unforgettable music from Jerome Kern and Oscar Hammerstein, the musical is based on Edna Ferber's novel. Stars include Kathryn Grayson, Howard Keel, and Ava Gardner in this 1951 film classic. Songs from the musical include "Can't Help Lovin' that Man of Mine," "Ole' Man River," and "We Could Make Believe."

It is always advised to preview a film and obtain parental consent before showing it to students.

5-10 MARDI GRAS MASKS

For the Teacher

Materials Needed:

- copies of Activity 5-10
- lightweight cardboard
- glue
- scissors
- paper plates
- stapler

- feathers, sequins, glitter, or bric-a-brac
- black markers
- (*optional*) colored markers and pencils
- (*optional*) colored construction paper
- popsicle sticks or tongue depressors

Teacher Preparation:

- Reproduce Activity 5-10, *Mardi Gras Masks*, as needed and organize materials. Eye Stick Masks are suggested for the girls and Clown Masks are recommended for the boys. Ask students to bring in any scraps of the bric-a-brac items they may have from home.

- Pass out the activity and go over the information with students.

- Distribute the materials and allow time for students to develop their Mardi Gras Masks.

- When they are finished, display them around the room.

- Ask the art teacher to judge the most creative and/or funniest submissions and award prizes.

Extended Activity:

- As an alternative, contact the art teacher in your building well in advance and coordinate a mask-making project while your classes are participating in a Mardi Gras celebration.

Photo 5-1 *Cardboard stick mask, collection of the author.* Many sizes and shapes of masks were developed during a mask-making activity in art class. This student-made version was created on lightweight cardboard. The basic designs on the mask were outlined in black marker, then colored in with yellow, orange, and red markers.

5-10 MARDI GRAS MASKS

A Mardi Gras celebration isn't a celebration without masks. During carnival time, as well as throughout the year, many shapes and sizes are for sale. In fact, masks are one of the most frequently purchased items by tourists when they visit New Orleans.

Costumed participants create much of the fun and charm of Mardi Gras in New Orleans. Women favor the colorful stick masks because of the many varieties possible. Clown masks, on the other hand, are generally worn by men. Create your own mask versions by following these easy-to-make directions.

Eye Stick Masks

Look at the illustration below. Then cut your own basic eye mask shape from lightweight cardboard. Cut out eye shapes. Then decorate the mask with yarn, feathers, sequins, glitter, or flashy bric-a-brac. After you have finished, staple or tape a popsicle stick or tongue depressor to the back.

Clown Masks

Clown masks, generally worn by males, dot the Mardi Gras. To make your own clown mask, look at the illustration below. Then cut two slits (about 2" on each side of a paper plate. Overlap the slits and staple shut. Cut out eye shapes. Decorate the masks with cutout, colored construction paper shapes for the mouth, nose, hat, hair, and neck dress or tie. When you are finished, staple or tape a popsicle stick or tongue depressor to the back.

5-11 BASICS OF CREOLE COOKING

For the Teacher

Materials Needed:

- copies of Activity 5-11
- pencils

Teacher Preparation:

- Reproduce Activity 5-11, *Basics of Creole Cooking*, as needed.
- Pass out the activity and allow time for students to read the information and complete the worksheet. (Answers are given below.) When they are finished, review the Creole food basics.

Answer Key:

Part One:

Seafood: crawfish; shrimp; crab; oysters

Fish specialties: shrimp creole; seafood gumbo

Meats: beef; lamb; pork; chicken

Creole meat specialty: jambalaya

Vegetables: beans; rice; okra; turnips; spinach; eggplant; green beans; mustard greens

Vegetable dish: black beans and rice

Seasonings: file; Louisiana hot sauce

Desserts: beignets; pecan pralines; New Orleans bread pudding

Part Two:

Creole cuisine: a unique culinary art developed in Louisiana by cooking techniques of French, Spanish, African, and Choctaw Indians

Roux: a mixture of flour and shortening to use as a thickener

Crawfish: a spiny lobster

Okra: a green pod vegetable

File: a powdered seasoning made from bay leaves and peppers

Louisiana hot sauce: a tomato-and-pepper-based sauce

Shrimp creole: shrimp with a tomato-based sauce served with rice

Seafood gumbo: a thick soup using shrimp, crab, and okra

Jambalaya: ham, chicken, sausage, or seafood with tomatoes and rice

Beignets: French doughnuts

Pecan pralines: caramel and pecan candy

Extended Activity:

- Encourage students to collectively develop a Creole cookbook. Divide classes into groups and assign specific topics to each group. Approximate topics include Soups, Breads, Vegetables, Meats, Seafood, and Desserts. After students have collected their recipes, duplicate their submissions and allow each person to organize a cookbook of his or her own.

5-11 BASICS OF CREOLE COOKING

Creole cuisine is a unique culinary art developed in New Orleans and other sections of Louisiana by the combined cooking techniques of the French and Spanish settlers with modifications from African and Choctaw Indian cooks. This regional cooking has gained acceptance throughout the United States. Many large cities have restaurants that serve Creole food.

ROUX

One of the most important parts of Creole cooking is the use of roux. Roux is a creamed mixture of flour and shortening that acts as a thickener. The roux sauce is the basis for many seafood, soup, and meat recipes.

SEAFOOD

Creole cooks use an abundance of local seafood from the Gulf waters that surround Louisiana. *Crawfish, shrimp, crab,* and *oysters* reign supreme with many sophisticated and distinct methods of preparation. Crawfish is a spiny lobster-type of fish. Two famous fish specialties include *shrimp creole* (shrimp with a tomato-based sauce served with rice), and *seafood gumbo* (a thick soup using shrimp, crab, and okra).

MEATS

Beef, lamb, pork, and *chicken* are all used by Creole cooks. Perhaps the most famous of all Creole specialties is *jambalaya.* This famous dish combines ham, chicken, sausage, or seafood with tomatoes and rice.

VEGETABLES

Beans, rice, okra, turnips, mustard greens, spinach, green beans, and *eggplant* are all used in Creole cooking. *Black beans and rice* is a typical Louisiana "common folks" food. It is the South's equivalent to Italy's spaghetti and tomato sauce dishes. Okra is a green pod vegetable that is used by many Creole cooks to create soups and gumbos.

SEASONING

File is a powdered seasoning made from a combination of bay leaves and a variety of peppers. Most of the flavorful Creole dishes are highly seasoned with file. Another seasoning used by Creole cooks is *Louisiana hot sauce,* a tomato-and-pepper-based sauce that should be used cautiously.

DESSERTS

Desserts are a special treat to southern cooks. Especially popular in New Orleans are *beignets, pecan pralines,* and *New Orleans bread pudding.* Beignets are French doughnuts. A popular New Orleans tradition is to begin or end the day with chicory coffee and fresh beignets. Pecan pralines are caramel and pecans mixed together to form sweet candy patties.

5-11 BASICS OF CREOLE COOKING

Part One: Use the boxes below to outline some of the food basics of Creole cooking.

Seafood: _____ _____

_____ _____

Two fish specialties: _____

_____

Meats: _____ _____

_____ _____

Creole meat specialty: _____

Vegetables: _____ _____

_____ _____

_____ _____

_____ _____

Famous vegetable dish: _____

Seasonings: _____

_____

New Orleans desserts: _____

_____

_____

_____

5-11 BASICS OF CREOLE COOKING *(continued)*

Part Two: Write the definitions of the foods listed below.

Creole cuisine _____

_____

Roux _____

_____

Crawfish _____

_____

Okra _____

_____

File _____

_____

Louisiana hot sauce _____

_____

Shrimp creole _____

_____

Seafood gumbo _____

_____

Jambalaya _____

_____

Beignets _____

_____

Pecan pralines _____

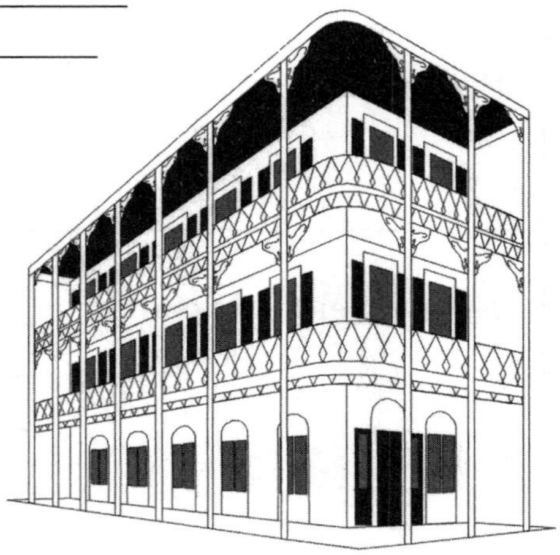

_____

5-12 PATOUT'S OF NEW ORLEANS RESTAURANT

For the Teacher

Hint: It is helpful to complete Activity 5-11, *Basics of Creole Cooking*, before participating in this one.

Materials Needed:

- copies of Activity 5-12
- pencils or pens

Teacher Preparation:

- Reproduce Activity 5-13, *Patout's of New Orleans Restaurant*, as needed.
- Pass out the activity. Then allow students time to read the menu and make their dinner selections. When they are finished, lead a discussion to compare and contrast a Creole dinner to a typical special-occasion dinner of their own.

Extended Activity:

- Ask students to bring in some simple or ready-prepared food items popular in New Orleans. Appropriate choices include French doughnuts, pecan logs, sugared pecans, petit fours, and fruit punch.

You are at a restaurant called **Patout's of New Orleans**. Look over the menu carefully. Then make your dinner selections on the activity sheet provided. (*This menu is compliments of Patout's.*)

APPETIZERS

FRIED PICKLES
Deep fried in our special batter. ....

ONION RING BASKET
Hand dipped in Patout's secret batter. ....

SPINACH & ARTICHOKE DIP
Served warm with celery and
carrot sticks. ....

ALLIGATOR SAUSAGE
Homemade sausage served
over rice in it's own gravy. ....

JAZZY WINGS
Cajun spicy wings served with celery & carrot
sticks with creamy Italian dressing. ....

OYSTER GI GI - AWARD WINNER
Fresh Oysters wrapped in bacon and
battered in Italian bread crumbs
& Patout seasoning then fried ....

CAJUN POPCORN
Delicious Louisiana Crawfish Tails
fried in a special batter. ....

COMBO PLATTER (SERVES TWO)
Alligator sausage, Cajun Popcorn and
Fried Pickles...

GUMBO

CHICKEN & SAUSAGE GUMBO
Voted # 1 in New Orleans. C'est Bon .... Cup
Bowl

FRENCH MARKET FRESH SALADS

Our signature salad dressing is our Mother's Creole Mustard Dressing.
1000 Island, Buttermilk Ranch, Creamy Italian, Cajun Catalina, Roquefort, Vinaigrette
Fat Free selections: Light Italian, Honey Dijon, 1000 Island

CAJUN GRILLED CHICKEN SALAD
A spicy chicken breast atop a variety of
lettuce greens with onions, mushrooms,
carrots, tomatoes, fresh croutons.
Served with warm Honey Dijon. ....

GRILLED CHICKEN SALAD
Grilled chicken atop a variety
of lettuce greens with onions, mushrooms,
carrots, tomatoes croutons and
Parmasean Cheese. ....

SHRIMP SALAD - LA LOUISIANA
A variety of mixed greens with your choice of
Fried Shrimp or Boiled Shrimp topped with
mushrooms and tomatoes ....

CAESAR SALAD/
GRILLED CHICKEN CAESAR
Fresh Romaine lettuce topped with croutons,
Parmasean Cheese and Caesar Dressing. ....
Add 2.00 for Grilled Chicken topping

BLACKENED CHICKEN SALAD
A spicy combination of Blackened chicken
breast on a bed of mixed greens with mushrooms,
carrots, tomatoes, onions and croutons – served
with warm Honey Dijon...........................

SALAD ACADIANA (CHEF SALAD)
Diced tender Ham and Turkey with
Monterey Jack and Mild Cheddar cheeses
on a bed of variety of greens with tomatoes,
mushrooms, onions and croutons
with your choice of dressing. ....

CRAWFISH SALAD
Choice of Boiled or Fried Crawfish Tails atop
a variety of salad greens with mushrooms,
tomatoes and croutons ....

SHRIMP REMOULADE
A savory creole mustard and
celery dressing tossed in boiled shrimp
atop a variety of greens. ....

PO-BOY SANDWICHES

A classic New Orleans sandwich served on French bread
and is at it's best dressed all the way with lettuce, creole mustard, pickles and tomatoes.
Served with chips.   Substitute for Fries only 1.00 extra.

Oyster Po-Boy .... Half .... Full
Shrimp Po-Boy .... Half .... Full
Catfish Po-Boy .... Half .... Full
Cochon De Lait (Roast Pork) .... Half .... Full
Chicken Breast Po-Boy .... Half .... Full

OUR SANDWICH PANTRY

All sandwiches are served with chips. Substitute Fries

1/2 LB. BOURBON STREET HAMBURGER

Hand patted and grilled to absolute perfection
garnished with lettuce, tomato, onion
and pickles. ....

BREADED PORK TENDERLOIN

Deep fried loin served with
onions, lettuce, tomato an pickles. ....

CAJUN HAMBURGER

Hand patted 1/2 pound seasoned with Patout's
seasonings patted and grilled to perfection .....

BACON CHEESEBURGER SUPREME

1/2 pound burger with bacon and Mild Cheddar
cheese tops this one with lettuce, tomato, red
onion and pickles on a fresh bun. ....

N'AWLINS FAVORITES

All served with bread & butter

RED BEANS & SAUSAGE

Red beans cooked slowly with
onions, bell peppers and sausage
served over rice. ....

JAMBALAYA

Slowly cooked chicken, sausage with onions
and bell peppers in a dark roux base,
tossed with Louisiana rice. ....

SHRIMP CREOLE

A New Orleans Classic, with tomatoes
and herb sauce, fresh shrimp seasoned
just right and served over rice. ....

COCHON DE LAIT

Slowley roasted pork in it's natural gravy
with rice and Sweet Potato topped
with Praline topping. ....

DESSERT

Bread pudding w/Whiskey Sauce – house speciality ....
Ice cream - Lemon Yogurt. ....
Pecan pie topped with ice cream – a Louisiana favorite ....
Chocolate Suicide ....

©1997 by The Center for Applied Research in Education

Name _____ **Date** _____ **Period** _____

5-12 PATOUT'S OF NEW ORLEANS RESTAURANT

After you have looked over the menu from **Patout's New Orleans Restaurant,** make your dinner selections in the appropriate spaces below. When making your choices, name the food item and then describe it (if a description is listed). When you are finished, outline a typical special-occasion dinner you might have at your house. Are there any differences? Are there similarities?

New Orleans Dinner

Appetizer _____

_____

Gumbo _____

French Market Fresh Salads _____

_____

Choose one from the following:

Po-Boy Sandwiches _____

Our Sandwich Pantry _____

N'Awlins Favorites _____

Patout's Favorites _____

Dessert _____

_____

American Dinner

Appetizer _____

_____

Soup or Salad _____

_____

Main Course _____

_____

Vegetables _____

_____

Bread _____

_____

Dessert _____

_____

5-13 PECAN PRALINES

For the Teacher

Equipment Needed:

- copies of Activity 5-13
- 2-quart saucepan
- measuring cups
- candy thermometer
- wooden spoon
- teaspoon
- cookie sheet
- container with lid

Supplies Needed:

- white sugar
- brown sugar
- corn syrup
- evaporated milk
- vanilla
- pecan halves
- waxed paper

Teacher Preparation

- Reproduce Activity 5-13, *Pecan Pralines*, as needed and organize equipment and supplies.
- Give a demonstration on making candy as students follow along with the recipe. Follow up with a candy treat day.
- **ALTERNATIVE**: Go over the recipe with students. Then make an out-of-class assignment for students to make the pralines at home and bring them to school for a special New Orleans treat day. Encourage students to ask for adult supervision when making the candy.

Extended Activity:

- Contact the Consumer and Family Living teacher well in advance to coordinate a Creole lunch or dessert lab activity while your classes are learning about the Mississippi Valley.

5-13 PECAN PRALINES

Pecan Pralines is a New Orleans tradition. Visitors seldom visit without taking home some of these deliciously sweet candied nuts. Like many other dishes connected to New Orleans, the origin of the recipe is French. In fact, the candy was named after a French aristocrat, Cesar du Plessis-Pralin. This recipe makes 30 small pralines.

You need:

1-1/2	cups white sugar
1-1/2	cups brown sugar
3	tablespoons corn syrup
1	cup evaporated milk (such as Pet®)
1	teaspoon vanilla
2	cups pecan halves

What to do:

1. In a saucepan, combine white sugar, brown sugar, corn syrup, and milk.
2. Bring mixture to a boil while stirring with a wooden spoon.
3. Reduce to medium heat and clip a candy thermometer to side of pan. Cook to soft-ball stage while stirring occasionally.
4. Cool 10 minutes.
5. Add vanilla and pecan halves.
6. Beat by hand until mixture loses its gloss.
7. Drop by teaspoons onto waxed paper. If candy becomes too stiff, add a few drops of hot water.
8. Cool. Then store in air-tight container.

5-14 PRALINE SUNDAES

For the Teacher

Equipment Needed:

- copies of Activity 5-14
- saucepan
- measuring cup
- spoon
- jar with lid

Supplies Needed:

- brown sugar
- dark corn syrup
- chopped pecans
- ice cream

Teacher Preparation:

- Reproduce Activity 5-14, *Praline Sundaes*, as needed and organize equipment and supplies.

- Give a demonstration on making the topping as students follow along with the recipe. Follow up with a praline sundae taste treat.

- **ALTERNATIVE:** Go over recipe with students. Then make an out-of-class assignment for students to make the topping at home and bring it to school for a special sundae treat day. Encourage students to ask for adult supervision when making the sundae topping.

Extended Activity:

- A New Orleans tradition is visiting **Cafe du Monde** for a cup of cafe au lait and beignets (French doughnuts). Cafe au lait is chicory coffee (traditionally served with equal amounts of coffee and milk). For a special New Orleans treat, make and serve chicory coffee and beignets. Chicory coffee and beignet mixes can be purchased from Cafe du Monde in New Orleans.

5-14 PRALINE SUNDAES

Pecans and pecan recipes are popular throughout the South, with pralines reigning supreme. In this delightful New Orleans dessert, praline syrup is poured over vanilla ice cream for a deliciously satisfying sweet dessert. This recipes serves 6 to 8.

You need:

1/4	cup boiling water
1/3	cup brown sugar
1	cup dark corn syrup
1	cup chopped pecans
1	quart vanilla ice cream

What to do:

1. In a saucepan, combine water, sugar, and corn syrup.

2. Bring mixture to a full boil, then remove from heat.

3. Add chopped pecans.

4. Cool, then pour syrup into a jar. Mixture will thicken as it cools.

5. Serve chilled praline sauce over ice cream.

5-15 BREAD PUDDING

For the Teacher

Equipment Needed:

- copies of Activity 5-15
- toaster
- 1-1/2-quart baking dish
- mixing bowl
- hand mixer
- measuring cup
- measuring spoons
- 1-1/2-quart saucepan

Supplies Needed:

- white bread
- margarine
- raisins
- eggs
- brown sugar
- white sugar
- cinnamon
- vanilla
- milk

Teacher Preparation:

- Reproduce Activity 5-15, *Bread Pudding*, as needed and organize equipment and supplies.

- Give a demonstration on making the pudding as students follow along with the recipe. Follow up with a bread pudding taste treat.

- **ALTERNATIVE:** Go over the recipe with students. Then make an out-of-class assignment for students to make the pudding at home and bring it to school for a special New Orleans treat day. Encourage students to ask for adult supervision when making the pudding.

5-15 BREAD PUDDING

The French call Bread Pudding *Pain Perdu* which means "lost bread." The pudding was named Pain Perdu because it is prepared with bread that is old and might have gone to waste if not used in a pudding. This very popular dessert in New Orleans has many versions. For simplification, this one uses white bread; however, in Creole country, day-old French bread would be used. Bread pudding is especially delicious when topped with praline syrup (see Activity 5-14). This recipe serves 6 to 8.

You need:

4	slices white bread
2	tablespoons margarine, softened
1/3	cup raisins
2	eggs, beaten
1/3	cup brown sugar
1/3	cup white sugar
1	teaspoon vanilla
1/2	teaspoon cinnamon
2-1/2	cups milk, heated
	(*optional*) praline syrup (see Activity 5-14)

What to do:

1. Heat oven to 350°.

2. Coat sides and bottom of baking dish with margarine.

3. Toast bread slices. Spread with margarine.

4. Cut toast into bite-sized pieces and arrange in baking dish. Then sprinkle with raisins.

5. In a mixing bowl, beat eggs. Then add brown sugar, white sugar, vanilla, and cinnamon. Mix thoroughly.

6. In a saucepan, heat milk. Then *slowly* stir egg mixture into milk.

7. Pour into baking dish, covering the bread and raisins.

8. Bake for about 45 minutes or until an inserted knife comes out clean.

9. Serve warm or cool.

10. (*optional*) Top with praline syrup.

BIBLIOGRAPHY FOR THE MISSISSIPPI VALLEY

Children's Fiction

York, Carol Beach. *Mike Fink*. Mahwah, NJ: Troll Associates, 1980.

Children's Nonfiction

Carson, Robert. *America the Beautiful: Mississippi*. Chicago: Children's Press, 1993.

Heinrichs, Ann. *America the Beautiful: Arkansas*. Chicago: Children's Press, 1992.

Kent, Deborah. *America the Beautiful: Louisiana*. Chicago: Children's Press, 1988.

McNair, Sylvia. *America the Beautiful: Kentucky*. Chicago: Children's Press, 1992.

McNair, Sylvia. *America the Beautiful: Tennessee*. Chicago: Children's Press, 1993.

Cookbooks

Darling, Jennifer and Shelli McConnell. *Better Homes and Gardens Heritage of America Cookbook*. Des Moines: Meredith Corporation, 1993.

New Orleans Restaurants. *Favorite New Orleans Recipes*. New Orleans: Express Publishing Co., Inc.

Music

Staff. *Academic American Encyclopedia, Volumes 1 & 3*. Danbury, CT: Grolier Inc., 1996.

Pastimes

The National Society of the Colonial Dames of America. *To a King's Taste*. The National Society of the Colonial Dames of America, New Orleans, 1987.

Travel

Brochure. *The Delta Queen Steamboat Company*. New Orleans: Delta Queen Steamboat Co., 1996.

Editors. *Mobil 1995 Travel Guide, Southeast*. New York: Fodor's Travel Publications, 1995.

Editors. *Mobil 1995 Travel Guide, Southwest & South Central*. New York: Fodor's Travel Publications, 1995.

THE BECKONING WEST

Section 6, The Southwest—After Texas won its independence from Mexico, many pioneers began to settle the southwest part of America. This large region included the present-day states of Texas and most of New Mexico plus a smaller section of Arizona. Although there is some variance on what states are considered to be today's southwest, this version includes the states of Texas, New Mexico, and Arizona.

Although you will learn about all of the southwest states in Section 6, it will feature **San Antonio, Texas**. This colorful city represents an important historical part of Texas. It was, after all, at the battle of the **Alamo** where a small band of Americans fought bravely for independence from Mexico. In San Antonio, as well as other parts of the southwest, Spanish, Indian, and American cultures blended together and produced a unique region in America. In fact, some visitors who visit the southwest feel like it is a country of its own.

Section 7, The Northwest—At about the same time the southwest was being settled, pioneers began to journey beyond the Rocky Mountains into the northwest. This region consists of the present-day states of Washington, Oregon, Idaho, Montana, and Wyoming.

Although you will learn about all the northwest states, Section 7 will journey to the northwest along **the Oregon Trail**.

Section 8, The West—In 1848 Mexico and the United States signed a peace treaty. As a result America gained the land that makes up the present-day states of California, Utah, Nevada, and Colorado plus parts of New Mexico and Arizona. Although there is some variance on what states are considered part of the west, this version includes the present-day states of California, Nevada, Utah, and Colorado.

In Section 8 you will learn about all of the western states. However, the focus will be on **the California Gold Rush** near Sacramento.

SECTION 6

THE SOUTHWEST

Below is an outline of the interdisciplinary activities included in this section. They are designed to bring a broad range of hands-on cultural lessons and activities into the social studies classroom. Pick and choose the ones that best fit into your program.

Social Studies

Mathematics

Language Arts

Physical Education

Music

Art

Consumer and Family Living

Bibliography for the Southwest

MAP OF THE SOUTHWEST

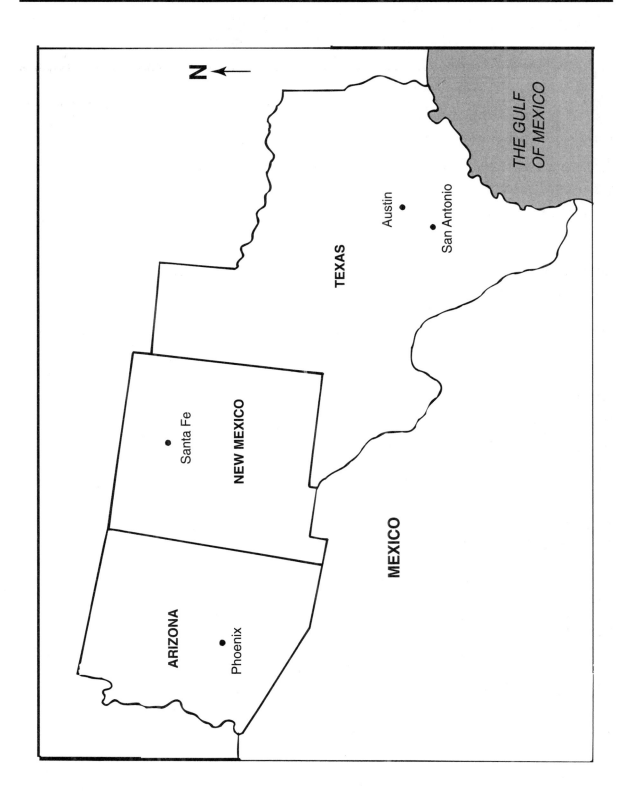

6-1 GETTING TO KNOW THE SOUTHWEST

For the Teacher

Materials Needed:

- copies of Activity 6-1
- labeled map of the Southwest (enlarged on opaque projector)
- copies of unlabeled map of the Southwest
- colored pencils

Teacher Preparation:

- Reproduce Activity 6-1, *Getting to Know the Southwest*, as needed. Also reproduce copies of the unlabeled map of the Southwest as needed.
- Pass out the activity and map to each student. Then allow time for students to locate and label the Southwest as outlined in the activity. When they are finished, review the geography with them.

Extended Activities:

- Reproduce additional copies of the unlabeled map and have students identify other features of southwestern states, such as early settlements, population distribution, land use, or climate. PC Globe® computer program can provide much of the information needed for this activity. Consult your school's media person for assistance, too.
- Reproduce the chart of *The Fifty States* (at back of book) as needed. Pass out the chart and have students make a list of the Southwest states, date they entered the Union, order of entry, capital, and largest city. *List states in order they entered the union.* Answers should appear as follows:

State	Date Entered Union	Order of Entry	Capital	Largest City
Texas	1845	28	Austin	Houston
New Mexico	1912	47	Santa Fe	Albuquerque
Arizona	1912	48	Phoenix	Phoenix

6-1 GETTING TO KNOW THE SOUTHWEST

Use the map provided to locate and label the following features:

State: Arizona
Capital: Phoenix

State: New Mexico
Capital: Santa Fe

State: Texas
Capital: Austin
Early settlement: San Antonio

Bordering body of water: Gulf of Mexico
Bordering country: Mexico

6-1 GETTING TO KNOW THE SOUTHWEST

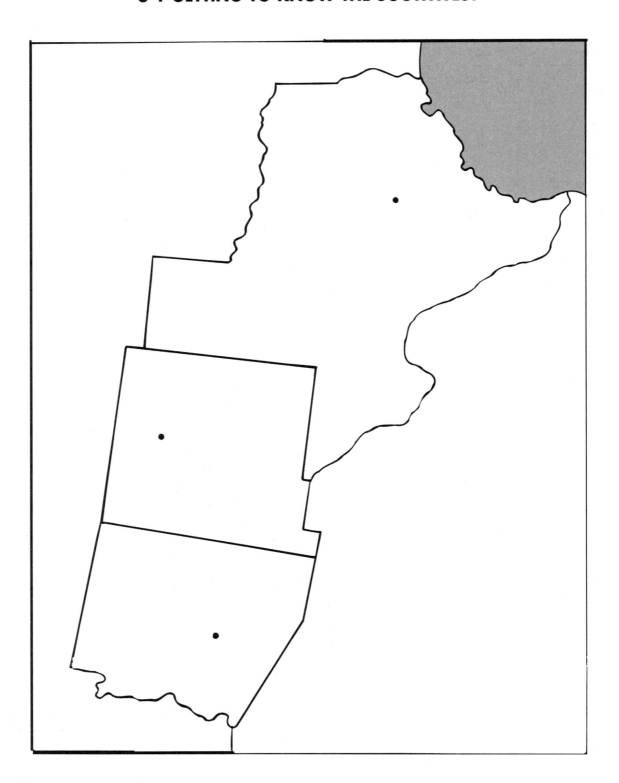

6-2 PEOPLE OF THE SOUTHWEST

For the Teacher

Materials Needed:

- copies of Activity 6-2
- pencils
- research materials

Teacher Preparation:

- Reproduce Activity 6-2A and 6-2B, *People of the Southwest*, as needed.
- Pass out the activity and allow enough time for students to complete the word search puzzle. When they are finished, review the answers (given below) with them.

Answer Key:

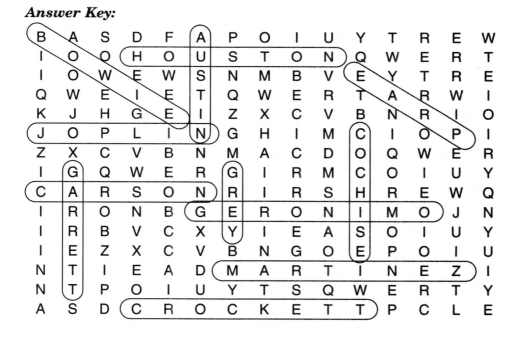

Extended Activities:

- Encourage students to pick one of the famous people in the puzzle (or another person from the southwest who has made a contribution to America) and assign research papers on his or her life and contributions. Use the outline provided in Activity 6-2B to develop the reports.
- Films have been made about some of the famous people in the puzzle. Select one and show it to your classes.

6-2A PEOPLE OF THE SOUTHWEST

The story of the southwest is one of cultures blending together. For many years the American Indians and Spanish descendants occupied the general area of America known today as the Southwest. During the late 1800s the southwest grew in size with white settlers of European descent. Like other settlers pushing westward, they came to make a better life.

Listed below are some people who lived in or had some influence on the development of the Southwest region. In the word search puzzle, locate and circle the names of these famous people. **Hint:** When locating the names, look for the *last name only*. You will find them across, diagonal, or down. After completing the puzzle, choose one of the famous persons and write a report on his or her life and accomplishments.

Houston

©1997 by The Center for Applied Research in Education

Stephen F. Austin   (1793–1836) pioneer; "Father of Texas"

Sam Houston   (1793–1863) soldier, first president of Republic of Texas

Scott Joplin   (1868–1917) musician; originator of ragtime music

Wyatt Earp   (1848–1929) frontier lawman; marshal of Tombstone in 1881

Geronimo   (1829–1909) Apache chief who resisted white settlers

Zane Grey   (1872–1939) wrote novels with western themes from Arizona

Kit Carson   (1809–1868) frontiersman, explorer, Indian agent

Cochise   (1812–1874) Apache chief in Arizona

Maria Martinez   (1887–1980) Indian pueblo potter

Pat Garrett   (1850–1908) cowboy, Texas Ranger, lawman

Jim Bowie   (1796–1836) pioneer from Kentucky; defender of the Alamo

Davy Crockett   (1786–1836) pioneer from Tennessee; defender of the Alamo

Bowie

```
B   A   S   D   F   A   P   O   I   U   Y   T   R   E   W
I   O   O   H   O   U   S   T   O   N   Q   W   E   R   T
I   O   W   E   W   S   N   M   B   V   E   Y   T   R   E
Q   W   E   I   E   T   Q   W   E   R   T   A   R   W   I
K   J   H   G   E   I   Z   X   C   V   B   N   R   I   O
J   O   P   L   I   N   G   H   I   M   C   I   O   P   I
Z   X   C   V   B   N   M   A   C   D   O   Q   W   E   R
I   G   Q   W   E   R   G   I   R   M   C   O   I   U   Y
C   A   R   S   O   N   R   I   R   S   H   R   E   W   Q
I   R   O   N   B   G   E   R   O   N   I   M   O   J   N
I   R   B   V   C   X   Y   I   E   A   S   O   I   U   Y
I   E   Z   X   C   V   B   N   G   O   E   P   O   I   U
N   T   I   E   A   D   M   A   R   T   I   N   E   Z   I
N   T   P   O   I   U   Y   T   S   Q   W   E   R   T   Y
A   S   D   C   R   O   C   K   E   T   T   P   C   L   E
```

6-2B PEOPLE OF THE SOUTHWEST

Use the outline below to research and write about one of the famous people of the Southwest listed in Activity 6-2A.

Name of famous person_____

Profession _____

Write a summary about his or her family and personal life.

_____

_____

_____

_____

_____

_____

_____

_____

_____

Summarize what this person contributed to make him or her famous.

_____

_____

_____

_____

_____

_____

_____

_____

Bowie

Houston

6-3 LIFE IN EARLY TEXAS

For the Teacher

Materials Needed:

- copies of Activity 6-3
- pencils

Teacher Preparation:

- Reproduce Activity 6-3, *Life in Early Texas,* as needed.
- Pass out the activity and allow time for students to complete the story. When they are finished, review the answers (given below) with them.

Answer Key:

(1) Arkansas	(11) Germany
(2) Louisiana	(12) England
(3) Mississippi	(13) Belgium
(4) farmers	(14) Ireland
(5) ranchers	(15) Scandinavia
(6) rebellion	(16) Czechoslovakia
(7) Davy Crockett	(17) France
(8) Jim Bowie	(18) Mexico
(9) the Alamo	(19) white
(10) San Jacinto	(20) Hispanic

(11)–(14) } any order

Extended Activity:

- There are many historic sites and landmarks throughout the Southwest. This activity focuses on early life in Texas, especially San Antonio where so much colorful history took place. Although San Antonio has evolved into a modern, prosperous city, much of the flavor of the past has remained. Develop an exhibit on San Antonio and The Alamo as well as the Battle of San Jacinto. Contact the Visitor Information Center, 317 Alamo Plaza, San Antonio, Texas 78205 and the Greater Houston Convention Center and Visitors Bureau, 801 Congress, Houston, Texas 77002 for orientation and bulletin board materials.

©1997 by The Center for Applied Research in Education

6-3 LIFE IN EARLY TEXAS

Read the story carefully. Then fill in the blanks with words from the WORD BANK that best complete the sentences. **Hint:** Each dash in a blank represents one letter. Therefore, if there are five dashes in a blank, for example, choose the best word available that has five letters.

WORD BANK

Hispanic	Arkansas	white
Louisiana	Mexico	Mississippi
France	farmers	Czechoslovakia
ranchers	Scandinavia	rebellion
Davy Crockett	Ireland	Jim Bowie
Belgium	the Alamo	England
San Jacinto	Germany	

Spain had ruled Mexico and the southwestern section of the United States since the 1500s. In 1821 Mexico won its independence from Spain and gained all the Spanish land in North America including Texas. However, few people lived in Texas at that time. The Mexican government encouraged people from Mexico to resettle, but because it was so far away most Mexicans did not want to move. Therefore, the Mexican government gave a large section of Texan land to an American named Stephen Austin.

In the 1820s Stephen Austin brought settlers to Texas. Most of the settlers were from nearby southern states close to Texas. Some southern states near Texas include

(1) _ _ _ _ _ _ _ _, (2) _ _ _ _ _ _ _ _ _, and (3) _ _ _ _ _ _ _ _ _ _ _. The settlers came to

Texas to start a new life. Many grew crops, so they earned a living as (4) _ _ _ _ _ _ _.

Others raised cattle and were called (5) _ _ _ _ _ _ _ _.

Soon the Mexican government realized the mistake they made in allowing so many Americans to settle their land. However, they had waited too long. There were already too many American farmers and ranchers in Texas. The settlers began to rebel and they talked openly of gaining independence from Mexico.

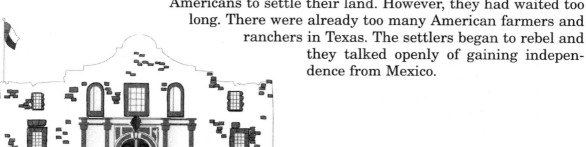

6-3 LIFE IN EARLY TEXAS (continued)

General Santa Anna was the dictator and president of Mexico. He decided to lead his army into Texas and crush the American rebellion. A (6) _ _ _ _ _ _ _ _ is an open defiance and opposition to one of authority. Santa Anna and his army marched toward the settlement of San Antonio, Texas. San Antonio was defended by a small group of Texans under the command of Colonel William Travis. Also among the group defending San Antonio were several famous pioneer Americans. Two of them included (7) _ _ _ _ _ _ _ _ _ _ _ and (8) _ _ _ _ _ _ _ _.

Colonel Travis and his men could have fled to safety from Santa Anna. Instead, they decided to stay and defend (9) _ _ _ _ _ _ _ _, a Spanish mission in San Antonio. On February 23, 1836, Santa Anna and his army of 4,000 soldiers attacked the Alamo where William Travis and his group of less than 200 men took shelter. The small group of Americans fought bravely but after twelve days the men were exhausted. On the thirteenth day of the battle, the Mexican troops stormed the Alamo and defeated the Americans. This battle sparked the cry, "Remember the Alamo!"

General Sam Houston was the leader of about 800 Texan troops. The general knew the future of Texas rested on his shoulders. Although greatly outnumbered, General Houston and his troops defeated Santa Anna and his army in the battle of San Jacinto. (10) _ _ _ _ _ _ _ _ _ _ is a river in southern Texas. As Texan troops went into battle, they shouted "Remember the Alamo!" For the price of his freedom, Santa Anna agreed to withdraw his troops and grant Texas independence.

Under the leadership of Sam Houston, Texas grew and prospered. Many immigrants from Europe came to Texas seeking a better way of life. They came from many countries in Europe, including (11) _ _ _ _ _ _ _, (12) _ _ _ _ _ _ _, (13) _ _ _ _ _ _ _, (14) _ _ _ _ _ _ _, (15) _ _ _ _ _ _ _ _ _ _, (16) _ _ _ _ _ _ _ _ _ _ _ _ _ _, and (17) _ _ _ _ _ _. Also many Hispanics immigrated from (18) _ _ _ _ _ _. Today the population of Texas is about 75% Caucasian or (19) _ _ _ _ _ and 25% Mexican or (20) _ _ _ _ _ _ _ _.

Because of the history that surrounds the city, San Antonio is the heart and soul of Texas. The Alamo remains one of the most visited historical sites. There is an old saying in Texas: "All Texans have two homes—the one they live in and the other, San Antonio."

6-4 TAKE A TRIP TO THE SOUTHWEST

For the Teacher

Materials Needed:

- copies of Activity 6-4
- travel agency pamphlets
- travel books (such as *Mobil Travel Guide*)

Note:

There is some variance on which states are considered the Southwest. This version includes the states of Arizona, New Mexico, and Texas.

Teacher Preparation:

- Reproduce Activity 6-4, *Take a Trip to the Southwest*, as needed and organize reference materials.
- Divide classes into small groups and assign specific states or regions of a state for students to visit. Instruct classes to center their trips around historical places and events when possible.
- Pass out travel materials and the journal activity. Then allow time for students to complete the activity. Encourage the inclusion of photographs or illustrations, if possible. When students are finished, allow time for groups to share their journals with the rest of the class.

Extended Activities:

- Show classes a travel video on one or more of the southwestern states. Sources for travelogue tapes include educational channel television, video stores, or libraries.
- Encourage students to learn more about the economy of the state they are visiting. What products or services does the state make or provide? What are the major types of jobs in the state? Information on a state's economy can be found in encyclopedias.

6-4 TAKE A TRIP TO THE SOUTHWEST

DESTINATION _____

For each day, describe the location, place visited, and special activity (such as art, music, food, or holiday).

DAILY ITINERARY

Day 1 _____
_____
_____

Day 2 _____
_____
_____

Day 3 _____
_____
_____

Day 4 _____
_____
_____

Day 5 _____
_____
_____

Day 6 _____
_____
_____

Day 7 _____
_____
_____

6-5 WHAT WILL IT COST?

For the Teacher

Materials Needed:

- copies of Activity 6-5
- travel books
- pencils or pens

Teacher Preparation:

- Reproduce Activity 6-5, *What Will It Cost?*, as needed.
- Pass out the activity and allow time for students to solve the problems. When they are finished, review the answers (given below) with them.

Answer Key:

1. $20.95
2. $9.50
3. $20.30
4. $38.35
5. $13; $1.30; $11.70
6. $23.80; $3.57; $27.37
7. $20.95; $9.50; $20.30; $38.35; $11.70; $27.37; $128.17

Extended Activity:

- Have students estimate the costs for one day of *their* destination for a family of four (2 adults and 2 students). Approximate hotel and dining expenses can be found in most travel books. Other expenses can be estimated. Although Activity 6-5 can be used as a guide, encourage students to make other selections on how the family will spend the day.

Name _____ Date _____ Period _____

6-5 WHAT WILL IT COST?

A family of four (2 adults and 2 children) are visiting the Southwest. One of their stops is *San Antonio, Texas*. Listed below are some places they visit. Solve the problems to see how much money they will spend for the day.

1. The first place the family visits is *the Alamo*. There is no admission charge, but the family purchases the following souvenirs from the museum shop: 1 Republic of Texas flag $4.50, 1 book on the heroes of the Alamo $8.95, and 6 postcards for $1.25 each.

   What is the total cost for all items? $_____

2. The next place the family visits is *Pioneer Hall*. Admission charge is $2 for adults and $1.50 for students. There is an additional charge of $1 for adults and $.25 for students for a guided tour. The family needs admissions for 2 adults and 2 students.

   What is the total cost for admissions and tours? $_____

3. The family decides to have lunch at a nearby cafeteria. Lunch costs are as follows: $3.50, $4.85, $5.25, and $6.70.

   What is the total cost for lunch? $_____

4. After lunch the family visits *La Villita*, a 250-year-old Spanish settlement, where they make the following purchases: 1 piñata for $5.95 and 1 piñata for $8.95, 1 box of Mexican candy for $3.50, and 1 Mexican weaving for $19.95.

   What is the total cost for all items? $_____

5. The family attends an early performance of a Mariachi Band and Spanish dancers. Tickets for the show are $4 for adults and $2.50 for students. The family needs 2 adult and 2 student tickets. They have received a coupon for a 10% discount.

   What is cost for the tickets? $_____

   Less the 10% discount. $_____

   What is the final cost for the tickets? $_____

6. The family eats dinner at a Mexican restaurant called *Casa Rio*. Specialties of the house include chicken enchiladas, fajatas, and quesadillas. Dinner costs are 2 at $3.95 each, 1 at $6.95, and 1 at $8.95.

   What is the cost for all meals? $_____

   Add a 15% tip. $_____

   What is the total cost for all meals? $_____

7. Add all the expenses to see how much money the family has spent.

   Total cost for #1. $_____

   Total cost for #2. $_____

   Total cost for #3. $_____

   Total cost for #4. $_____

   Total cost for #5. $_____

   Total cost for #6. $_____

   Total cost for the day. $_____

6-6 SOUTHWEST TERMS

For the Teacher

Materials Needed:

- copies of Activity 6-6
- copies of *Glossary of Terms* (at back of book)

Teacher Preparation:

- Reproduce Activity 6-6, *Southwest Terms,* as needed. Also reproduce copies of the *Glossary* as needed.

- Pass out the activity and allow time for students to complete the matching definitions. When they are finished, review the answers (given below) with them.

Answer Key:

f.	Apache	r.	mission
d.	adobe	g.	Navajo
o.	canyon	a.	panhandle
l.	chili	p.	park
k.	battle	b.	pueblo
s.	desert	c.	Pueblo Indians
h.	drought	e.	reservation
m.	Hispanic	q.	rodeo
t.	mesa	j.	saguaro
n.	mestizo	i.	yucca

Extended Activity:

- Use some of the southwest terms listed in the activity as ideas for further research. Appropriate titles include The Grand Canyon, The Apache Indians of the Southwest, The Navajo Indians of the Southwest, The Missions of the Southwest, The Alamo, The Battle of San Jacinto, and The Deserts of the Southwest.

6-6 SOUTHWEST TERMS

Expand your vocabulary by learning some terms often used in the American Southwest. Match the correct definitions to the words.

_____Apache   a.   a narrow piece of land attached to a larger part that looks similar to a handle (as in Oklahoma or Texas)

_____adobe   b.   a communal dwelling consisting of flat-topped adobe houses in groups, sometimes several stories high

_____canyon   c.   a group of Indians in New Mexico who live in pueblos and are famous for making pottery

_____chili   d.   a sun-baked brick made of clay used to make pueblos

_____battle   e.   land set aside for a specific group of American Indians on which to live

_____desert   f.   a group of American Indians of the Southwest noted for resisting white settlers; Geronimo was a leader

_____drought   g   a group of American Indians who live in New Mexico and Arizona who are famous for making weavings

_____Hispanic   h.   a period of prolonged dryness in an area, causing excessive damage to crops

_____mesa   i.   the state flower of New Mexico which is a plant of the lily family with long leaves and white blossoms

_____mestizo   j.   the state flower of Arizona which is a type of tall cactus that bears white flowers and edible fruit

_____mission   k.   an extended struggle or controversy between two or more persons

_____Navajo   l.   a thick soup of meat and chilies; the state dish of Texas

_____panhandle   m.   people who are descendants of the Spanish culture

_____park   n.   people of mixed Spanish and Indian heritage

_____pueblo   o.   a large and deep valley with steep sides

_____Pueblo Indians p.   a tract of land maintained in its natural state that can be visited by the general public

_____reservation   q.   a contest where cowboys compete at a variety of riding and roping events with horses and cattle

_____rodeo   r.   a church and fort built by the Spanish of the early southwest and west

_____saguaro   s.   a large, very dry region

_____yucca   t.   a flat-topped terrace on top of a mountain or hill

6-7 FOLKTALES AND LITERATURE

For the Teacher

Materials Needed:

- copies of Activity 6-7
- practice paper and pencils
- drawing paper and pens
- (*optional*) black markers and/or colored pencils

Teacher Preparation:

- Reproduce Activity 6-7, *Folktales and Literature*, as needed and organize materials.

- Pass out the activity and allow students time to read the story. When they are finished, instruct them to create their own cowboy folktale. They can develop a Pecos Bill story or create a folk hero of their own.

- Using drawing paper and pens, have students rewrite their stories in their best printing or writing.

- (*optional*) Encourage students to illustrate their stories with markers and/or colored pencils.

Extended Activity:

- Set aside time for reading folktales or literature that relate to the Southwest. Contact the media person in your building or community for assistance in gathering appropriate titles. When possible, take classes to the library for this activity. There are a number of books available that tell stories about the southwest. A brief list follows that will help you get started. **Note**: Remember, this is merely a list of some options. Regional differences may vary, so use whatever is available in your area.

FOLKTALES

American Tall Tales by Mary Pope Osborne (New York: Random House, 1991). This book is about some of America's favorite heroes. From the Southwest there is Pecos Bill, the greatest cowboy who ever lived.

CHILDREN'S LITERATURE

Waterless Mountain by Laura Adams Armer (New York: Knopf, 1993). This author received the Newbery Medal in 1932 for this children's story about the Indians of Arizona.

Wait for Me, Watch for Me, Eula Bee by Patricia Beatty (New York: Morrow, 1990). Lewallen and Eula Bee are the only survivors after an Indian raid on their Texas farm. Lewallen struggles to rescue his four-year-old sister from the Comanches.

CLASSIC LITERATURE *(suggested for older students)*

The Adventures of Big-Foot Wallace by John C. Duval (Temecula, CA: Reprint Service, 1993) and *Early Times in Texas* by John C. Duval (Temecula, CA: Reprint Service, 1993). The author combines crisp writing and frontier action in these adventure books of the cowboy era in Texas. Duval is often hailed as the "Father of Texas literature."

Giant by Edna Ferber (Cutchogue, NY: Buccaneer Books, 1991). This popular novel set in Texas was also made into a 1956 movie starring Elizabeth Taylor and Rock Hudson.

Lonesome Dove by Larry McMurtry (New York: Simon & Schuster, 1985). This Texas cowboy story won the 1986 Pulitzer Prize for literature and was made into a popular television mini-series.

Texas by James Michener (New York: Fawcett, 1987). Although not from Texas, Michener wrote a best-selling novel about the state. When asked why he wrote about Texas, Michener replied, "Because there are so many exciting stories there."

The Last of the Plainsmen and *The Call of the Canyon* by Zane Grey (various editions available). The author fashioned his thrilling tales of western novels in Arizona settings.

The Sea of Grass by Conrad Richter (Athens: Ohio University Press, 1992). This novel tells about the plight of a frontier family from New Mexico.

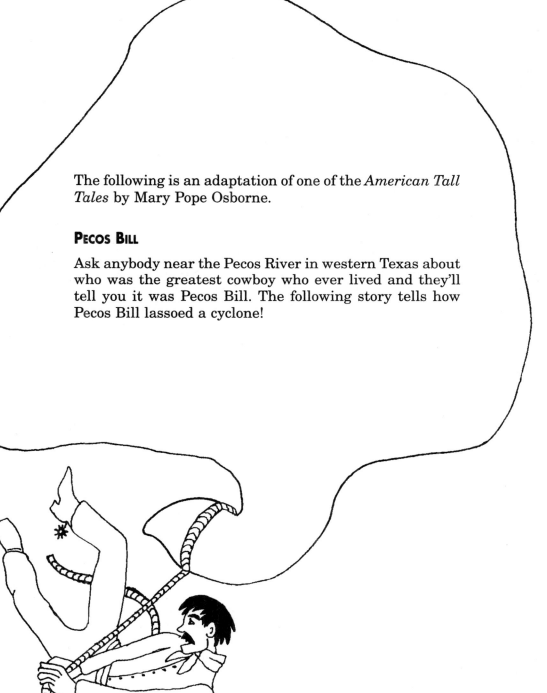

The following is an adaptation of one of the *American Tall Tales* by Mary Pope Osborne.

Pecos Bill

Ask anybody near the Pecos River in western Texas about who was the greatest cowboy who ever lived and they'll tell you it was Pecos Bill. The following story tells how Pecos Bill lassoed a cyclone!

6-7 FOLKTALES AND LITERATURE *(continued)*

Pecos Bill's friends were some of the toughest, meanest bunch of fellers who ever lived. They were called "The Hell's Gate Gang." With the help of the gang, Pecos Bill developed the biggest ranch in the southwest. It was so big that New Mexico was the corral and Arizona was the pasture.

Things were going real well until Texas suffered from the worst drought in history. Rivers turned into powdery dust and parched grass was catchin' on fire. For a spell Bill and the gang managed by lassoing water from the Gulf of Mexico. No matter how hard Pecos Bill and The Hell's Gate Gang tried, though, they couldn't lasso enough water to keep the ranch goin'. The horses and cows were all dryin' up and blowin' away.

Just when things looked horrible, the sky turned into a dark shade of purple. The mountains began to tremble and a huge black funneled cyclone appeared and headed straight for Pecos Bill's ranch. The Hell's Gate Gang got so scared that they jumped on their horses and headed toward New Mexico.

Pecos Bill wasn't a bit scared of a big ole' cyclone. He just hollered "Yahoo!" and swung his long rope around the varmit's neck. Bill hung on to the rope tight as he got drawn up into the middle of the swirlin' cyclone. As the cyclone roared, Pecos Bill grabbed it by the ears and pulled himself on its back. Then he let out another "Yahoo!" and headed the cyclone straight out of Texas. The wild cyclone bucked and screamed like a bronco, but Bill just held on. As the cyclone moved across Texas Pecos Bill wrung the rain out of it. All across Texas, New Mexico, and Arizona Bill wrung the rain out of the cyclone. Alas, the terrible drought was past and Pecos Bill became the hero who brought rain to the southwest.

6-8 PASTIMES AND GAMES

For the Teacher

Materials Needed:

• copies of Activity 6-8

• items mentioned in "Teacher Preparation"

Teacher Preparation:

• Reproduce Activity 6-8, *Pastimes and Games*, as needed.

• Pass out the activity and go over the pastimes outlined. If possible, *allow students to help make choices on which activities will be selected. Then set aside some time for participation.*

• If they choose the *piñata* game, ask for volunteers to bring in goodies to fill it. Use ready-made piñatas or have students make their own as outlined in Activity 6-10.

• If there is interest in seeing a *rodeo,* tape a televised performance and show it to your classes. Consult your local sports channel for times and availability.

• For those interested in learning more about one of the many legends of the Southwest or a Texas historical story, select one of the films made on the subject and set aside some class time to view it. A few options are listed in the activity, but there are many titles available. Use your own taste and discretion about selections. Resources for films include television, libraries, or video stores. **Note**: This activity is particularly useful for older students, but parental consent is suggested for showing any film. The films listed in the activity are all about 2 hours long with the exception of *Texas,* which is about 3 hours in length.

Photo 6-1 Inexpensive ready-made piñatas, such as the one shown in this photo, can be purchased in many specialty shops across America. If your students prefer to make their own, check Activity 6-10. Additional fiesta ideas for music and food can be found in activities 6-9 and 6-14.

6-8 PASTIMES AND GAMES

Attending fiestas and rodeos are two favorite pastimes in the Southwest. Also Texans, in particular, take pride in telling or seeing stories about their history. Look at the pastimes listed for the Southwest and decide which ones you would enjoy.

FIESTAS

Fiestas are celebrated in Mexico, Central America, and South America. Because the southwest part of the United States has a large Hispanic population, Mexican fiestas are frequent celebrations in Texas as well. Games, food, music, and dancing are all part of a fiesta.

A favorite fiesta pastime is the piñata (peen-YAH-tah) game. A piñata is a hollow container that has been decorated with tissue. The container is filled with candy and small toys and hung from the ceiling. Then children are blindfolded and take turns striking the piñata with a stick until it breaks. When the piñata finally bursts, revelers scramble for the treats hidden inside. For those who want to make their own piñatas, follow the easy-to-make instructions in Activity 6-10.

RODEOS

Rodeos are a popular sporting event enjoyed throughout the Southwest. The rodeo was born many years ago when cowhands gathered to display their skills at roping calves, wrestling steers, riding wild broncos, and branding cattle. Modern rodeos feature clowns and music along with the cowboy skills. Some rodeos are so popular that they are televised.

THE WILD WEST ERA

Stories about the folk heroes of the Southwest are plentiful. Some include the adventures and misadventures of Kit Carson, Wyatt Earp, Doc Holiday, and Billy the Kid. Several stories about men who spent time in the Southwest have been made into movies. A few are listed below. Can you think of others?

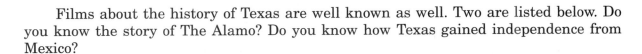

Tombstone (1993), stars Kurt Russell and Val Kilmer, tells the adventures and misadventures of the Earp brothers and Doc Holiday in the lawless Tombstone, Arizona region.

Wyatt Earp (1994) stars Kevin Costner and Gene Hackman. Kevin Costner plays the famous lawman of the Wild West in a gritty, complex portrayal hailed as a classic performance. Gene Hackman plays Earp's best friend, Doc Holiday.

Geronimo: An American Legend (1993) stars Robert Duvall, Gene Hackman, and Wes Studi. Studi gives a stunning performance as the fearless Indian leader Geronimo who was the last Indian leader to surrender to the white man. The story is a journey through the heart of an Indian warrior.

Films about the history of Texas are well known as well. Two are listed below. Do you know the story of The Alamo? Do you know how Texas gained independence from Mexico?

The Alamo (1960) stars John Wayne as Davy Crockett. John Wayne stars, produces, and directs this bigger-than-life chronicle of one of the most famous battles in American history. At the Alamo (a crumbling mission) 185 men bravely joined together to stand firm against Mexican leader Santa Anna and his huge army and willingly gave their lives for freedom. This film was nominated for seven Oscar nominations.

Texas (1994) stars Stacy Keach as Sam Houston and Patrick Duffy as Stephen Austin. The film is based on the epic Pulitzer Prize-winning story by James A. Michener. It is a larger-than-life epic of the heroic men and women who dreamed of and fought for new lives in the untamed land of present-day Texas. Set against the backdrop of America's turbulent frontier, *Texas* tells a dazzling story of conflict, romance, and adventure as Texans fight for freedom and statehood.

6-9 SOUNDS OF THE SOUTHWEST

For the Teacher

Materials Needed:

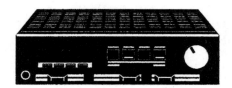

- CD or cassette
- audio equipment

Teacher Preparation:

- Songs of the lonesome cowboy often symbolize music from the Southwest. Songs like "Home on the Range" and "Bury Me Not on the Lone Prairie" are cowboy favorites and have been passed down from one generation to another. The guitar is the musical instrument of cowboy and western music. For listening to cowboy songs, consider the following option:

  Cowboy Hymns and Prayers
  featuring Don Edwards, Waddie Mitchell, Michael Martin Murphy, Mark O'Conner, Sons of the San Joaquin, and Red Steagall (Warner Brothers, Burbank, CA, 1996)

- Two popular contemporary western musicians include *Willie Nelson* and *Waylon Jennings*. Both were born in Texas and often perform together. For an opportunity to listen to specific titles on one or both artists, check your local library or record store. Availability may vary from region to region.

- Scott Joplin (1868–1916) was born in Texarkana, Texas. Joplin is considered the father of "ragtime" music. This brilliant black musician wrote more than one hundred pieces of music as well as a ballet and two operas. For opportunities to listen to music by Scott Joplin, consider the following titles: *Marches and Rags of Scott Joplin, The Entertainer, Scott Joplin's Piano Works,* and *The Greatest Ragtime of the Century.*

- Another Southwestern Musical favorite is the *Mexican Mariachi Band* as well as a Texas-Mexican music called *conjunto*. Conjunto developed in the 1800s from lively German polkas. In modern times Flaco Jimenez performs music that stems from the Texas border region. Although specific Mexican Mariachi Band or conjunto recordings are readily available in the southwest, they may or may not be available in other areas of the United States. Check your local library or record store for availability.

6-10 PIÑATAS

For the Teacher

Materials Needed:

- copies of Activity 6-10
- materials listed on activity sheet

Teacher Preparation:

- Although ready-made piñatas can be purchased rather inexpensively, many students prefer to have the experience of making their own. The activity of making piñatas is ideal for an outside-the-classroom assignment. Finished piñatas may serve as classroom decorations or can be used to play piñata games. Make copies of the materials needed and the easy directions for making piñatas for interested students and assign extra credit for those who participate.

Extended Activity:

- *Tinware* is a popular craft sold in the Mexican markets of the Southwest. In some areas, masks are a particular favorite form of tinware. Consult the art person in your building for a Mexican-style art project while your classes are learning about the Southwest.

Photo 6-2 *Mexican tin mask, collection of the author.* Brightly painted tin masks represent one of the types of crafts made by Mexicans or Mexican-Americans in or near the southwest. These masks provide a source of inspiration for art students who want to experiment with a project in mask making—Mexican style.

Photo 6-3 *Paper mask, collection of the author.* Inexpensive and safer versions of Mexican-style masks can be made from paper. In this photo, the student used a brown paper bag to create the mask. Then scissors and a hole puncher were used for the cut-outs. For more colorful versions, colored construction paper can be used to develop the masks.

6-10 PIÑATAS

Piñatas are hollow containers that have been decorated with tissue and filled with candy and small toys. Piñatas are hung from the ceiling. Then blindfolded party goers take turns trying to break them with sticks. When the piñata breaks, revelers scramble for the treats that have scattered to the floor. You can make your own piñata by following the easy directions below.

Materials Needed:

- balloons
- newspapers
- liquid laundry starch
- twine or strong string
- colored tissue paper
- school glue (such as Elmer's® Glue-all)
- scissors

Steps to Making a Piñata:

1. Blow up a balloon and tie a firm knot in the end.

2. Tear newspaper into strips about 2 inches wide and 4 inches long. Sizes may vary, but making the strips too large makes them difficult to glue to the balloon. Tearing the paper allows the rough edges to stick together better than cutting.

3. One at a time dip strips into liquid laundry starch and cover the balloon. Reinforce the balloon by placing three or four layers of dipped newspaper over the balloon.

4. Cut an opening in the top so that treats may be added later.

5. Allow piñata to dry.

6. Stuff treats inside the piñata.

7. Seal piñata shut. Then punch two holes and string the piñata for hanging.

8. Decorate the piñata with colored crepe paper strips that have been curled at the ends. Use thinned-down school glue to attach crepe paper. Hang the piñata and allow to completely dry.

6-11 NAVAJO RUG DESIGNS

For the Teacher

Materials Needed:

- copies of Activity 6-11
- 12" × 18" drawing paper
- pencils
- black and gray markers
- (*optional*) red or gold colored pencils or markers

Teacher Preparation:

- Reproduce Activity 6-11, *Navajo Rug Designs*, as needed and organize materials. Inexpensive school-grade white drawing paper is suggested for this activity. Although 12" × 18" is recommended, other sizes may be used as well.
- Pass out the activity and go over it with students.
- Distribute drawing paper and allow time for students to develop a Navajo rug design.
- When they are finished, pass out black and gray markers to darken in part of their designs.
- (*optional*) Encourage students to add color to their designs. Red is the traditional color used by the Ganada weavers, although other colors can be selected as well.
- When students are finished, display some of the designs around the room.

Extended Activity:

- As an alternative or in conjunction with Activity 6-11, contact the Art teacher in your building well in advance and coordinate a *fabric weaving* project while your classes are learning about the Southwest.

Photo 6-4 *Navajo weaving, collection of the author.* The Navajo weaving shown in this photo is from the Ganada area of the Navajo Indian Reservation in Arizona. The stair-stepped diamond shape is typical of the type of design used by Ganada weavers. Many of the weavers use white, gray, black, and red in their weavings.

Photo 6-5 *Student weaving, collection of the author.* Art students used Navajo weavings as inspiration to develop fabric weavings while social studies classes were learning about the southwest. This student made a small pouch from her weaving.

6-11 NAVAJO RUG DESIGNS

THE NAVAJO INDIANS

The Navajo Indians live on a reservation that is mostly in Arizona, although it extends into New Mexico and Utah. To survive in the southwest region of little water, the Navajos became farmers. They also took up the art of weaving. Some of the regions on the reservation have become very famous for the special designs and colors they use to make the weavings. One of these regions is called *Ganada*.

GANADA NAVAJO DESIGNS

The Navajo Indians in the Ganada region of the reservation have developed rugs that use their own special style of designs. The most common type of Ganada design is the *serrate* or stair-stepped diamond. Sometimes the serrate is one large diamond stretching from end to end. Other serrate designs include two or three adjoining diamonds.

GANADA NAVAJO DESIGN COLORS

The traditional colors used by Ganada weavers are white, gray, and black with areas of red. Sometimes golds are used in place of red, but the basic colors are nearly always neutrals of white, gray, and black.

NAVAJO RUG DESIGN

The Navajo rug design below shows how the Indians develop a design from a single serrate or diamond shape. Notice how the stair-steps begin at one end, then angle toward the middle and start to recede to the opposite end. (**This design is from *Southwestern Indian Designs* by Madeleine Orban-Szontagh, Dover Design Library.**)

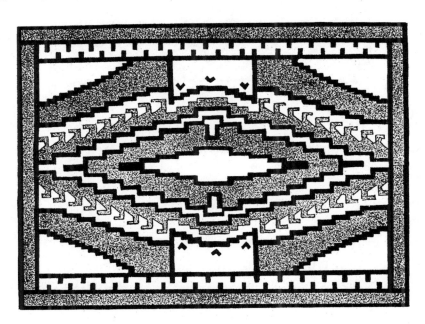

NAVAJO RUG DESIGN

The Navajo rug design below shows how a double serrate design is formed. Although it is more difficult to make a two- or three-stair-step diamond shape, these weavings are more valuable and bring higher prices to the weaver. (**This design is from *Southwestern Indian Designs* by Madeleine Orban-Szontagh, Dover Design Library.**)

Steps to Making a Navajo Rug Design

1. On a scrap piece of paper, develop a serrate in a stair-step fashion. Use the illustrations shown to get an idea of how to develop a serrate. Then create your own version.

2. On a piece of white drawing paper, carefully plan and sketch your Ganada-style Navajo design.

3. Use black and gray markers to color in parts of the design.

4. (*optional*) Choose a bright shade to add color to the black, gray, and white design. Although the Navajo weavers usually select red or gold, you can choose any color you like.

6-12 BASICS OF SOUTHWEST COOKING

For the Teacher

Materials Needed:

- copies of Activity 6-12
- pencils

Teacher Preparation:

- Reproduce Activity 6-12, *Basics of Southwest Cooking*, as needed.
- Pass out the activity and allow time for students to read the information and complete the worksheet. (Answers are given below.) When they are finished, review the food basics of the Southwest.

Answer Key:

Part One:

Basic foods: corn; beans; rice; chilies

Meats: beef; pork; chicken

Bread: tortillas

Tortilla specialties: tacos; burritos; chimichangas; quesadillas

Sides: beans; rice

Types of beans: red; pinto; black; kidney

Sauces: red or green chile; taco sauce

Garnishes: cheese; onions

Desserts: flan; tea cakes; buñuelos

Favorite Texas ways with beef: steaks; barbecue; chili

Part Two:

Tortilla: a round, flat bread

Taco: a pocket-shaped, crisp-fried, tortilla shell filled with meat, garnishes, and sauce

Burrito: a soft tortilla filled with variations of beef, beans, cheese, garnishes, and sauce

Chimichanga: a flour tortilla with various fillings, then deep-fried

Quesadilla: a flour tortilla filled with cheese

Flan: a caramel-topped egg custard

Mexican tea cakes: rich, buttery cookies rolled in powdered sugar

Buñuelos: crisp, puffy dough coated with sugar and cinnamon

Bowl o' red: Texas chili

Extended Activity:

• Encourage students to collectively develop a Southwest cookbook. Divide classes into groups and assign specific topics to each group. Appropriate topics include Soups, Breads, Vegetables, Meats, and Desserts. After students have collected their recipes, duplicate their submissions and allow each person to organize a cookbook of his or her own.

6-12 BASICS OF SOUTHWEST COOKING

The cooking of the southwest region is influenced by Mexican and Indian foods. The tasty dishes based on these two cultures have developed a regional style of cooking called Tex-Mex. Tex-Mex cooking has gained wide acceptance throughout the United States. In addition to Tex-Mex cooking, the southwest (particularly Texas) is known as beef country. Listed below are a few Tex-Mex and Texas food basics.

TEX-MEX BASIC FOODS

Originally many Tex-Mex dishes were improvised by natives who had limited cooking facilities and used what foods they had on hand: *corn, beans, rice,* and *chilies*. The meats used along with the food basics include *beef, pork,* and *chicken*.

TACOS AND BURRITOS

The traditional bread of Mexico and the Tex-Mex southwest is the *tortilla*, a round, flat bread. This versatile unleavened bread is rolled or folded, then heated, fried, or baked in a variety of ways.

Tacos are, perhaps, the most popular Tex-Mex tortilla sandwich. They are pocket-shaped, crisp-fried, tortilla shells filled with meat, garnishes, and sauce. *Burritos*, another favorite, are soft tortillas filled with variations of beef, beans, cheese, garnishes, and sauce. Other tortilla specialties are variations of the taco or burrito. Two include *chimichangas*, flour tortillas with various fillings then deep fried, and *quesadillas,* flour tortillas filled with cheese.

SIDE DISHES

Beans, served mashed and refried, appear at almost all Tex-Mex meals. Types of beans used include *red, pinto, black*, and *kidney*. Although beans are the most popular vegetable in Tex-Mex meals, *rice* is highly favored as well.

ACCOMPANIMENTS

Red or green chili sauce and *taco sauce* represent the two main sauces that accompany many Tex-Mex dishes. Other garnishes include *cheese* and *onions*.

DESSERTS

Puddings and custards are most characteristic of Tex-Mex desserts. The most common one is *flan*, a caramel-topped egg custard. Two other dessert favorites include *Mexican tea cakes* (rich, buttery cookies rolled in powdered sugar), and *buñuelos* (crisp, puffy dough coated with sugar and cinnamon).

TEXAS FOOD BASICS

Texas is cattle country with *beef* reigning supreme. Three favorite methods of preparing and eating beef are as follows:

1. Texans love *steaks* served large and grilled.

2. *Barbecue* and Texas go together with anything from hamburgers to whole steers skillfully grilled or baked and sauced.

3. *Chili,* the state dish of Texas, is enjoyed by most all Texans. Each year many festivals throughout Texas have chili contests and applaud the cook who comes up with the best recipe for their Texas version of chili. In Texas, chili is called "bowl o' red."

6-12 BASICS OF SOUTHWEST COOKING

Part One: Use the boxes below to outline some of the food basics of the Southwest.

Basic Tex-Mex foods: _____ _____

_____ _____

Meats: _____ _____

_____

Traditional bread: _____

Tortilla specialties: _____ _____

_____ _____

Side dishes: _____ _____

Types of beans: _____ _____

_____ _____

Sauces: _____

_____

Garnishes _____ _____

Desserts: _____ _____

_____

Favorite Texas
ways to use beef: _____

_____

_____

6-12 BASICS OF SOUTHWEST COOKING *(continued)*

Part Two: Write the definitions of the foods listed below.

Tortilla_____

_____

Taco _____

_____

Burrito_____

_____

Chimichanga _____

_____

Quesadilla_____

_____

Flan _____

_____

Mexican tea cakes_____

_____

Buñuelos _____

_____

Bowl o' red _____

_____

6-13 CASA RIO MEXICAN RESTAURANT

For the Teacher

Hint: It is helpful to complete Activity 6-12, *Basics of Southwest Cooking,* before participating in this one.

Materials Needed:

- copies of Activity 6-13
- pencils or pens

Teacher Preparation:

- Reproduce Activity 6-13, *Casa Rio Mexican Restaurant,* as needed.
- Pass out the activity. Then allow students time to read the menu and make their dinner selections. When they are finished, lead a discussion to compare and contrast a Tex-Mex dinner to a typical special-occasion dinner of their own.

Extended Activity:

- Ask students to bring in some simple or ready-prepared food items popular in the Tex-Mex region of the southwest. Appropriate snack choices include taco chips and refried bean or salsa dip. Fresh fruit options include a colorful assortment of papaya, mango, pineapple, and banana.

6-13 CASA RIO MEXICAN RESTAURANT

You are at a Tex-Mex restaurant called **Casa Rio**. Look at the menu items **carefully**. Then make your dinner selections on the activity sheet provided. **(This menu is compliments of Casa Rio Mexican Restaurant, San Antonio, Texas.)**

Mexican Restaurant

Appetizers

Nachos (Served with Jalapeños)
Cheese . . . .
Bean & Cheese . . . .
Beef Nachos . . . .
Deluxe Nachos . . . .
 Beef, Cheese, Guacamole, Beans
 Sour Cream and Pico de Gallo

Chili Con Queso . . . .
Guacamole Dip . . . .

Flautas (6) . . . .
 Crisp rolled chicken filled corn
 tortillas served with guacamole,
 sour cream and Pico de gallo

From The Grill

All dinners include homemade corn tortillas, chips and hot sauce
No substitutions please.

POLLO ASADO
Guacamole Salad
Charbroiled Boneless Chicken Breast
with Red Santa Anna Sauce,
Spanish Rice,
Whole Beans, Pico de Gallo

**FAJITAS
TACO SALAD**
Charbroiled Beef or Chicken
Lettuce, Tomato,
Cheese and Guacamole

FAJITAS
Beef or * Chicken
Flour Tortillas, Guacamole,
Pico de Gallo, Onions,
Rice and Whole Beans

CARNE ASADA
Guacamole Salad
Charbroiled Beef Tenderloin
with Red Santa Anna Sauce,
Spanish Rice,
Whole Beans, Pico de Gallo

TACO SALAD
Picadillo Meat,
Lettuce, Tomato,
Cheese and Guacamole

FAJITAS COMBO
Beef and Chicken
Flour Tortillas, Guacamole,
Pico de Gallo, Onions,
Rice and Whole Beans

A La Carte

ENCHILADAS
Cheese Enchiladas (2) . . .
 with Chili . . . .

Beef Enchiladas (2) . . . . . .
 Topped with Chili . . . . . .

Enchilada and Chalupa
 Compuesta . . . .

CHALUPAS
Lettuce, Tomato, Refried Beans,
Cheese on Crisp Tortilla
Chalupas (2) . . . .
 Compuestas (w/guacamole)

Beef Chalupas (2) . . . .

Chicken Chalupas (2) . . . . .
 Compuestas (w/guacamole)

TACOS
Crispy Beef Tacos (2) . . . .

Soft Beef Tacos
 (corn tortillas) (2) . . . . . .

Crisp Chicken Tacos (2) . .

* Soft Chicken Tacos (2)
 (corn tortillas) . . . .

Entree Selections

All dinners include homemade corn tortillas, chips and hot sauce. No substitutions please.

REGULAR (Our Original Plate) . . . . .

Enchilada, Tamale, Chili, Rice, Beans

EL SOMBRERO (Linda's Favorite) . .

Enchilada, Rice, Taco, Chalupa

GREEN CHICKEN ENCHILADAS . . . .

Guacamole Salad, (2) Soft Rolled Corn Tortillas
With Chicken topped with Monterey Jack,
Tomatillo Sauce, Sour Cream,
Spanish Rice and Beans

CASA RIO DELUXE DINNER (Lupe's Special) . .

Guacamole Salad, Taco
Chili Con Queso, Enchilada, Tamale
Beans, Rice, Chili

CHEESE ENCHILADA SPECIAL . . . .

Two Cheese Enchiladas, Rice, Beans
Lettuce, Tomato Slice

or Beef Enchiladas . . . .

LA SENORA . . . .

Guacamole Salad, Chili Con Queso
Enchilada, Rice, Beans

EL RIO . . . .

Guacamole Salad, Taco
Enchilada, Rice, Beans, Chili

CHICKEN CON SALSA . . . .

Chicken Fried Chicken, Red Santa
Anna Sauce, Rice, Beans

CARNE CON QUESO (Bill's Choice) :

Hamburger Steak Topped with Chili Con Queso
and Pico de Gallo, Spanish Rice and Beans.

12 AND UNDER   CHILD'S PLATES

Enchilada, Rice, Beans   Taco, Rice Beans   Chicken Nuggets, French Fries

Casa Rio Cantina

BEVERAGES

Iced Tea . . . .

Hot Tea . . . .

Coffee . . . .

Milk . . . .

Soft Drinks . . . .

Lemonade . . . .

6-13 CASA RIO MEXICAN RESTAURANT

After you have looked over the menu of the **Casa Rio Mexican Restaurant**, make your dinner selections in the appropriate spaces below. When making your choices, name the food item and then describe it (if a description is listed). When you are finished, list a typical special-occasion dinner your family might serve. Compare and contrast the two menus.

Tex-Mex Dinner

Appetizer _____

_____

From the Grill _____

_____

A La Carte _____

Entree Selections _____

_____

Beverage _____

American Dinner

Appetizer _____

_____

Soup or Salad _____

Main Course _____

_____

Vegetables _____

_____

Bread _____

_____

Dessert _____

_____

6-14 MEXICAN TEA CAKES

For the Teacher

Equipment Needed:

- copies of Activity 6-14
- mixing bowl
- measuring cup
- measuring spoons
- hand mixer
- cookie sheets
- shallow pan
- sifter

Supplies Needed:

- butter
- powdered sugar
- vanilla
- chopped pecans
- flour

Teacher Preparation:

- Reproduce Activity 6-14, *Mexican Tea Cakes,* as needed and organize equipment and supplies.

- Give a demonstration on making the cookies as students follow along with the recipe. Follow up with a cookie treat day.

- **ALTERNATIVE**: Go over the recipe with students. Then make an out-of-class assignment for students to make the cookies at home and bring them to school for a special Tex-Mex treat day. Encourage students to ask for adult supervision when making the cookies.

Extended Activity:

- Contact the Consumer and Family Living teacher well in advance to coordinate a Southwest lunch or dessert lab activity while your classes are learning about the region.

6-14 MEXICAN TEA CAKES

Mexican tea cakes, called *pasteles de boda*, are actually cookies. While they are still warm, the cookies are coated with powdered sugar. These sweet treats have been a popular dessert in Mexico and the southwest for many years. In recent years, they have gained wide acceptance in other areas of America as well. The cookies, often served at special occasions, are sometimes called Mexican Wedding Cakes. This recipe makes about 2-1/2 dozen cookies.

You need:

1	cup butter, softened
1/2	cup powdered sugar
1	tablespoon vanilla
2	cups all-purpose flour
2	cups finely chopped pecans
1	cup powdered sugar

What to do:

1. Preheat oven to 275°.
2. In a mixing bowl, cream butter, powdered sugar, and vanilla until light and fluffy.
3. Gradually add flour and nuts to make a soft dough that you can work with your hands.
4. Wash your hands with soap and water and dry completely.
5. Pinch off pieces of dough about the size of a walnut and roll between your hands to form a ball (about the size of a large walnut).
6. Place balls on ungreased cookie sheets and bake for about 40 minutes or until *very lightly* browned.
7. Remove from oven and allow cookies to cool a few minutes.
8. Put 1 cup of powdered sugar in a small bowl and roll each cookie until completely coated.
9. Place cookies in a shallow pan. Then sift remaining powdered sugar over the tea cakes and cool completely.
10. Store in a covered container.

6-15 BOWL O' RED CONTEST

For the Teacher

Equipment Needed:

- large frypan or dutch oven with lid
- measuring cup
- measuring spoons
- large spoon

Supplies Needed:

- chili meat (coarsely ground round)
- onions
- tomato sauce
- chili powder
- oregano
- cumin
- 4-ounce can mild green chiles
- salt, pepper, garlic
- crackers

Teacher Preparation:

- Reproduce Activity 6-15, *Bowl o' Red Contest*, as needed and organize equipment and supplies.
- Give a demonstration on making the chili as students follow along with the recipe.
- **ALTERNATIVE**: Go over the recipe with students. Then make an outside-the-classroom assignment for them to make the chili at home and bring it to school for a special chili treat day. Encourage students to ask for adult supervision when making the chili.
- Most everyone has his or her own version of making chili. Encourage your classes to use the recipe as a base to create their own bowl o' red special. Invite a panel of judges (teachers, students, and parents) to declare contest winners and award prizes to the winners.

6-15 BOWL O' RED CONTEST

Bowl o' red is what Texans call chili. Many claims have been made to the origin of chili. Generally, it is accepted that it originated in Mexico and contains ground beef, chilies, and beans. Many Texans, however, do not add beans to their bowl o' red. There are as many versions of chili as there are cooks. The one in this activity came from San Antonio. Develop your own special recipe for the hearty meal and then bring it to school for a chili cook-off contest. This recipe serves 4.

You need:

1	pound chili meat (coarsely ground round steak)
1	large onion, chopped
1	15-ounce can tomato sauce
1	cup water
2	teaspoons chili powder
1	teaspoon oregano
1	teaspoon cumin powder
1	4-ounce can mild green chiles, diced
	salt, pepper, and garlic to taste
	(*optional*) crackers

What to do:

1. Saute meat in a large heavy frypan or dutch oven until lightly browned.
2. Skim off fat.
3. Add remaining ingredients and bring to boil.
4. Reduce heat and allow chili to simmer for 30–40 minutes.
5. (*optional*) Serve piping hot with crackers.

BIBLIOGRAPHY FOR THE SOUTHWEST

Art

Orban-Szontagh, Madeleine. *Southwestern Indian Designs.* New York: Dover Publications, Inc., 1992.

Children's Fiction

Osborne, Mary Pope. *American Tall Tales.* New York: Random House, 1991.

Children's Nonfiction

Heinrichs, Ann. *America the Beautiful: Arizona.* Chicago: Children's Press, 1991.

Stein, Conrad. *America the Beautiful: New Mexico.* Chicago: Children's Press, 1988.

Stein, Conrad. *America the Beautiful: Texas.* Chicago: Children's Press, 1989.

Cookbooks

Editors. *Mexican Cook Book.* Menlo Park, CA: Lane Publishing Company, 1989.

Textbooks

Bass, Herbert J. *People in Time and Place: Our Country.* Parsippany, NJ: Silver Burdett & Ginn, 1993.

Davidson, James West and John E. Batchelor. *The American Nation.* Englewood Cliffs, NJ: Prentice Hall, 1993.

Travel

Editors. *Mobil 1995 Travel Guide, California and the West.* New York: Fodor's Travel Publications, 1995.

Editors. *Mobil 1995 Travel Guide, Southwest and South Central.* New York: Fodor's Travel Publications, 1995.

THE NORTHWEST

Below is an outline of the interdisciplinary activities included in this section. They are designed to bring a broad range of hands-on cultural lessons and activities into the social studies classroom. Pick and choose the ones that best fit into your program.

Social Studies

7-1   Getting to Know the Northwest
7-2   People of the Northwest
7-3   Life on the Oregon Trail
7-4   Take a Trip to the Northwest

Mathematics

7-5   What Will It Cost?

Language Arts

7-6   Northwest Terms
7-7   Folktales and Literature

Physical Education

7-8   Pastimes and Games

Music

7-9   Sounds of the Northwest

Art

7-10   Totem Poles
7-11   Salmon Designs

Consumer and Family Living

7-12   Basics of Northwest Cooking
7-13   Potlatch and Oregon Trail Menus
7-14   Wild Rice with Blueberries
7-15   Black Walnut Cream Pie

Bibliography for the Northwest

MAP OF THE NORTHWEST

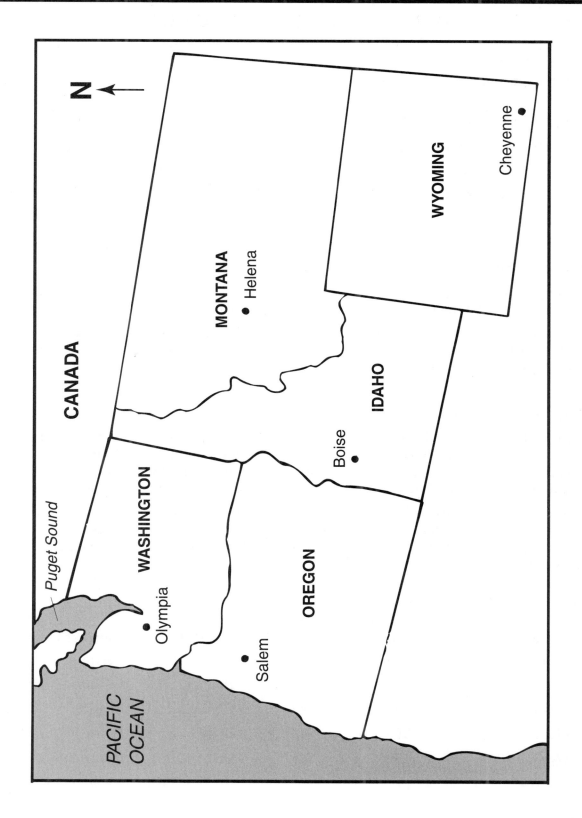

7-1 GETTING TO KNOW THE NORTHWEST

For the Teacher

Materials Needed:

- copies of Activity 7-1
- labeled map of the Northwest (enlarged on opaque projector)
- copies of unlabeled map of the Northwest
- (colored) pencils

Teacher Preparation:

- Reproduce Activity 7-1, *Getting to Know the Northwest*, as needed. Also reproduce copies of the unlabeled map of the Northwest as needed.
- Pass out the activity and map to each student. Then allow time for students to locate and label the Northwest as outlined in the activity. When they are finished, review the geography with them.

Extended Activities:

- Reproduce additional copies of the unlabeled map and have students identify other features of northwestern states, such as early settlements, population distribution, land use, or climate. PC Globe® computer program can provide much of the information needed for this activity. Consult your school's media person for assistance, too.
- Reproduce the chart of *The Fifty States* (at back of book) as needed. Pass out the chart and have students make a list of the Northwest states, date they entered the Union, order of entry, capital, and largest city. *List states in order they entered the Union.* Answers should appear as follows:

State	Date Entered Union	Order of Entry	Capital	Largest City
Oregon	1859	33	Salem	Portland
Montana	1889	41	Helena	Billings
Washington	1889	42	Olympia	Seattle
Idaho	1890	43	Boise	Boise
Wyoming	1890	44	Cheyenne	Cheyenne

Name _____ **Date** _____ **Period** _____

7-1 GETTING TO KNOW THE NORTHWEST

Use the map provided to locate and label the following features:

State: Washington
Capital: Olympia
Body of water: Puget Sound

State: Oregon
Capital: Salem

State: Montana
Capital: Helena

State: Idaho
Capital: Boise

State: Wyoming
Capital: Cheyenne

Bordering body of water: Pacific Ocean

7-1 GETTING TO KNOW THE NORTHWEST

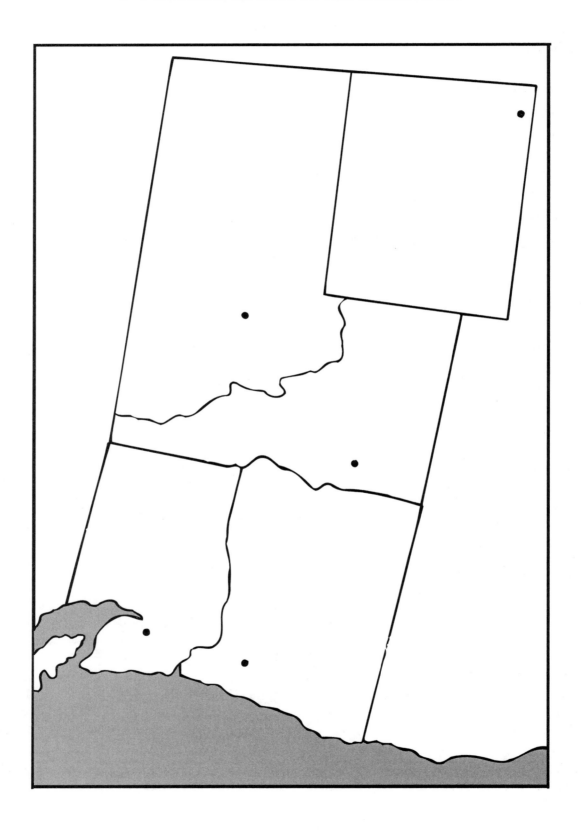

7-2 PEOPLE OF THE NORTHWEST

For the Teacher

Materials Needed:

- copies of Activity 7-2
- pencils
- research materials

Teacher Preparation:

- Reproduce Activity 7-2A and 7-2B, *People of the Northwest*, as needed.
- Pass out the activity and allow enough time for students to complete the word search puzzle. When they are finished, review the answers (given below) with them.

Answer Key:

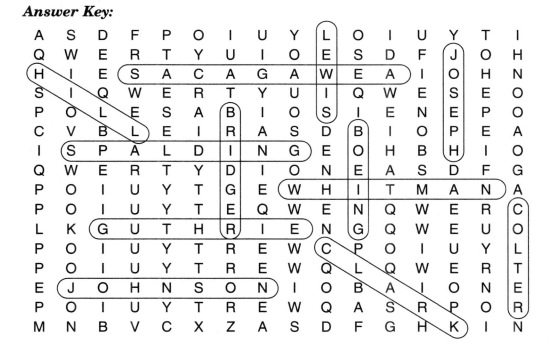

Extended Activities:

- Allow students to pick one of the famous people in the puzzle (or another person from the Northwest region who has made a contribution to America) and assign research papers on his or her life and contributions. Use the outline in Activity 7-2B to develop the reports.
- Films have been made about some of the famous people (or their work) in the puzzle. Select one and show it to your classes.

7-2A PEOPLE OF THE NORTHWEST

The story of America is a story of people moving westward. Leading the way to the Pacific Northwest were Indians, explorers, mountain men, trappers, missionaries, and pioneer farmers.

Listed below are some people who lived in or had some influence in the development of the Northwest region. In the word search puzzle, locate and circle the names of these famous people. **Hint:** When locating the names, look for the *last name only*. You will find them across, diagonal, or down. After completing the puzzle, choose one of the famous persons and write a report on his or her life and accomplishments.

James Jerome Hill   (1838–1916) founded the Great Northern Railway

Chief Joseph   (1840–1904) Nez Perce Indian chief

Narcissa Prentiss Whitman   (1808–1847) pioneer, missionary; one of the first two white women to journey across the Oregon Trail

Eliza Hart Spalding   (1807–1851) pioneer, missionary; one of the first two white women to cross the Rockies into the Oregon Territory

John Colter   (1775–1813) explorer; first white man in Yellowstone Park

William Clark   (1770–1838) explored northwest region of Louisiana Purchase with Meriwether Lewis

Clark

Meriwether Lewis   (1774–1809) explored northwest region with William Clark

James (Jim) Bridger   (1804–1881) pioneer, mountain man

Alfred Bertram (A.B.) Guthrie   (1901–) wrote *The Big Sky, The Way West*

Sacagawea   (1786–1812) Shoshone Indian woman who served as a guide for Lewis and Clark expedition in 1805

Dorothy M. Johnson   (1905–1984) wrote *A Man Called Horse* and *The Man Who Shot Liberty Valance* (both made into movies)

Lewis

William Edward Boeing   (1881–1956) engineer who pioneered aerospace technology

```
A  S  D  F  P  O  I  U  Y  L  O  I  U  Y  T  I
Q  W  E  R  T  Y  U  I  O  E  S  D  F  J  O  H
H  I  E  S  A  C  A  G  A  W  E  A  I  O  H  N
S  I  Q  W  E  R  T  Y  U  I  Q  W  E  S  E  O
P  O  L  E  S  A  B  I  O  S  I  E  N  E  P  O
C  V  B  L  E  I  R  A  S  D  B  I  O  P  E  A
I  S  P  A  L  D  I  N  G  E  O  H  B  H  I  O
Q  W  E  R  T  Y  D  I  O  N  E  A  S  D  F  G
P  O  I  U  Y  T  G  E  W  H  I  T  M  A  N  A
P  O  I  U  Y  T  E  Q  W  E  N  Q  W  E  R  C
L  K  G  U  T  H  R  I  E  N  G  Q  W  E  U  O
P  O  I  U  Y  T  R  E  W  C  P  O  I  U  Y  L
P  O  I  U  Y  T  R  E  W  Q  L  Q  W  E  R  T
E  J  O  H  N  S  O  N  I  O  B  A  I  O  N  E
P  O  I  U  Y  T  R  E  W  Q  A  S  R  P  O  R
M  N  B  V  C  X  Z  A  S  D  F  G  H  K  I  N
```

7-2B PEOPLE OF THE NORTHWEST

Use the outline below to research and write about one of the famous people of the Northwest listed in Activity 7-2A.

Name of famous person_____

Profession _____

Write a summary about his or her family and personal life.

_____

_____

_____

_____

_____

_____

_____

_____

_____

Summarize what this person contributed to make him or her famous.

_____

_____

_____

_____

_____

_____

_____

_____

Lewis

Clark

7-3 LIFE ON THE OREGON TRAIL

For the Teacher

Materials Needed:

- copies of Activity 7-3
- pencils

Teacher Preparation:

- Reproduce Activity 7-3, *Life on the Oregon Trail*, as needed.

- Pass out the activity and allow time for students to complete the story. When they are finished, review the answers (given below) with them.

Answer Key:

(1) Missouri

(2) Oregon

(3) prairie schooner

(4) sun

(5) rainstorms

(6) oxen

(7) cow

(8) flour (or sugar)

(9) sugar (or flour)

(10) baking powder

(11) apples

(12) rifle

(13) blankets

(14) kettles

(15) fifteen

(16) twenty

(17) rabbit

(18) deer

(19) buffalo

(20) tag

(21) hide-and-seek

(22) strawberries (or blackberries)

(23) blackberries (or strawberries)

(24) blueberries

Extended Activity:

- Every Memorial Day weekend, a group called the Westmont Wagoners celebrate the pioneer spirit with a wagon train journey. The trip takes place in southern Montana and travels through the Flathead Indian Reservation. Encourage students to learn more about the modern pioneers by reading *West by Covered Wagon—Retracing the Pioneer Trails* by Dorothy Hinshaw Patent.

7-3 LIFE ON THE OREGON TRAIL

Read the story carefully. Then fill in the blanks with words from the WORD BANK that best complete the sentence. **Hint:** Each dash in a blank represents one letter. Therefore, if there are five dashes in a blank, choose the best word available that has five letters.

WORD BANK		
blueberries	Missouri	blackberries
Oregon	strawberries	tag
hide-and-seek	kettles	blankets
rainstorms	sun	prairie schooner
apples	oxen	rabbit
rifle	baking powder	fifteen
twenty	sugar	flour
cow	buffalo	deer

In the 1800s wagon trains creaked over a long trail that led to Oregon Territory. The journey began in Independence, (1) _ _ _ _ _ _ _ _ and ended in the Willamette Valley near present-day Portland, (2) _ _ _ _ _ _. Between Missouri and Oregon lay grassy plains, hot deserts, and rugged mountains. It would take about five months to reach Oregon. However, at the end of the journey, pioneers were promised rich, green land.

Travelers on the Oregon Trail were a mixed crowd. Some came from the New England states while others hailed from the newer states in the Midwest. One group from Kentucky and Indiana organized a caravan of thirty wagons. In the group were sixty men, thirty-four women, and seventy children. Each family had its own wagon. It was called a (3) _ _ _ _ _ _ _ _ _ _ _ _ _ _. A prairie schooner was a sturdy wagon with side-boards and iron-rimmed wheels. Above the wagon was an arched canvas hood. The canvas protected the families from the hot (4) _ _ _ and the wet (5) _ _ _ _ _ _ _ _ _ _. The animals used to pull the wagons were (6) _ _ _ _, yoked in pairs. Oxen were used instead of mules or horses because they stood the trip better.

7-3 LIFE ON THE OREGON TRAIL *(continued)*

Each family took along a (7) _ _ _ to provide milk during the long journey. Basic supplies for the long journey included bacon, beans, cornmeal, salt, coffee, and tea. Other supplies used for baking included (8) _ _ _ _ _, (9) _ _ _ _ _, (10) _ _ _ _ _ _ _ _ _ _ _ _, and dried (11) _ _ _ _ _ _. Other items included a churn (for making butter), an axe, a saw, a shovel, rope, and a (12) _ _ _ _ _ (for hunting and protection). Also, there were (13) _ _ _ _ _ _ _ _ (to keep warm) and large (14) _ _ _ _ _ _ _ (to cook meals).

A typical day on the Oregon Trail began at 4:00 A.M. After breakfast women and children milked the cows and loaded the wagons. The oxen were yoked by 7:00 A.M. and the wagon train was ready to roll another day. Each day averaged between (15) _ _ _ _ _ _ _ and (16) _ _ _ _ _ _ miles. Only small babies and the sick rode in the wagons. Women and older children walked. Most of the men rode horses. The men often left the wagon train to scout or hunt animals to eat. Some of the animals included (17) _ _ _ _ _ _, (18) _ _ _ _, and (19) _ _ _ _ _ _ _.

At sunset the wagon train formed a circle. Sometimes while the evening meal was being prepared, children played games of (20) _ _ _ or (21) _ _ _ _ - _ _ _ - _ _ _ _. Often they gathered wood for the fire or looked for patches of wild berries. The berries included (22) _ _ _ _ _ _ _ _ _ _ _ _, (23) _ _ _ _ _ _ _ _ _ _ _ _, or (24) _ _ _ _ _ _ _ _ _ _. After dinner there may have been a little time to relax around the campfire to tell stories or sing a few songs. However, bedtime came soon because 4:00 A.M. would roll around quickly.

Many hardships and problems arose. There were diseases, accidents, and Indians that troubled every group. There were also weather-related concerns such as intense heat or heavy rainstorms. The hardest of all was, however, crossing the mountains. For many the green meadows of the Willamette Valley in Oregon finally came into view. Do you think most of the pioneers felt the long journey was worth it?

7-4 TAKE A TRIP TO THE NORTHWEST

For the Teacher

Materials Needed:

- copies of Activity 7-4
- travel agency pamphlets
- travel books (such as *Mobil Travel Guides*)

Note: There is some variance on which states are considered the Northwest. This version includes the states of Washington, Oregon, Montana, Idaho, and Wyoming.

Teacher Preparation:

- Reproduce Activity 7-4, *Take a Trip to the Northwest*, as needed and organize reference materials.
- Divide classes into small groups and assign specific states or regions of the Northwest for students to visit. Instruct classes to center their trips around historical places and events when possible.
- Pass out travel materials and the journal activity. Then allow time for students to complete the activity. Encourage the inclusion of photographs or illustrations, if possible. When students are finished, allow time for groups to share their journals with the rest of the class.

Extended Activities:

- Show classes a travel video on one or more states from the Northwest. Sources for travelogue tapes include educational channel television, video stores, or libraries.
- Encourage students to learn more about the economy of the states they are visiting. What products or services does the state make or provide? What are the major types of jobs in the state? Information on a state's economy can be found in encyclopedias.

7-4 TAKE A TRIP TO THE NORTHWEST

DESTINATION _____

For each day, describe the location, place visited, and special activity (such as art, music, food, or holiday).

DAILY ITINERARY

Day 1 _____
_____
_____

Day 2 _____
_____
_____

Day 3 _____
_____
_____

Day 4 _____
_____
_____

Day 5 _____
_____
_____

Day 6 _____
_____
_____

Day 7 _____
_____
_____

7-5 WHAT WILL IT COST?

For the Teacher

Materials Needed:

- copies of Activity 7-5
- travel books
- pencils

Teacher Preparation:

- Reproduce Activity 7-5, *What Will It Cost?*, as needed.
- Pass out the activity and allow time for students to solve the problems. When they are finished, review the answers (given below) with them.

Answer Key:

1. $28
2. $24.80; $2.48; $27.28
3. $162
4. $42.31
5. $38; $27.28; $162; $42.31; $259.59

Extended Activity:

- Have students estimate the costs for one day of *their* destination for a family of four (2 adults and 2 students). Approximate hotel and dining costs can be found in most travel books. Other expenses can be estimated. Although Activity 7-5 can be used as a guide, encourage students to make other selections on how the family will spend the day.

7-5 WHAT WILL IT COST?

A family of four (2 adults and 2 students) are visiting the Northwest. One of their stops is *Seattle, Washington*. Listed below are some places they visit. Solve the problems to see how much money they will spend for the day.

1. The family's first visit is to the *Seattle Aquarium* featuring exhibits of Pacific seals and sea otters. Admission is $8 for adults and $6 for students. The family needs 2 adult and 2 student tickets.

    What is the total cost of the tickets? $_____

2. Next the family visits *Pioneer Square*, the restored area of early Seattle. They have lunch at one of the restaurants that specializes in Northwest seafood. Lunches are 2 at $6.95, 1 at $4.95, and 1 at $5.95.

    What is the cost of all 4 lunches? $_____

    Add a 10% tip. $_____

    What is the total cost for lunch? $_____

3. In the afternoon and early evening the family takes a ferry trip to *Tillicum Village* on Blake Island. The excursion includes a narrated harbor cruise, a Northwest Coast Indian salmon dinner in an Indian long house, and a Northwest Indian stage show. Cost for the trip is $48.50 for adults and $32.50 for students. The family needs 2 adult and 2 student tickets.

    What is the total cost of the tickets? $_____

4. During the day the family makes the following purchases: 1 Northwest Coast Indian totem pole at $18, 4 cans of Pacific Salmon at $2.39 per can, 1 poster of Seattle and Puget Sound at $6.95, and 4 packages of dried berries at $1.95 each.

    What is the total cost for all items? $_____

5. Add all the expenses to see how much money the family has spent.

    Total cost for #1. $_____

    Total cost for #2. $_____

    Total cost for #3. $_____

    Total cost for #4. $_____

    Total cost for the day. $_____

©1997 by The Center for Applied Research in Education

7-6 NORTHWEST TERMS

For the Teacher

Materials Needed:

- copies of Activity 7-6
- copies of *Glossary of Terms* (at back of book)

Teacher Preparation:

- Reproduce Activity 7-6, *Northwest Terms*, as needed. Also reproduce copies of the *Glossary* as needed.
- Pass out the activity and allow time for students to complete the activity. When they are finished, review the terms (answers given below) with them.

Answer Key:

e.	Louisiana Purchase	o.	missionaries
g.	expedition	p.	pioneer
i.	Lewis and Clark	m.	prairie schooner
l.	Sacagawea	q.	Oregon Trail
a.	Continental Divide	f.	Willamette Valley
b.	Rocky Mountains	h.	Northwest Coast Indians
n.	Oregon Country	j.	potlatch
r.	Puget Sound	d.	long house
c.	mountain men	k.	totem pole

Extended Activity:

- Use some of the terms in the activity as topics for further research. Appropriate titles include The Louisiana Purchase, The Lewis and Clark Expedition, The Oregon Trail, The Pioneer Era in the Oregon Country, and The Northwest Coast Indians.

7-6 NORTHWEST TERMS

Expand your vocabulary by learning some terms often associated with the Northwest region. Match the correct definitions to the words.

_____Louisiana Purchase

_____expedition

_____Lewis and Clark

_____Sacagawea

_____Continental Divide

_____Rocky Mountains

_____Oregon Country

_____Puget Sound

_____mountain men

_____missionaries

_____pioneer

_____prairie schooner

_____Oregon Trail

_____Willamette Valley

_____Northwest Coast Indians

_____potlatch

_____long house

_____totem pole

a. principal watershed boundary in North America separating streams that flow into Pacific Ocean from those that flow into the Atlantic Ocean

b. great chain of mountains extending from Canada to New Mexico and bordered by Great Plains

c. refers to the trappers and fur traders of the 1800s who lived in the Rocky Mountains

d. a communal dwelling of the Northwest Coast Indians often decorated with elaborate carvings

e. large area of land between Mississippi River and Rocky Mountains purchased from France in 1803

f. rich valley in Oregon and destination for many pioneers who traveled along the Oregon Trail

g. a journey taken for a specific purpose such as to explore

h. refers to the Indian tribes who lived along the rugged west coast from Oregon to Alaska

i. men who led the expedition to explore the Northwest territory of the Louisiana Purchase

j. a social event of the Northwest Coast Indians noted for feasting and gift-giving

k. a tall carved log made by Northwest Indians that tells a story

l. Shoshone Indian woman who helped Lewis and Clark's expedition

m. a sturdy wagon with side-boards, iron-rimmed wheels, and an arched canvas hood

n. refers to the large area of land between the Rocky Mountains and the Pacific Ocean in the 1800s

o. persons undertaking a religious mission

p. a person or group that opens up or settles a new territory

q. the trail pioneers followed in the 1800s that started in Missouri and ended in Oregon

r. a body of water that separates the Olympic Peninsula from the state of Washington

©1997 by The Center for Applied Research in Education

7-7 FOLKTALES AND LITERATURE

For the Teacher

Materials Needed:

- copies of Activity 7-7

- practice paper and pencils

- drawing paper and pens

- (*optional*) black markers and/or colored pencils

Teacher Preparation:

- Reproduce Activity 7-7, *Folktales and Literature*, as needed and organize materials.

- Pass out the activity and allow students time to read the story. When they are finished, instruct them to write a legend of their own, preferably one with a "Northwest Coast Indian" or "Along the Oregon Trail" setting.

- Using drawing paper and pens, have students rewrite their story in their best printing or writing.

- (*optional*) Encourage students to illustrate their tales with markers and/or colored pencils.

Extended Activity:

- Set aside time for reading stories that relate to the Northwest region. Contact the media person in your building or community for assistance in gathering appropriate titles. When possible, take classes to the library for this activity. There are a number of books available that tell stories about the first Americans of the Northwest or those who followed. A brief list follows that will help get you started. **Note**: Remember, this is merely a list of some options that are available. Regional differences may vary, so use whatever is available in your area.

FOLKTALES

Totem Pole by Diane Hoyt-Goldsmith (New York: Holiday House, 1990). This book, seen through the eyes of David (a young member of the Tsimshian tribe), tells about the relationship with his father, a wood-carver who learned the traditions of the "old ways" of their ancestors. David also relates his favorite tale (which is retold in this activity).

Star Tales by Gretchen Will Mayo (New York: Walker & Co., 1987). This is a collection of favorite stories among the North American Indians about the stars, moon, and night-time sky.

The Girl Who Married a Ghost and other Tales from the North American Indian by Edward S. Curtis (New York: Four Winds Press, 1978). This book gives a collection of first-hand narratives from Indians gathered during the early 1900s from the Northwest, California, the Plains, and Southwest.

CHILDREN'S LITERATURE

Bound for Oregon by Jean Van Leeuwen (New York: Dial Books, 1994). This story is a fictionalized account of nine-year-old Mary Ellen Todd and her family making the journey from their home in Arkansas westward over the Oregon Trail in 1852.

Wolf at the Door by Barbara Corcoran (New York: Simon & Schuster Children's, 1993). The setting for the story is Montana. Lee, who is living in the shadow of her beautiful and talented sister, takes care of a wolf pack that needs protection from the cattle ranchers.

Spirit Quest by Susan Sharpe (New York: Simon & Schuster Children's, 1991). Eleven-year-old Aaron is vacationing on an old Indian Reservation off the coast of Washington. Aaron becomes friends with Robert, a Quileute Indian who is preparing for his spirit quest.

The Haymeadow by Gary Paulsen (New York: Dell, 1994). A fourteen-year-old boy named John, tending his father's sheep, gains confidence during the summer he spends in the mountains of Wyoming. This is a different kind of survival story.

Wild Horse Running by Sam Savitt (New York: Dodd Mead, 1973). This story is based on fact. The setting is present-day Montana where there has been a struggle to keep the wild horses running free.

Bonanza Girl by Patricia Beatty (New York: Morrow, 1993). A widow and her two children set out for the gold rush territory in Idaho hoping to find a new life.

Sarah and Me and the Lady from the Sea by Patricia Beatty (New York: Morrow, 1989). The story takes place in 1894 during a flood. The family's dry goods business goes bankrupt. Sarah's family is forced to sell their Portland, Oregon home and move to their summer home on the Washington Peninsula.

Across the Wide and Lonesome Prairie: The Oregon Trail Diary of Hattie Campbell (New York: Scholastic, 1997). Scholastic Publishing has released a new "Dear America" series for young readers. The diary series splices fact and fabrication, revealing the drudgery of everyday life as history explodes around them.

7-7 FOLKTALES AND LITERATURE

The following is an adaptation from a Tsimshian Indian tale as retold from *Totem Pole* by Diane Hoyt-Goldsmith.

THE TALE OF THE EAGLE AND THE YOUNG CHIEF

Once upon a time there was a young Indian chief from the Tsimshian tribe named Gikwah. One day Gikwah was walking on a beach near his village. Suddenly, he heard a loud noise in the wooded area nearby. As Gikwah grew closer, he could see there was a magnificent eagle trapped in some bushes.

The young chief began to free the great eagle. Carefully and cautiously he loosened the knotted branches and cleared away the vines that trapped the bird. Soon, the bird was free and flew away. The young chief did not know that his kind deed would one day be rewarded.

A few years passed and times became hard for Gikwah and his village. Food became scarce and many people in his tribe were going hungry. The young chief was very worried because he didn't want his people to starve. One day, while walking on the beach as Gikwah often did, a beautiful salmon fish dropped from the sky near his feet. When he looked up he saw a beautiful eagle flying away.

Every day, for the next months, the eagle brought fresh fish to the beach for Gikwah to collect and feed the villagers. Eventually, the bad season of scarce food passed and the Indians began to find food again.

So you see, all this was done because Gikwah had performed a good deed. This tale is passed from one generation to the next among the Tsimshian tribe. When one performs a kind deed, it is often paid back a hundred fold.

7-8 PASTIMES AND GAMES

For the Teacher

Materials Needed:

- copies of Activity 7-8

- items mentioned in "Teacher Preparation"

Teacher Preparation:

- Reproduce Activity 7-8, *Pastimes and Games,* as needed.

- Pass out the activity and go over the pastimes outlined. If possible, *allow students to help make choices on which activities will be selected. Then set aside some time for participation.*

- If there is interest in pioneer activities along the Oregon Trail, organize *simple games* or gather around for *campfire-style stories.*

- For those interested in participating in a *potlatch*, pick and choose the activities that best fit your situation.

Extended Activity:

- Most of the Northwest Coast Indians of today live in Canada. However, some still reside in the Northwest region. One area that offers a look into the past is near Seattle. *The Tillicum Village*, on Blake Island, offers tours from Seattle to an Indian long house as well as an authentic Northwest Coast Native American feast and entertainment. Included in the meal is baked salmon, Indian fry bread, corn on the cob, and berry pies. Develop an exhibit on the Northwest Coast Indians for your classroom while students are learning about the Northwest. Write to Seattle Convention & Visitor Bureau, 520 Pike Street, Suite 1300, Seattle, Washington, 98101 for information or consult the media specialist in your building for assistance.

7-8 PASTIMES AND GAMES

PIONEER PASTIMES

Games and social activities along the Oregon Trail were minimal. Most of the time was spent on the demands of making the journey. However, a few activities were enjoyed. Simple games of *tag* or *hide-and-seek* were played. A favorite pastime was *telling stories* around the campfire before bedtime.

A POTLATCH

One of the most elaborate pastimes of the Indians of the Northwest Coast was hosting a *potlatch*. A potlatch is a great celebration given in honor of a birth, marriage, death, or any other reason to entertain. To host your own potlatch, consider the following.

TOTEM POLES

Often tribes would carve a totem pole to display in honor of the special event. A totem pole is a long, carved, and painted log that tells a story or shows a family history. Make your own designs by following the directions in Activity 7-10, *Totem Poles*. When the totem poles are complete, hang them around the room. You might want to stack them by group to tell a totem pole story. Ask the Art teacher to judge the best or most creative submissions and award prizes to winners.

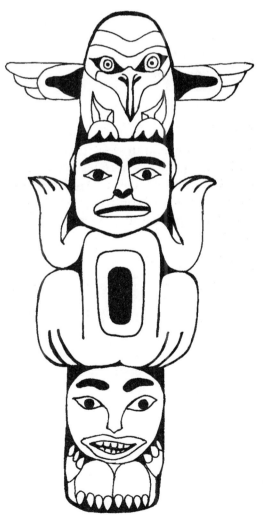

POTLATCH FOOD

As visitors to potlatches arrived, drums would beat and dancing began. Soon bowls of food were served and a feast began. The feast started with servings of salmon and other fish and meats. Other offerings included fresh and dried berries (blueberries, blackberries, strawberries) and various nutmeats. In modern times, at *Tillicum Village*, on Blake Island near Seattle, the Northwest Coast American Indians serve visitors a native feast that includes baked salmon, corn-on-the-cob, Indian fry bread, and berry pies and tarts. For your potlatch, choose some ready-made or simple-to-prepare Northwest Coast Indian-style foods. Appropriate choices include salmon and crackers, and fresh or dried blueberries, blackberries, and/or strawberries. With a little extra effort you can make *wild rice with blueberries* as outlined in Activity 7-14.

A POTLATCH TRADITION

The Indian word *potlatch* means "give away." At a potlatch celebration it was customary for the host to give every guest a gift. After the feasting ended, the host stood and made many toasts, then proceeded to give away some of his most prized possessions. One special gift was a piece of copper that had been elaborately decorated with designs. Other articles given away included decorated blankets, carved bowls, painted masks, large carved canoes, and baskets filled with various types of fishes, meats, berries, and nuts. For your potlatch "give away" celebration, exchange wrapped gift items with classmates. Inexpensive candy, fruit, or nut items make appropriate choices, although other items can be selected as well. With a little extra effort, create a salmon design as shown in Activity 7-11 and use it as wrapping paper for your gift exchange.

POTLATCH STORYTELLING

Another activity at potlatches included telling stories. Of the many stories told, those about the Raven were the most popular. The Raven was known as being sly and cunning. Therefore, stories about the Raven told of ways he fooled the sea creatures and forest animals. Create your own Northwest Coast Indian-style story. Refer to Activity 7-7 to get the storytelling started.

7-9 SOUNDS OF THE NORTHWEST

For the Teacher

Materials Needed:

- CD, cassette, or film
- audio-visual equipment

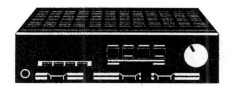

Teacher Preparation:

- There was precious little time for the pioneers who traveled along the Oregon Trail to participate in activities that involved music. However, on occasion, a member of the wagon train would bring out his fiddle around the evening campfire and entertain folks.

  After the pioneer families settled in Oregon country, social events centered around church socials and community dances. *Square dancing* was a favorite kind of dance. A local fiddler played the tunes while a caller led the dancers through the steps. For opportunities to listen to square dance music, check with your local library, record store, or music teacher. Encourage your students to learn one or two square dances. The Physical Education and Music teachers may be able to help you with this.

- The Northwest Coast Indians enjoyed their own style of music that included drums, chants, and dancing. Although there are regional differences among Indian tribes, almost every area of America has some type of Indian music. For opportunities to listen to Native American music, check your local library or record store. Also consider the following options:

  Creations Journey (Smithsonian Folkways Recordings, Washington, D.C., 1994).
  This recording celebrates the ceremonial, social, and contemporary music of Native Americans.

  All One Earth, Songs for the Generations (Luna Blu, Norwich, VT, 1994).
  The recording features Michael J. Cadutato and the sounds of the Indians of North America.

- For an opportunity to view a musical film production relating to the Oregon territory, consider the following option:

  Seven Brides for Seven Brothers
  This 1950s musical is a dancing and singing spectacle about seven backwoods brothers from the Oregon Territory during the 1850s and their quest to obtain brides. It stars Jane Powell as Molly and Howard Keel as Adam Pontipee. When Molly marries Adam, she soon discovers he has six unruly brothers and decides to teach them some manners so that they can fetch some brides of their own.

7-10 TOTEM POLES

For the Teacher

Materials Needed:

- copies of Activity 7-10
- white drawing paper
- black markers
- (*optional*) colored markers

Teacher Preparation:

- Reproduce Activity 7-10, *Totem Poles*, as needed and organize materials.
- Pass out the activity and go over it with your students.
- Divide classes into small groups. Then pass out the materials and allow time for groups to develop three or four totem designs.
- When they are finished, display them around the room (stacked by groups to give a totem pole appearance). Ask the Art teacher to judge the most creative or interesting submissions. Award prizes to winners.

Extended Activity:

- Stimulate interest in Native American Indian cultures by cutting and assembling masks while your classes are learning about the Northwest. An excellent source is *Cut and Make North American Indian Masks* by A. G. Smith and Josie Hazen (Dover Publications, Mineola, NY, 1989.) The book provides eight full-color masks that are based on authentic Indian designs. They are ready to cut out and assemble and provide ideal attention-getting visual aids for your classroom.

This illustration is a bear mask, Kwakiuti tribe, Northwest Coast Indians, *North American Indian Design Coloring Book* by Paul E. Kennedy (Dover Publications). It is similar to one of the cut-out masks recommended.

7-10 TOTEM POLES

The Northwest Coast Indians lived along the rugged shores of North America in the present-day states of Oregon and Washington in the United States and British Columbia in Canada. These tribes developed a culture that was unique to this part of the world. They lived near the water which provided them with an abundance of seafood. Nearby forests provided additional food. Today, some tribes still live in the Northwest, although many reside in Canada.

The Northwest Coast tribes developed a sophisticated culture and became very skilled fishermen and carvers. They lived in villages along the coast in "long houses" that were big enough for entire extended families. Nearby was a totem pole. A *totem pole* is a long, carved log that tells a story, records history, or identifies a family. Long before writing was used, the Indians created a system of symbolic designs for the totem poles.

TOTEM POLE SYMBOLS

The most popular symbols used by the Native Americans included the eagle, bear, whale, frog, and raven. In fact, the eagle (or Thunderbird) remains the most widely used design of all totem pole characters.

TOTEM POLE DESIGNS

The illustration below shows how to develop a totem pole story using symbols and designs similar to those used by the Northwest Coast Indians. This story tells about the tribe leader (bottom) who sends out a hunter in search of the bear (middle) for food. As the hunter departs, the leader wishes him good luck. The Thunderbird (top) represents the good fortune of the hunter as he brings back the bear to the tribe.

At the top of many totem poles is the Thunderbird, which represents good luck and good fortune. In this tale, it has brought the hunter fortune by showing him where the bear is hidden in the woods.

The middle figure is that of a bear. This is a good symbol because it is the one that provides fur for warmth, food to eat, and teeth and claws for good-luck charms.

The bottom figure represents an Indian leader or head of the family clan. He stands for wisdom and leadership. In this totem, he sends out a tribesman to hunt for bear.

7-10 TOTEM POLES (continued)

Look at the totem pole on the previous page carefully. As you can see, the designs are created in geometric shapes. Circles, squares, and rectangles are used throughout the designs. Notice how the designs are created in sections. Will you start from the inside section and work outward? Will it be easier to begin at the top and work down? Choose the place to begin that feels the most comfortable, but remember to work in sections.

Steps to Creating a Totem Pole

1. Begin by dividing into groups of three to four people. Within the group decide what symbolic story you will tell. You may use the basic shapes outlined below to get started; however, expand the story with your own symbols and ideas.

2. When the group has decided on a story, select three or four symbols that will represent the totem pole story. Within the group have each person draw and design one symbol on white drawing paper.

3. First, outline the basic shapes of your drawing as well as your designs within the drawing. Remember to work in sections when you are creating the designs.

4. (*optional*) Use markers to add color to the totem pole designs.

5. When each member of the group has finished, stack the designs in the appropriate order of the story and hang them on the wall.

Below are two basic shapes often used to create totem pole stories. They are the Thunderbird and a masked figure. Use one or both of these designs to get started at creating your own totem pole story. Remember, these are *basic shapes only*. It is up to you to finish them with your own geometric and symbolic illustrations. Add additional basic shapes of your own to add to the story. What animal would you choose to create a symbolic story? Why?

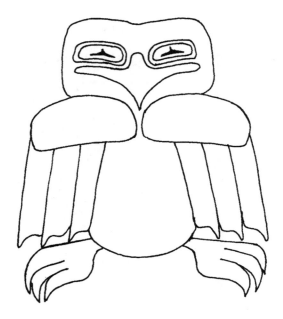

7-11 SALMON DESIGNS

For the Teacher

Materials Needed:

- copies of Activity 7-11
- white drawing paper, 9" x 12" or 12" x 18"
- black markers

Teacher Preparation

- Reproduce Activity 7-11, *Salmon Designs*, as needed and organize materials.
- Pass out the activity and go over it with your students.
- Distribute the materials and allow time for students to complete the salmon drawings.
- When they are finished, display them around the room.

Extended Activity:

- Use the salmon designs to wrap gifts for the potlatch as described in Activity 7-8, *Pastimes and Games*.

7-11 SALMON DESIGNS

The most famous works of art created by the Northwest Coast Indians were the carved totem poles that told stories or related historical events. The Indians were also well known for decorating other items. They carved or painted storage boxes, canoes, platters, tools, masks, drums, and large panels (used to decorate walls inside homes).

Salmon designs were a popular drawing motif used on the decorative items created by the Indians. The salmon represented a vital source of food for the people. In addition, salmon oil was used for cooking, heating, and a source for light during long winter nights. Because the salmon was so important, fish designs were used on many art objects.

Like the totem pole drawings, the salmon designs were very geometric. Circles, squares, and rectangles were used throughout. Create your own salmon drawing by following the steps below.

Steps to Creating Salmon Designs

1. Begin by drawing a basic fish shape. Look at the shape of the fish shown to get started. Then be creative and draw your own version.

2. Divide the fish into two, three, or four sections. Within each section create geometric shapes and patterns. Use repeat patterns in the design whenever appropriate.

3. When you are finished, display the drawings around the room.

7-12 BASICS OF NORTHWEST COOKING

For the Teacher

Materials Needed:

- copies of Activity 7-12
- pencils

Teacher Preparation:

- Reproduce Activity 7-12, *Basics of Northwest Cooking*, as needed.
- Pass out the activity and allow time for students to read the information and complete the worksheet. (Answers are given below.) When they are finished, review the food basics of the pioneers and the first Americans.

Answer Key:

Part One: Basic Foods of the Northwest Coast Indians

Fish: salmon; cod; halibut; flounder; sole

Shellfish: clams; oysters; crabs

Methods of cooking: baked; barbecued; steamed; dried

Meats: bear; deer; rabbit; squirrel; fox; beaver

Vegetables (for stews): parsnips; onions; seaweed; potatoes; rice

Fruits: blackberries; blueberries; strawberries

Types of tea: mint; blackberry; strawberry; huckleberry

Other beverage: berry punch

Part Two: Basic Foods along the Oregon Trail

Basic supplies: bacon; beans; cornmeal; salt; flour; sugar; baking powder; lard; apples; dried apples

Beverages: tea; coffee

Animal taken: cow (for milk and butter)

Meats: buffalo; deer; rabbit; squirrel

Berries: strawberries; blackberries; blueberries

Nuts: black walnuts; hickory nuts

Basic meals: cornmeal mush with milk; beans and biscuits; meat stews and biscuits

Special treats: blackberry pie; black walnut cream pie

Extended Activity:

- Encourage students to collectively develop a pioneer and Northwest Coast Indian cookbook. Divide classes into groups and assign some to develop pioneer recipes and others to develop Indian recipes. Appropriate topics include Soups, Main Meals, Desserts, and Beverages. After students have collected their recipes, duplicate their submissions and allow each person to organize a cookbook of his or her own.

7-12 BASICS OF NORTHWEST COOKING

BASIC FOODS OF THE NORTHWEST COAST INDIANS

Seafood: The Indians depended heavily on fish as their food source. Although *salmon* was the most important, *cod, halibut, flounder,* and *sole* were also eaten. Equally important were various types of *shellfish* including *clams, oysters*, and *crabs*. Cooks were inventive in the way they prepared seafood. Methods of cooking included *baked, barbecued, steamed,* and *dried.*

Meats: Various types of meat were part of the Indians' diet as well. Large animals eaten were *bear* and *deer*. Smaller animals included *rabbit, squirrel, fox,* and *beaver*.

Soups and Stews: Fish and animal meats were often used in soups and stews. Vegetables used in stews included *parsnips, onions*, and *seaweed* as well as wild *potatoes* and harvested wild *rice*.

Fruits: Indian women looked forward to the berry season. Special berry baskets were made to pick berries. Among the most popular were *blackberries, blueberries,* and *strawberries*. These were eaten fresh or dried for the long winter months.

Beverages: The Northwest Indians enjoyed a variety of *teas*. Among them were *mint, blackberry, strawberry* and *huckleberry*. A sweet *berry punch* was also made from berries and honey.

BASIC FOODS ALONG THE OREGON TRAIL

Basic supplies: Each man, woman, and child who joined a wagon train for the long journey to Oregon was expected to bring along some basic food items. These foods included *bacon, beans, cornmeal, salt, flour, sugar, baking powder, lard, apples, dried apples*, as well as *tea* and *coffee*. In addition, each family brought along one or more *cows* for milk and butter along the way.

Meats: As you can imagine, the basic supplies gave cooks the bare minimum with which to use. Along the trail, meat was added to the meals when the men hunted for game. Among them were *buffalo, deer, rabbit*, and *squirrel*.

Berries: Along the trail, the pioneers often collected wild berries that were a welcome sweet treat. They included wild *strawberries, blackberries* and *blueberries*.

Nuts: Nutmeats were also often collected along the way. Two of them included *black walnuts* and *hickory nuts*.

Basic meals: With a minimum amount of food supplies, cooks prepared the daily meals along the Oregon Trail. The trip lasted for four to five months, so inventiveness was necessary to spark up the menus. Basic meals consisted of the following: *cornmeal with milk* (for breakfast), and *beans and biscuits* or *meat stews and biscuits* for the main meals. Sunday was a day of rest from the trail and a time to prepare special treats. A fresh *wild blackberry pie* or a *black walnut cream pie* would be welcome desserts.

7-12 BASICS OF NORTHWEST COOKING

Part One: Use the boxes below to outline some of the food basics of the Northwest Coast Indians.

Fish: _____   _____
_____   _____
_____

Shellfish: _____   _____
_____

Methods of cooking: _____   _____
_____   _____

Meats: _____   _____
_____   _____
_____   _____

Vegetables: _____   _____
(used in stews) _____   _____
_____

Fruits: _____
_____
_____

Types of teas: _____   _____
_____   _____

Other beverage: _____

7-12 BASICS OF NORTHWEST COOKING *(continued)*

Part Two: Use the boxes below to outline some of the food basics of the pioneers along the Oregon Trail.

Basic Supplies: _____   _____

_____   _____

_____   _____

_____   _____

_____   _____

Beverages: _____

What animal was every family expected   _____

to bring and what foods did it supply?   _____

_____

Foods along the Oregon Trail

Meats: _____   _____

_____   _____

Berries: _____   _____

_____

Nuts: _____   _____

Basic trail meals: _____

_____

_____

Special treats: _____

_____

7-13 POTLATCH AND OREGON TRAIL MENUS

For the Teacher

Hint: It is helpful to complete Activity 7-12, *Basics of Northwest Cooking*, before participating in this one.

Materials Needed:

- copies of activity 7-13
- pencils or pens

Teacher Preparation:

- Reproduce Activity 7-13, *Potlatch and Oregon Trail Menus*, as needed.
- Pass out the activity. Then allow students time to read the menus and make their dinner selections. When they are finished, lead a discussion to compare and contrast the meals of the Indians to those of the pioneers. Then contrast the foods of both to a special-occasion meal at their house.

Extended Activities:

- Ask students to bring in some simple or ready-prepared food items appropriate for a potlatch. Appropriate choices include salmon and crackers; beef jerky; dried or fresh blueberries, blackberries, or strawberries; fruit teas, and berry punch.
- Ask students to bring in some simple or ready-prepared food items appropriate for an Oregon Trail treat. Appropriate choices include dried apples; apple pie; biscuits and jam; nutmeats; and fresh or dried blueberries, blackberries, or strawberries.

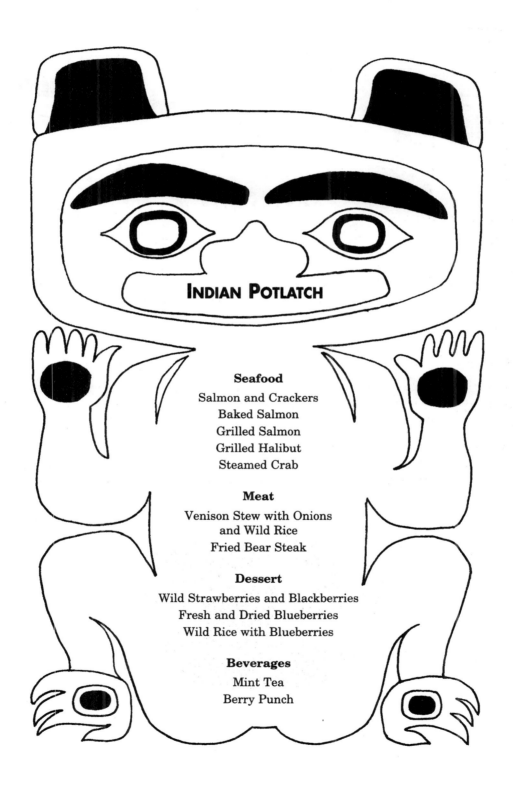

INDIAN POTLATCH

Seafood
Salmon and Crackers
Baked Salmon
Grilled Salmon
Grilled Halibut
Steamed Crab

Meat
Venison Stew with Onions
and Wild Rice
Fried Bear Steak

Dessert
Wild Strawberries and Blackberries
Fresh and Dried Blueberries
Wild Rice with Blueberries

Beverages
Mint Tea
Berry Punch

OREGON TRAIL MENU

Meat
Buffalo Burgers on Biscuits
Rabbit Stew with Gravy over Biscuits

Other Dishes
Pork and Beans with Biscuits
Cornmeal Pudding

Desserts
Wild Berry Pie
Black Walnut Cream Pie
Fried Apple Rings

Beverages
Tea
Coffee
Wild Berry Punch

7-13 POTLATCH AND OREGON TRAIL MENUS (continued)

After you have looked over the menus for the Indian potlatch and the Oregon Trail, choose which menu you want to try. From the menu you have selected, choose as many food items as you want. After you have made your choices, list a typical evening meal at your home. When you are finished, compare the potlatch or Oregon Trail meal with your own.

Potlatch Menu

Seafood

_____

_____

_____

_____

_____

Meat

_____

_____

Desserts

_____

_____

_____

Beverages

_____

_____

_____

Oregon Trail Menu

Meat

_____

_____

_____

Other Dishes

_____

_____

Desserts

_____

_____

_____

Beverages

_____

_____

_____

American Dinner

Appetizer _____

Soup or Salad _____

Main Course_____

Vegetables_____

Bread _____

Dessert _____

Beverage _____

7-14 WILD RICE WITH BLUEBERRIES

For the Teacher

Equipment Needed:

- copies of Activity 7-14
- 1-1/2-quart saucepan with lid
- measuring cup
- measuring spoons
- bowl
- strainer

Supplies Needed:

- wild rice or long-grain white rice
- milk
- sugar
- salt
- margarine
- vanilla
- blueberries

Teacher Preparation:

- Reproduce Activity 7-14, *Wild Rice with Blueberries*, as needed and organize equipment and supplies.
- Give a demonstration on making rice as students follow along with the recipe. Follow up with a rice and blueberry taste treat.
- **ALTERNATIVE:** Go over the recipe with students. Then make an out-of-class assignment for students to make the recipe at home and bring it to school for a special Northwest Coast Indian treat day. Encourage students to ask for adult supervision when preparing the rice.

Extended Activity:

- Contact the Consumer and Family Living teacher well in advance and coordinate a Northwest Indian-type luncheon activity while your classes are learning about the Northwest.

7-14 WILD RICE WITH BLUEBERRIES

The Northwest Coast Indians did not serve many sweet desserts. They did, however, enjoy many kinds of fresh and dried berries. In addition, two dishes have been found in the cookbooks of the coastal Indians that may have served as desserts. One consisted of a bowl filled with whipped wild berries. Another is wild rice with blueberries. This version has adapted to 20th-century tastes by adding sugar to the rice. Have you ever eaten wild rice with blueberries? Is it hard to imagine that it was a special treat for the Northwest Coastal Indians? This recipe serves 4 to 6.

You need:

3-1/2	cups milk
2/3	cup wild rice or long-grain white rice (uncooked)
1/2	cup sugar
2	dashes of salt
2	tablespoons margarine
1	teaspoon vanilla
1	cup blueberries

What to do:

1. In a saucepan combine milk, rice, sugar, and salt. Let stand for 1 hour.

2. Bring to a boil. Then reduce heat and cook (uncovered) over medium-low heat until rice has softened and milk is absorbed—about 30 to 35 minutes. Stir rice frequently during the last ten minutes.

3. Remove from heat and stir in margarine and vanilla.

4. Cover and cool.

5. In a strainer, wash blueberries and drain completely.

6. Serve rice topped with blueberries.

7-15 BLACK WALNUT CREAM PIE

For the Teacher

Equipment Needed:

- copies of Activity 7-15
- 8" pie pan
- 1-1/2-quart saucepan with lid
- measuring cup
- spoon

Supplies Needed:

- ready-made pie crust
- vanilla pudding/pie filling (not instant)
- milk
- black walnuts
- whipped cream or whipped topping

Teacher Preparation:

- Reproduce copies of Activity 7-15, *Black Walnut Cream Pie*, as needed and organize equipment and supplies.
- Give a demonstration on making the pie as students follow along with the recipe. Follow up with a pie taste treat.
- **ALTERNATIVE:** Go over the recipe with students. Then make an out-of-class assignment for students to make the pie at home and bring it to school for a special Pioneer treat day. Encourage students to ask for adult supervision when preparing the pie at home.

Extended Activity:

- Contact the Consumer and Family Living teacher well in advance and coordinate a pioneer on-the-trail-type luncheon activity while your classes are learning about the Northwest.

7-15 BLACK WALNUT CREAM PIE

The pioneer women who traveled the Oregon Trail lacked many cooking ingredients that were available to them before their journey. These resourceful women, however, developed several delicious recipes using nutmeats and wild berries they gathered along the trail. *Black walnut cream pie* and *cream pie with fresh strawberries** represent two of them. This easier version takes advantage of some of our modern conveniences. Remember, if you were on the Oregon Trail, it would take much longer to prepare and the pie would be reserved for a very special treat. This recipe serves 6 to 8.

You need:

1	ready-made pie crust
1	3-ounce box vanilla pudding/pie filling (not instant)
2	cups milk
2/3	cup black walnuts (chopped)**
	whipped cream or whipped topping

What to do:

1. Set oven at 400°.
2. Follow directions on pie crust package to make a *baked shell for pudding*.
3. Cool thoroughly.
4. Empty pudding/pie filling powder in a saucepan.
5. Slowly add milk to powder, stirring to keep mixture smooth.
6. Cook and stir over medium heat until mixture comes to a full boil.
7. Remove from heat, cover pan with lid and cool 10 minutes.
8. Stir black walnuts into pudding. Then pour into pie shell.
9. Cover with plastic wrap and thoroughly chill pie.
10. Top with whipped cream or whipped topping and serve.

* For *cream pie with strawberries*, delete black walnuts and top pie with fresh strawberries and whipped cream after pie has thoroughly chilled.

** The pioneers used many kinds of nuts—including hickory nuts, walnuts, pecans, and hazelnuts—so most any kind of nutmeat can be substituted for black walnuts.

BIBLIOGRAPHY FOR THE NORTHWEST

Art

Hoyt-Goldsmith, Diane. *Totem Pole*. New York: Holiday House, 1990.

Smith, Tom. *Northwest Coast Indians Coloring Book*. Los Angeles: Price Stern Sloan, Inc., 1993.

Children's Nonfiction

Heinrichs, Ann. *America the Beautiful: Montana*. Chicago: Children's Press, 1991.

Heinrichs, Ann. *America the Beautiful: Wyoming*. Chicago: Children's Press, 1992.

Kent, Zachary. *America the Beautiful: Idaho*. Chicago: Children's Press, 1990.

Stein, Conrad. *America the Beautiful: Oregon*. Chicago: Children's Press, 1989.

Stein, Conrad. *America the Beautiful: Washington*. Chicago: Children's Press, 1992.

Cookbooks

Barchers, Suzanne I. and Patricia Marden. *Cooking Up U.S. History*. Englewood, CO: Teacher Ideas Press, 1991.

Batdorf, Carol. *Northwest Native Harvest*. Blaine, WA: Hancock House Publishers, 1990.

Editors. *Better Homes and Gardens Heritage Cook Book*. Des Moines, IA: Meredith Corporation, 1985.

Pastimes

Beck, Mary Giraudo. *Potlatch*. Seattle: Alaska Northwest Books, 1993.

Patent, Dorothy Hinshaw. *West by Covered Wagon—Retracing the Pioneer Trails*. New York: Walker and Company, 1995.

Social Studies

Bass, Herbert J. *Our Country*. Parsippany, NJ: Silver Burdett and Ginn, 1991.

Travel

Editors. *Mobil 1995 Travel Guide, Northwest and Great Plains*. New York: Fodor's Travel Publications, 1995.

SECTION 8

THE WEST

Below is an outline of the interdisciplinary activities included in this section. They are designed to bring a broad range of hands-on cultural lessons and activities into the social studies classroom. Pick and choose the ones that best fit into your program.

Social Studies

8-1   Getting to Know the West
8-2   People of the West
8-3   The California Gold-Rush Days
8-4   Take a Trip to the West

Mathematics

8-5   What Will It Cost?

Language Arts

8-6   Far West Terms
8-7   Tall Tales and Literature

Physical Education

8-8   Pastimes and Games

Music

8-9   Sounds of the West

Art

8-10   Gold-Nugget Jewelry

Consumer and Family Living

8-11   Basics of Old West Cooking
8-12   Mining Camp and Boom Town Menus
8-13   Caramel-Pecan Campfire Biscuits
8-14   Boom Town Lemon Pie
8-15   Blackberry Cobbler

Bibliography for the West

MAP OF THE WEST

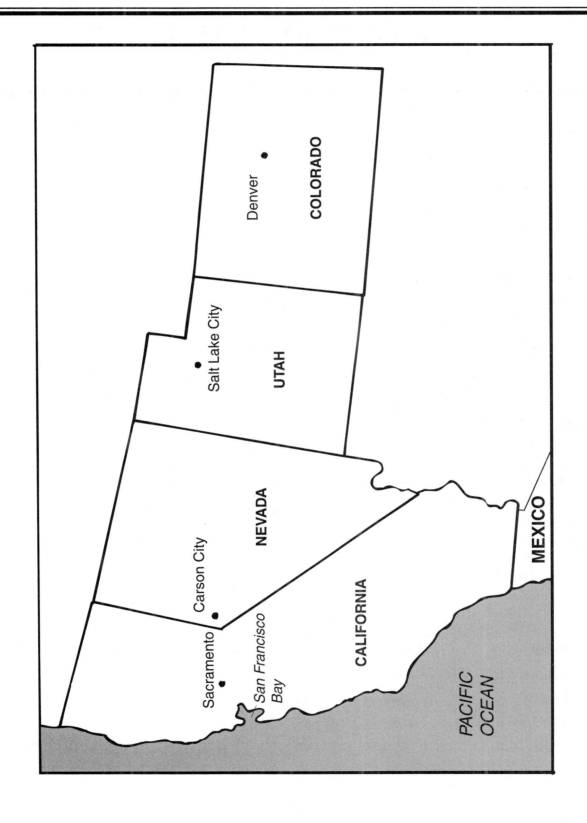

8-1 GETTING TO KNOW THE WEST

For the Teacher

Materials Needed:

- copies of Activity 8-1
- labeled map of the West (enlarged on opaque projector)
- copies of unlabeled map of the West
- (colored) pencils

Teacher Preparation:

- Reproduce Activity 8-1, *Getting to Know the West*, as needed. Also reproduce copies of the unlabeled map of the West as needed.

- Pass out the activity and map to each student. Then allow time for students to locate and label the West as outlined in the activity. When they are finished, review the geography with them.

Extended Activity:

- Reproduce additional copies of the unlabeled map and have students identify other features of the western states, such as population distribution, land use, or climate. PC Globe® computer program can provide much of the information needed for this activity. Consult your school's media person for assistance, too.

- Reproduce the chart of *The Fifty States* (at back of book) as needed. Pass out the chart and have students make a list of the West states, date they entered the Union, order of entry, capital, and largest city. *List states in order they entered the Union.* Answers should appear as follows:

State	Date Entered Union	Order of Entry	Capital	Largest City
California	1850	31	Sacramento	Los Angeles
Nevada	1864	36	Carson City	Las Vegas
Colorado	1876	38	Denver	Denver
Utah	1896	45	Salt Lake City	Salt Lake City

8-1 GETTING TO KNOW THE WEST

Use the map provided to locate and label the following features:

State: California
Capital: Sacramento
Body of water: San Francisco Bay

State: Nevada
Capital: Carson City

State: Utah
Capital: Salt Lake City

State: Colorado
Capital: Denver

Bordering body of water: Pacific Ocean
Bordering country: Mexico

8-1 GETTING TO KNOW THE WEST

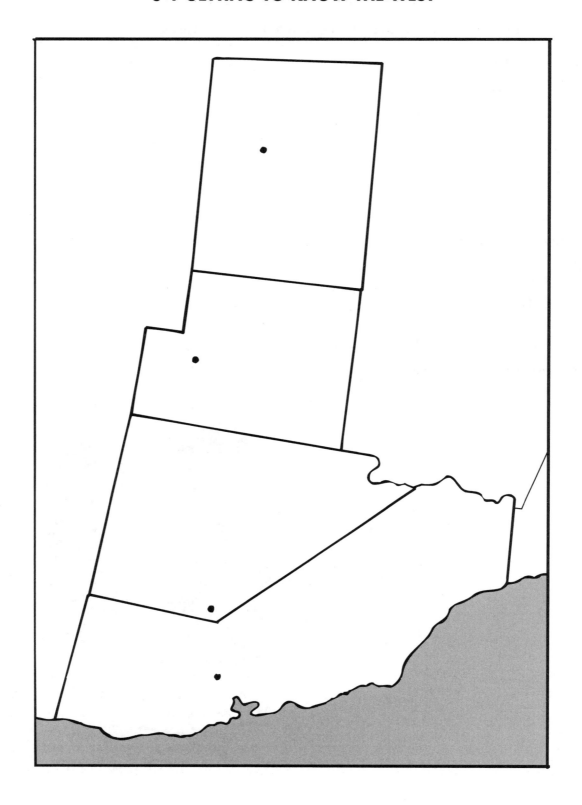

8-2 PEOPLE OF THE WEST

For the Teacher

Materials Needed:

- copies of Activity 8-2
- pencils
- research materials

Teacher Preparation:

- Reproduce Activity 8-2A and 8-2B, *People of the West*, as needed.
- Pass out the activity and allow enough time for students to complete the word search puzzle. When they are finished, review the answers (given below) with them.

Answer Key:

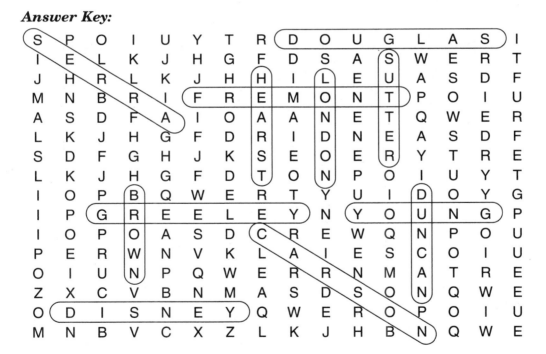

Extended Activities:

- Allow students to pick one of the famous people in the puzzle (or another person from the West region who has made a contribution to America) and assign research papers on his or her life and contributions. Use the outline in Activity 8-2B to develop the reports.
- Films have been made about some of the famous people in the puzzle. Select one and show it to your classes.

8-2A PEOPLE OF THE WEST

Listed below are some people who lived in or had some influence in the development of the West region. In the word search puzzle, locate and circle the names of these famous people. **Hint:** When locating the names, *look for last names only.* You will find them across, diagonal, or down. After completing the puzzle, choose one of the famous persons and write a report on his or her life and accomplishments.

Christopher (Kit) Carson (1809–1868) frontiersman; helped guide pioneers to California

Walt Disney (1901–1966) pioneer motion-picture animator and producer

Donald Douglas (1892–1981) aircraft manufacturer

Isador Duncan (1878–1927) dancer; created interpretive dancing

John Fremont (1813–1890) explorer; helped bring California into the Union

William Randolph Hearst (1863–1951) journalist and publisher

John (Jack) London (1876–1916) novelist; wrote *The Call of the Wild*

John Sutter (1803–1880) California pioneer; the 1848 gold strike was at his mill

Junipero (Miguel Jose) Serra (1713–1784) Franciscan missionary and founder of several missions in California

Brigham Young (1801–1877) Mormon leader in Utah

Margaret Tobin (Molly) Brown (1873–1932) Colorado mining-era pioneer

Horace Greeley (1811–1872) political and social reformer; reportedly said, "Go west, young man"

Carson

Young

```
S P O I U Y T R D O U G L A S I
I E L K J H G F D S A S W E R T
J H R L K J H H I L E U A S D F
M N B R I F R E M O N T P O I U
A S D F A I O A A N E T Q W E R
L K J H G F D R I D N E A S D F
S D F G H J K S E O E R Y T R E
L K J H G F D T O N P O I U Y T
I O P B Q W E R T Y U I D O Y G
I P G R E E L E Y N Y O U N G P
I O P O A S D C R E W Q N P O U
P E R W N V K L A I E S C O I U
O I U N P Q W E R R N M A T R E
Z X C V B N M A S D S O N Q W E
O D I S N E Y Q W E R O P O I U
M N B V C X Z L K J H B N Q W E
```

8-2B PEOPLE OF THE WEST

Use the outline below to research and write about one of the famous people of the West listed in Activity 8-2A.

Name of famous person _____

Profession _____

Write a summary about his or her personal life.

_____
_____
_____
_____
_____
_____
_____
_____
_____

Summarize what this person contributed to make him or her famous.

_____
_____
_____
_____
_____
_____
_____
_____

Young

Carson

8-3 THE CALIFORNIA GOLD-RUSH DAYS

For the Teacher

Materials Needed:

- copies of Activity 8-3
- pencils

Teacher Preparation:

- Reproduce Activity 8-3, *The California Gold-Rush Days*, as needed.
- Pass out the activity and allow time for students to complete the story. When they are finished, review the answers (given below) with them.

Answer Key:

(1) gold nuggets	(13) pan
(2) gold fever	(14) beans
(3) forty-niners	(15) flour
(4) Poker Flat	(16) sugar } any order
(5) Poverty Place	(17) bacon
(6) Sacramento	(18) lard
(7) San Francisco	(19) restaurants
(8) Virginia City	(20) dance halls
(9) tents	(21) gambling houses
(10) shacks	(22) egg
(11) pickaxe	(23) potatoes
(12) shovel	(24) berry pie

Extended Activity:

- *Sacramento, California* is the gateway to Gold Country. A few highlights in or near Sacramento include *Sutter's Fort, Marshall Gold Discovery State Historic Park, Sutter Creek, Gold Bug Mine,* and *Empire Mine.* Show a film or develop an exhibit on The Gold-Rush Days in California. Contact the Visitor Information Center in Sacramento for specific orientation materials and programs.

8-3 THE CALIFORNIA GOLD-RUSH DAYS

Read the story carefully. Then fill in the blanks with words from the WORD BANK that best complete the sentence. **Hint:** Each dash in a blank represents one letter. Therefore, if there are five dashes in a blank, choose the best word available that has five letters.

WORD BANK		
berry pie	gold nuggets	pickaxe
shovel	shacks	Virginia City
beans	pan	gold fever
dance halls	restaurants	gambling houses
flour	sugar	bacon
lard	forty-niners	Poker Flat
Poverty Place	San Francisco	potatoes
Sacramento	tents	egg

John Sutter was a pioneer in California in the 1800s. He owned a sawmill near present-day Placerville (not far from Sacramento). One morning in January of 1848, Sutter's foreman, James Marshall, knocked on his door. Marshall unwrapped a cloth containing several (1) _ _ _ _ _ _ _ _ _ _ _. These gold nuggets would trigger the great California Gold Rush, the largest mass movement of people the world had seen.

(2) _ _ _ _ _ _ _ _ _ soon swept through California. Gold fever is the intense desire to find gold. In 1849 people came from all over to pan for gold. They were called (3) _ _ _ _ _ - _ _ _ _ _ _ because so many came in the year 1849. Many small mining camps were established. The camps had names like (4) _ _ _ _ _ _ _ _ _ or (5) _ _ _ _ _ _ _ _ _ _ _ _. Larger communities called "boom" towns sprang up near the present-day cities of (6) _ _ _ _ _ _ _ _ _ _ and (7) _ _ _ _ _ _ _ _ _ _ _ _ in California and (8) _ _ _ _ _ _ _ _ _ _ _ _ in Nevada.

8-3 THE CALIFORNIA GOLD-RUSH DAYS *(continued)*

Life in a mining camp was not easy. Miners were not interested in establishing a permanent residence. They came for gold and planned to leave as soon as the deposits were depleted. Most prospectors lived in canvas (9) _ _ _ _ _ or (10) rickety _ _ _ _ _ _. They owned few possessions. Among them were mining tools consisting of a (11) _ _ _ _ _ _ _, (12) _ _ _ _ _ _, and a shallow (13) _ _ _. The miners obtained supplies from the General Store in a mining town. Basic food supplies included (14) _ _ _ _ _, (15) _ _ _ _ _, (16) _ _ _ _ _, (17) _ _ _ _ _, and (18) _ _ _ _.

From time to time prospectors visited one of the nearest boom towns where there were (19) _ _ _ _ _ _ _ _ _ _ _, (20) _ _ _ _ _ _ _ _ _ _, and (21) _ _ _ _ _ _ _ _ _ _ _ _ _ _. In these places they could enjoy a good meal, be entertained by show girls, or play cards.

Storekeepers and businessmen in mining camps and boom towns often earned far more than the gold miners! There were few stores and thousands of customers, so prices were high. The practice of charging high prices to the miners was called "mining the miners." It was not uncommon to charge $3 for a single (22) _ _ _ (even today they are only about $1 per dozen), $1.25 for one pound of (23) _ _ _ _ _ _ _ _, or $5 for a fresh baked (24) _ _ _ _ _ _ _ _. One ingenious woman was reported to have made $12,000 in one year just by baking and selling pies and cakes!

The Gold Rush lasted a very short time. By 1859 the diggings were almost exhausted. However, between 1850 and 1860, the population of California had risen from about 100,000 to 400,000.

8-4 TAKE A TRIP TO THE WEST

For the Teacher

Materials Needed:

- copies of Activity 8-4

- travel agency pamphlets

- travel books (such as *Mobil Travel Guides*)

Teacher Preparation:

- Reproduce Activity 8-4, *Take a Trip to the West*, as needed and organize reference materials.

- Divide classes into small groups and assign specific states or regions of the West for students to visit. Instruct classes to center their trips around historical places and events when possible.

- Pass out travel materials and the journal activity. Then allow time for students to complete the activity. Encourage the inclusion of photographs or illustrations, if possible. When students are finished, allow time for groups to share their journals with the rest of the class.

Extended Activities:

- Show classes a travel video on one or more states from the West. Sources for travelogue tapes include educational channel television, video stores, or libraries.

- Encourage students to learn more about the economy of the state they are visiting. What types of products or services does the state make or provide? What are the major types of jobs in the state? Information on a state's economy can be found in encyclopedias.

8-4 TAKE A TRIP TO THE WEST

DESTINATION _____

For each day, describe the location, place visited, and special activity (such as art, music, food, or holiday).

DAILY ITINERARY

Day 1 _____
_____
_____

Day 2 _____
_____
_____

Day 3 _____
_____
_____

Day 4 _____
_____
_____

Day 5 _____
_____
_____

Day 6 _____
_____
_____

Day 7 _____
_____
_____

8-5 WHAT WILL IT COST?

For the Teacher

Materials Needed:

- copies of Activity 8-5
- travel books
- pencils or pens

Teacher Preparation:

- Reproduce Activity 8-5, *What Will It Cost?*, as needed.
- Pass out the activity and allow time for students to solve the problems. When they are finished, review the answers (given below) with them.

Answer Key:

1. $23.50
2. $17.00
3. $23.00
4. $27.95
5. $34.00
6. $28.90; $2.89; $31.79
7. $23.50; $17.00; $23.00; $27.95; $34.00; $31.79; $157.24

Extended Activity:

- Have students estimate the costs for one day of *their* destination for a family of four (2 adults and 2 students). Approximate hotel and dining expenses can be found in most travel books. Other expenses can be estimated. Although Activity 8-5 can be used as a guide, encourage students to make other selections on how the family will spend the day.

8-5 WHAT WILL IT COST?

A family of four (2 adults and 2 children) are visiting the West. One of their stops is *Sacramento, California*. Listed below are some places they visit. Solve the problems to see how much money they will spend for the day.

1. The family's first visit is to Placerville, near Sacramento, to *Marshall Gold Discovery State Historic Park* to see a replica of Sutter's Mill where gold was discovered in 1848. Admission is $10 per vehicle. Breakfast items at the concession stand are $13.50.

    What is the total cost for admission and food items? $_____

2. Next the family visits the *Gold Bug Mine* for a guided tour. Cost is $5 for adults and $3.50 for students. The family needs 2 adult and 2 student admissions.

    What is the total cost to visit the gold mine? $_____

3. For lunch the family visits *Lillian Russell Room Restaurant and General Store*. Lunches are $5.50, $3.85, $4.75, and $5.90.

    What is the cost for all lunches? $_____

    Add a 15% tip. $_____

    What is the total cost for all lunches? $_____

4. At the General Store the family makes the following purchases: gold nuggets for $12, miner's claim poster for $4, 3 beef jerky at $2 each, and a Boom Town Cookbook for $5.95.

    What is the total cost for all items? $_____

5. In the afternoon the family returns to Sacramento and visits Old Sacramento Historical District where they visit the *California State Railroad Museum*. Cost is $3 for adults and $2 for students. The family also attends a melodrama comedy play at *Old Eagle Theatre*. Admission is $8 for adults and $4 for students.

    What is the total cost for the railroad museum and theatre? $_____

6. For dinner the family eats at a local pizza restaurant. They order 2 pizzas at $10.95 and $12.95, plus 4 soft drinks at $1.25 each.

    What is the cost for pizza and drinks? $_____

    Add a 10% tip. $_____

    What is the total cost for dinner? $_____

7. Add all the expenses to see how much money the family has spent.

    Total cost for #1. $_____
    Total cost for #2. $_____
    Total cost for #3. $_____
    Total cost for #4. $_____
    Total cost for #5. $_____
    Total cost for #6. $_____
    Total cost for the day. $_____

©1997 by The Center for Applied Research in Education

8-6 FAR WEST TERMS

For the Teacher

Materials Needed:

- copies of Activity 8-6
- copies of *Glossary of Terms* (at back of book)

Teacher Preparation:

- Reproduce Activity 8-6, *Far West Terms*, as needed. Also reproduce copies of the *Glossary* as needed.
- Pass out the activity and allow time for students to complete the activity. When they are finished, review the terms (answers given below) with them.

Answer Key:

j.	Native Americans	g.	Sutter's Mill
o.	explorer	d.	claim
a.	missionaries	e.	prospector
l.	mission	f.	Mother Lode
k.	Spaniards	n.	mountain men
b.	mestizos	q.	Mormon
p.	ranches	m.	cliff dwellers
s.	cowboy	h.	boom town
r.	forty-niners	i.	ghost towns
c.	gold fever		

Extended Activity:

- Use some of the terms listed in the activity as topics for further research. Appropriate titles include The Mormons of Utah, The Missions of California, The Gold-Rush Days of California, The Mining Days of Colorado, Mountain Men of the West, The First Americans of the West, Mesa Verde National Park, and Yosemite National Park.

Name _____ **Date** _____ **Period** _____

8-6 FAR WEST TERMS

Expand your vocabulary by learning some terms associated with the far west region. Match the correct definitions to the words.

_____Native Americans

_____explorer

_____missionaries

_____mission

_____Spaniards

_____mestizos

_____ranches

_____cowboy

_____forty-niners

_____gold fever

_____Sutter's Mill

_____claim

_____prospector

_____Mother Lode

_____mountain men

_____Mormon

_____cliff dwellers

_____boom town

_____ghost towns

a. Catholic priests who built missions and converted natives to be Christians in the west and southwest

b. people of mixed Spanish and Mexican Indian bloodlines

c. an obsessive desire to find gold

d. a tract of land that is staked out for ownership

e. a person who stakes and mines a claim by himself or with a small group of partners

f. large region in California where much gold was found in the 1850s

g. name of place near Sacramento, California where James Marshall first discovered gold in 1848

h. larger communities that quickly sprang up near mining camps during the gold-rush days

i. communities abandoned by miners as soon as most of the gold was found

j. first inhabitants of the United States

k. a native of Spain; a group of explorers from Spain who invaded Mexico in the 1500s

l. a church and fort built by the Spaniards of the early west and southwest

m. bands of nomadic hunters who lived in caves in Colorado's mountains nearly 20,000 years ago

n. the brave and hardy fur traders who lived and blazed trails through the west

o. a person who travels in search of geographical information

p. a large farm for raising horses or cattle

q. a member of the Church of Jesus Christ of Latter-day Saints, many of whom live in Utah

r. one of thousands of men who set out for California in 1849 in search of gold

s. a person who tends cattle or horses on a ranch

©1997 by The Center for Applied Research in Education

8-7 TALL TALES AND LITERATURE

For the Teacher

Materials Needed:

- copies of Activity 8-7

- practice paper and pens

- (*optional*) black markers and/or colored pencils

Teacher Preparation:

- Reproduce Activity 8-7, *Tall Tales and Literature,* as needed and organize materials.

- Pass out the activity and allow time for students to read one of the tall tales commonly told among miners. When they are finished, instruct them to write a tall tale of their own.

- Using drawing paper and pens, have students rewrite their tall tale in their best printing or writing.

- (*optional*) Encourage students to illustrate their submissions with markers and/or colored pencils.

Extended Activity:

- Set aside some time for reading stories that relate to the West. Contact the media person in your building or community for assistance in gathering appropriate titles. When possible, take classes to the library for this activity. There are a number of books available that tell stories about the old west. A brief list follows that will help get you started. **Note:** Remember, this is merely a list of some options that are available. Regional differences may vary, so use whatever is available in your area.

TALL TALES

Rough and Ready Prospectors by A. S. Gintzler (Santa Fe, NM: John Muir Publications, 1994). This tells about the gold seekers in America, especially in California. It gives examples of tall tales as well as a practical joke told by miners. One of the tales is retold in this activity. The practical joke is retold in Activity 8-8, *Pastimes and Games.*

FOLKTALES

The Girl Who Married a Ghost and other Tales from the North American Indian by Edward S. Curtis (New York: Four Winds Press, 1978). This book gives a collection of first-hand narratives from Indians gathered during the early 1900s in California, Alaska, and Canada.

CHILDREN'S LITERATURE

California: The Rush for Gold by Linda R. Wade (Vero Beach, FL: Rourke Enterprises, 1991). This is from the series "Doors to America's Past." It begins when James Marshall finds gold at Sutter's Mill in 1848 and continues with the events that followed.

High Trail to Danger by Joan Lowery Nixon (New York: Bantam, 1991). In 1879 Sarah, age seventeen, travels from Chicago to Colorado in search of her missing father.

Vision Quest by Pamela F. Service (New York: Fawcett, 1990). Her father's death forces Kate Elliot and her mom to move to a small town in Nevada.

Let Them Speak for Themselves: Women in the American West 1849–1900 by Christiane Fischer (for older readers) (North Haven, CT: Shoe String, 1990). These 25 women's uncensored experiences of the West are taken from letters, diaries, and journals.

Moon Dancer by Margaret I. Rostkowski (for older readers) (San Diego: Harcourt Brace Jovanovich, 1995). Read about fifteen-year-old Miranda, who is both athletic and a nature lover, as she goes on a backpacking trip in southern Utah looking for Indian paintings in the canyons. Once there she feels a mystical connection with the women who were there before her.

8-7 TALL TALES AND LITERATURE

The following is an adaptation of a gold-rush tall tale taken from *Rough and Ready Prospectors* by A. S. Gintzler.

GOLD STRIKE IN A CEMETERY

Many miners who joined the Gold Rush of California in the 1850s had high hopes of striking it rich. Stories and tall tales of rich gold strikes spread throughout the mining camps. Tales about finding a 25-pound gold nugget were common. Many of these stories began with the prospectors as they sat around the campfire in the evening after a long day's work. Read one of the stories; then develop a tall tale of your own.

Back in the early days of the California Gold Rush, a miner could find gold just about everywhere. Once there was a small group of prospectors panning for gold around Rich Ravine near present-day Sacramento. One of the prospectors died of the fever. The other miners decided to give the dearly departed partner a proper burial.

The miners took the body to a cemetery. There they dug a grave with their pickaxes and shovels. When the hole was deep enough, they lowered the deceased into the grave. One of the men started reading some proverbs from the Bible while the others shed a few tears thinking about their departed friend.

Right in the middle of The Lord's Prayer, one miner saw a gold nugget. He cried out, "Hold it! Hold it! I see gold, boys!" He was correct. Right in front of their eyes in the dirt of the grave were several shining gold nuggets. So the prospectors dug up their friend's coffin, set it aside, and started digging for gold. They forgot all about the poor ol' deceased miner and spent the next weeks digging for gold nuggets. The miners were so excited in striking it rich that they never did bury their friend.

8-8 PASTIMES AND GAMES

For the Teacher

Materials Needed:

- copies of Activity 8-8
- items mentioned in "Teacher Preparation"

Teacher Preparation:

- Reproduce Activity 8-8, *Pastimes and Games*, as needed.

- Pass out the activity and go over the pastimes outlined. If possible, *allow students to help make choices on which activities will be selected. Then set aside some time for participation.*

- If there is interest in participating in a *practical joke* activity, divide the class into small groups. Have each group develop and write a practical joke of their own. When the groups are finished, have each group select one person to read the practical joke to the rest of the class. Assign prizes to the funniest or most original submissions.

- If students show an interest in *arm wrestling*, set up teams and organize a class competition.

- For those interested in *playing cards,* choose some educational-type games and set aside time for competitions. Three specific card games are suggested in the activity. There are several others available on the market. Check your local teacher educational store for availability. Perhaps you already have some favorite history-type games that your classes play.

8-8 PASTIMES AND GAMES

PROSPECTOR PASTIMES

Games and social activities in mining camps were minimal. Most of the time prospectors panned for gold six days a week. Although they picked and washed gravel most of the time, they were able to organize a few forms of amusement. One type of entertainment was to play a practical joke on a newcomer.

Have you ever played a practical joke on someone? Have you ever had a practical joke played on you? Read about one of the miners' jokes below; then see if you can create one of your own. Remember, practical jokes should be amusing or funny—*not* harmful or cruel.

A MINER'S PRACTICAL JOKE

Prospectors often played practical jokes on new miners who they referred to as "greenhorns." The following is an adaptation of a joke from *Rough and Ready Prospectors* by A. S. Gintzler.

In the old west when an "old timer" prospector saw a new miner arrive to the area, he sometimes played a joke on the "greenhorn." One of the most common practical jokes was to load gold flakes into a shotgun. Then the prospector would fire the gold flakes into the ground and spread the news of a new strike. Many greenhorns were tricked this way! Story has it that one prospector fired the gold flakes into several trees in the area. Then he went into camp and told a greenhorn that gold was so plentiful it was growing on trees!

COMPETITIVE ACTIVITIES

Arm Wrestling. Competitions were regularly held in mining towns. Fights were staged between roosters or other animals. In addition, men held competitions of arm wrestling to see who had the strongest arm. Have you ever arm wrestled with a friend? Would you like to participate in an arm-wrestling competition?

Playing Cards. Card playing was also a popular form of entertainment for miners. In mining camps and boom towns, card games were one of the most widely enjoyed forms of entertainment. To participate in this old west pastime favorite, choose card games that are educational as well as entertaining. There are several social studies types of cards available on the market. Two, authorized by the Smithsonian Institution are as follows: *Smithsonian American History Rummy©,* an educational card game featuring 40 paintings from The National Portrait Gallery, and *Smithsonian Presidential Rummy©,* an educational card game featuring 40 president paintings from The National Portrait Gallery. Both of these games are produced by Safari Ltd., Miami, FL.

Photo 8-1 *A Time for Native Americans©,* (1 to 4 players, age 8 and up), is another history-type card game. This biographical activity gives clues to place Native Americans in order, from the late 1400s to modern times. Flip over a card and the back reveals part of a giant map of North America giving hints to when and where the person lived. (Photo compliments of *Aristoplay,* Ann Arbor, MI.)

8-9 SOUNDS OF THE WEST

For the Teacher

Materials Needed:

- sheet music, CD, cassette, or film
- audio-visual equipment

Teacher Preparation:

- Many of the forty-niners were prospectors who left their families behind to try their luck at finding fame and fortune. Most of them found the "pickin's slim" or no gold at all. The miners often sang songs of broken dreams and weary bones or hard luck and bad habits. In boom towns, the homespun ballads of the miners found their way into music halls and theaters. Some favorites included "My Darling Clementine," "Oh Susanna," and "Sweet Betsy From Pike."

  Contact the music person in your school and ask for assistance in obtaining some sheet music of songs that were sung during the gold-rush days. Then organize a songfest. If a CD or cassette is available at your school or library with this type of music, set aside some time for listening to it.

- For an opportunity to view a musical film production relating to the old west, consider the following options. (It is always advised to preview a film and obtain parental consent before showing it to students.)

  The Unsinkable Molly Brown
  A delightful 1964 musical that stars Debbie Reynolds as Molly Brown, who finds fame and fortune in the mines of Colorado. Copies of the film can be borrowed or rented from your local library or video store.

  Paint Your Wagon (PG rating suggested for older students)
  This bawdy 1970 musical comedy tells the story of two California gold miners, played by Lee Marvin as Ben and Clint Eastwood as Partner, as they search for gold in a California mining-camp town. When rough- and-rowdy Ben weds a delicate Mormon lady, the partnership with Partner soon becomes complicated. The musical score by Lerner and Loewe includes "They Call the Wind Maria" and "I Talk to the Trees."

8-10 GOLD-NUGGET JEWELRY

For the Teacher

Materials Needed:

- copies of Activity 8-10
- 2" × 2" or 2" × 3" cardboard pieces
- various gold buttons, beads, sequins, and string
- glue
- pin backings

Teacher Preparation:

- Reproduce Activity 8-10, *Gold-Nugget Jewelry*, as needed and organize materials. Ask for volunteers to bring in an assortment of gold buttons, beads, and bric-a-brac. Pin backings can be purchased at craft stores.

- Pass out the activity and go over it with your students.

- Distribute the materials and allow time for students to develop a piece of "gold nugget" jewelry.

- When they are finished, glue pin backings to the back of the jewelry and allow it to dry overnight.

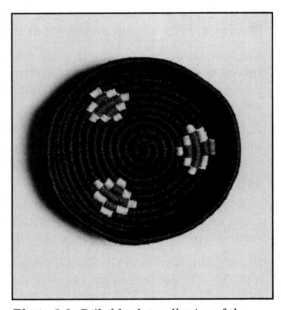

Photo 8-2 *Coiled basket, collection of the author.* After looking at some Indian baskets from the Pomo Indians of the west, art students developed coiled baskets of their own during the time social studies classes were learning about Native Americans. The coiled baskets were made with clothesline rope wrapped with yarn. Some students elected for thinner 4-ply yarns that make a more refined basket, while others chose heavier rug yarns to develop baskets faster.

Extended Activity:

- Basket weaving would make an appropriate cooperative education activity. Contact the Art teacher in your building and coordinate an Indian-style basket-weaving project while your classes are learning about the west.

8-10 GOLD-NUGGET JEWELRY

Photo 8-3 *Gold jewelry, collection of the author.*
Making jewelry from buttons, beads, sequins, and
scraps of gold string or bric-a-brac provides an excellent opportunity to create a craft in honor of the old
west during the Gold-Rush days. It's so easy! All you
need to do is gather some materials and then let your
imagination go! The gold pin shown in the photo was
created on a heart-shaped cardboard backing. Buttons
were carefully selected and then piled on top of one
another to create the gold pin.

Steps to Making Gold Nugget Jewelry

1. Begin by collecting many buttons, beads, and scraps of gold items. Be imaginative
   and see how many varieties you can gather. Sources for finding gold items include
   old beads, button box collections, or the jewelry section of second-hand stores.

2. Cut and organize a small shape from cardboard. The shape can be square, rectangle, round, triangle, or heart shaped.

3. Carefully organize and plan which gold items you will put on your backing.

4. Glue buttons to the basic cardboard shape. **Caution:** Be careful not to add too many
   gold items to the cardboard; otherwise, it will become heavy and difficult to wear.
   Also, be careful not to add too much glue as you are gluing the buttons; otherwise,
   unwanted and unsightly puddles appear.

5. When you are finished, allow the jewelry pieces to dry completely.

6. Glue a pin backing to the backside of the cardboard and allow to dry overnight.
   Jewelry pieces make nice gifts for friends or family.

8-11 BASICS OF OLD WEST COOKING

For the Teacher

Materials Needed:

- copies of Activity 8-11
- pencils

Teacher Preparation:

- Reproduce Activity 8-11, *Basics of Old West Cooking,* as needed.
- Pass out the activity and allow time for students to read the information and complete the worksheet. (Answers are given below.) When they are finished, review the food basics of the old west.

Answer Key:

Part One: Basic foods of mining camps
Basic foods: bacon; beans; beef jerky; flour; sugar; lard; canned fruit; coffee
Luxury items: beef; potatoes; eggs; onions
Meats: bacon; rabbit; beef
Stews: rabbit; beef
Bread: biscuits
Desserts: cherry cobbler; peach cobbler; blackberry cobbler
Beverage: coffee
Basic meals: beans and biscuits; biscuits and gravy; rabbit stew; beef pot roast

Part Two: Basic foods of restaurants in Boom Towns
Meat and fish: beef; crab; tuna; sole
Vegetables: corn; beans; tomatoes; peppers
Fruits: oranges; lemons; grapes; apricots; cherries; peaches
Wild fruits: blackberries; strawberries; raspberries; elderberries
Desserts: pies; cobblers; cakes; cookies
Basic meals: beef pot roast; country fried steak and potatoes; beef pot pie; fish chowder

Extended Activity:

- Encourage students to collectively develop an Old West cookbook. Divide classes into groups and assign specific topics to each group. Appropriate topics include Soups, Breads, Main Dishes, Vegetables, and Desserts. **Note:** The emphasis of this activity revolves around the foods of the mining camps and boom towns of the old west during the Gold-Rush days in California. Students can expand beyond that time to include cuisine from all of the western states. For example, the Mormons of Utah have contributed many fine recipes. After students have collected and submitted their recipes, duplicate them and allow each person to organize a cookbook of his or her own.

8-11 BASICS OF OLD WEST COOKING

BASIC FOODS OF MINING CAMPS

All mining towns had a General Store where miners stocked up on food items. *Basic foods* included *bacon, beans, beef jerky, flour, sugar, lard, canned fruit*, and *coffee*. Luxury items included *beef, potatoes, eggs*, and *onions*. Prices were outrageously high in gold country and stories of eggs at $3 each or onions for $2 each were common.

Meats: Although *bacon* was the most common meat used, sometimes the miners caught a *rabbit* or purchased some fresh *beef* to eat.

Stews: *Rabbit* and *beef* stews were boiled over open fires in heavy pots. Vegetables used in the soups included potatoes and onions.

Bread: *Biscuits, biscuits, biscuits!* Biscuits in the morning, biscuits in the evening, biscuits all the day-long time! And sourdough biscuits were the most common. An imaginative miner prepared several variations of the biscuits to fill his growling stomach.

Desserts were a luxury and it was a special treat, indeed, to have a campfire *cobbler*. Favorites included *cherry, peach,* and *blackberry*.

Beverage: *Coffee* was the main beverage made over an open campfire.

Basic Meals: *Beans and biscuits* or *biscuits and gravy* were the main meals, with an occasional *rabbit stew* or *beef pot roast*.

BASIC FOODS OF RESTAURANTS IN BOOM TOWNS

Larger communities, called "boom towns," sprung up in gold country. These cities were lined with restaurants, dance halls, and gambling houses to feed and entertain wealthy or weary prospectors. Miners were anxious to sit down to a good meal, so ingenious women soon learned they could make money by providing customers with a good meal.

Meat and Fish: Spain and Mexico had introduced the New World to cattle so large ranches provided *beef*. In addition, the waters of the Pacific Ocean produced a variety of fresh fish including *crab, tuna,* and *sole*.

Vegetables: The Franciscan missionaries introduced *corn, beans, tomatoes,* and *peppers* to California, so these vegetables were used by the rush of newcomers who came during the 1850s.

Fruits: The priests also introduced *oranges* and *lemons* to California. Soon *grapes, apricots, cherries,* and *peaches* were added to the fruit production.

Wild fruits: In addition to the fruits grown in the area or shipped from the east, ingenious cooks gathered wild fruits such as *blackberries, raspberries, strawberries,* and *elderberries*. Many wild berries were made into jams or found their way in all sorts of cobblers, cakes, pies, and cookies.

Desserts: The miners were especially eager to indulge in sweet treats. It was reported that one business-minded woman made over $12,000 in one year by providing baked goods to hungry prospectors! *Fresh baked pies and cobblers*, and various types of *cakes and cookies* were all popular.

Basic Meals: With the foods available plus additional shipments of other items from the east, restaurants and boarding houses were able to prepare and serve some tasty foods during the Gold-Rush days. No specific style of cuisine developed from this era but the foods served were hearty and simple. *Beef pot roast, country fried steak and potatoes, beef pot pie,* and *fish chowder* were some basic offerings.

8-11 BASICS OF OLD WEST COOKING

Part One: Use the boxes below to outline some of the foods of mining camps.

Basic supplies:	_____	_____
	_____	_____
	_____	_____
	_____	_____
Luxury items:	_____	_____
	_____	_____
Meats:	_____	_____
	_____	
Stews:	_____	
	_____	
Bread:	_____	
Desserts:	_____	
	_____	
	_____	
Beverage:	_____	
Basic meals:	_____	
	_____	
	_____	
	_____	

8-11 BASICS OF OLD WEST COOKING (continued)

Part Two: Use the boxes below to outline some of the basics of boom town restaurants.

Meat and fish:	_____ _____	_____ _____
Vegetables:	_____ _____	_____ _____
Fruits:	_____ _____ _____	_____ _____ _____
Wild fruits:	_____ _____	_____ _____
Desserts:	_____ _____	_____ _____
Basic meals:	_____ _____ _____ _____	

8-12 MINING CAMP AND BOOM TOWN MENUS

For the Teacher

Hint: It is helpful to complete Activity 8-11, *Basics of Old West Cooking*, before participating in this one.

Materials Needed:

• copies of Activity 8-12

• pencils or pens

Teacher Preparation:

• Reproduce Activity 8-12, *Mining Camp and Boom Town Menus*, as needed.

• Pass out the activity. Then allow students time to read the menus and make their dinner selections. When they are finished, lead a discussion to compare and contrast the meals of the miners to those of the boom towns. Then contrast the foods of both to the meals at their house.

Extended Activity:

• Ask students to bring in some simple or ready-prepared food items appropriate for a mining camp. Choices might include biscuits and jam, sourdough bread and jam, cherry or peach cobbler, and beef jerky.

• Ask students to bring in some simple or ready-prepared food items that might be available in a boom town. Appropriate choices may include fresh fruits such as grapes, oranges, apricots, cherries, or peaches. Since California has a history of growing citrus fruits, any cookies, cakes, or pies made from these fruits would make good choices. Lemon bars, apricot cookies, or orange-nut muffins are all options.

MINING CAMP MENU

Breakfast
Flapjacks and Syrup
Biscuits and Bacon
Caramel-Nut Biscuits
Sourdough Donuts

Main Meals
Pork and Beans with Biscuits
Biscuits and Gravy
Rabbit Stew
Beef Pot Roast with Potatoes
Bacon and Hash Brown Potatoes

Desserts
Campfire Cherry Cobbler
Campfire Peach Cobbler

Beverage
Coffee

BOOM TOWN RESTAURANT MENU

Dinners
Beef Pot Roast with Vegetables
Country Fried Steak with Fried Potatoes
Beef Pot Pie
Fish Chowder

Vegetables
Stewed Tomatoes
Corn
Baked Beans

Breads
Sourdough Rolls
Whole Wheat Bread

Desserts
Lemon Pie
Apricot Tarts
Blackberry Cobbler

Beverages
Coffee
Lemonade
Citrus Punch

8-12 MINING CAMP AND BOOM TOWN MENUS

After you have looked over the menus for the Mining Camp and Boom Town restaurant, choose which menu you want to try. On the menu you select, choose as many food items as you want. When you are finished, list a typical dinner you might have at your house. Then compare the 1850s' meal to your own.

Mining Camp Menu

Breakfast

_____
_____
_____
_____

Main Meal

_____
_____
_____
_____

Desserts

_____
_____

Beverage

_____

Boom Town Restaurant Menu

Dinners

_____
_____
_____
_____

Vegetables

_____
_____
_____

Breads

_____
_____

Desserts

_____
_____
_____

Beverages

_____
_____
_____

American Dinner

Appetizer _____
Soup or Salad _____
Main Course _____
Vegetables _____
Bread _____
Dessert _____
Beverage _____

8-13 CARAMEL-PECAN CAMPFIRE BISCUITS

For the Teacher

Equipment Needed:

- copies of Activity 8-13
- saucepan
- measuring cup
- measuring spoons
- large spoon
- 8" round cake pan or pie pan
- plate

Supplies Needed:

- margarine
- brown sugar
- corn syrup
- chopped pecans
- ready-to-bake biscuits (from the dairy case)

Teacher Preparation:

- Reproduce Activity 8-13, *Caramel-Pecan Campfire Biscuits*, as needed and organize equipment and supplies.
- Give a demonstration on making the biscuits as students follow along with the recipe. Follow up with a breakfast biscuit treat.
- **ALTERNATIVE:** Go over the recipe with students. Then make an out-of-class assignment for students to make the biscuits at home and bring them to school for a special miners' breakfast. Encourage students to ask for adult supervision when preparing the biscuits.

Extended Activity:

- Contact the Consumer and Family Living teacher well in advance and coordinate a Mining Town breakfast or lunch while your classes are learning about the West.

8-13 CARAMEL-PECAN CAMPFIRE BISCUITS

Miners often made sourdough biscuits. The necessary ingredient to make the biscuits is to have a basic dough made from yeast (called a starter). From that basic dough the cook always kept another starter for the next batch of biscuits. Because biscuits were eaten so often, the prospectors tried to think of different ways to serve them. Adding sugar and nuts was one method of perking them up a bit. This recipe has been simplified by using some of our modern conveniences. Remember, the forty-niners not only had to make the biscuits from scratch but they also had to bake them over a campfire as well. This recipe serves 6.

You need:

1/4	cup margarine
1/2	cup brown sugar, packed
2	tablespoons corn syrup
1/2	cup chopped pecans
1	small package of 6 ready-made biscuits (from the dairy case)

What to do:

1. Preheat oven to 400°.

2. In a saucepan heat margarine until melted.

3. Stir in brown sugar, corn syrup, and pecans. Then heat thoroughly.

4. Spread mixture in the bottom of an 8-inch round cake pan or pie pan.

5. Place biscuits on top of the caramel around the pan.

6. Bake for 10 to 15 minutes or until biscuits are golden brown.

7. Immediately invert pan on a plate. Let pan remain for a minute or two until caramel can drizzle over biscuits.

8-14 BOOM TOWN LEMON PIE

For the Teacher

Equipment Needed:

- copies of Activity 8-14
- 8" or 9" pie pan
- saucepan with lid
- measuring cup
- large spoon
- hand mixer
- small mixing bowl

Supplies Needed:

- ready-made pie crust
- lemon pie filling
- eggs
- sugar

Teacher Preparation:

- Reproduce copies of Activity 8-14, *Boom Town Lemon Pie*, as needed and organize equipment and supplies.
- Give a demonstration on making the pie as students follow along with the recipe. Follow up with a pie taste treat.
- **ALTERNATIVE:** Go over the recipe with students. Then make an out-of-class assignment for students to make the pie at home and bring it to school for a special California boom-town treat. Encourage students to ask for adult supervision when preparing the pie at home.

Extended Activity:

- Contact the Consumer and Family Living teacher well in advance and coordinate a California boom-town-type luncheon activity while your classes are learning about the West.

8-14 BOOM TOWN LEMON PIE

In California the Franciscan friars, who founded the missions in the 1700s, introduced the natives to many types of trees. Among them were lemon, orange, and apricot trees. In modern times California is a major producer of citrus fruit, but how many of you know they were grown as early as 1792? This lemon pie recipe has taken advantage of modern-day conveniences so you can enjoy Boom Town Lemon Pie the easy way. This recipe serves 6.

You need:

1	ready-made pie crust
1	3-ounce box lemon pie filling
1/2	cup sugar
2-1/4	cups water
2	egg yolks, slightly beaten
2	egg whites
1/4	cup sugar

What to do:

1. Set oven at 400°.
2. Follow directions on pie crust package to make a baked shell for pie filling.
3. Cool thoroughly.
4. Empty lemon pie powder in a saucepan.
5. Add 1/2 cup sugar and mix.
6. Gradually add water and slightly beaten egg yolks.
7. Cook over medium heat, stirring constantly, until mixture comes to a full boil.
8. Remove from heat, cover pan with lid, and cool while preparing meringue topping.
9. Reset oven to 425°.
10. In a small bowl, beat egg whites until foamy.
11. Gradually beat in 1/4 cup sugar until meringue forms peaks.
12. Pour lemon pie mixture into baked pie shell.
13. Spread meringue over pie filling. Be sure to seal the meringue to the crust around the edges.
14. Bake for about 5 minutes or until lightly brown.
15. Cool at room temperature for 1 hour. Then refrigerate 3 to 4 hours.

8-15 BLACKBERRY COBBLER

For the Teacher

Equipment Needed:

- copies of Activity 8-15
- mixing bowl
- measuring cup
- measuring spoons
- large spoon
- 8" round pie pan or square baking dish

Supplies Needed:

- flour
- sugar
- baking powder
- margarine
- milk
- blackberry pie filling
- (*optional*) ice cream

Teacher Preparation:

- Reproduce copies of Activity 8-15, *Blackberry Cobbler*, as needed and organize equipment and supplies.
- Give a demonstration on making the cobbler as students follow along with the recipe. Follow up with a cobbler taste treat.
- **ALTERNATIVE:** Go over the recipe with students. Then make an out-of-class assignment for students to make the cobbler at home and bring it to school for a special mining camp or boom town taste treat. Encourage students to ask for adult supervision when preparing the cobbler.

8-15 BLACKBERRY COBBLER

Early western boom town cooks depended heavily on a wide assortment of wild fruits that grew in the region. Some favorites included blackberries, elderberries, raspberries, and strawberries. From all these fruits, various cobblers, cakes, cookies, and pies were created. A cobbler is a deep-dish fruit dessert, usually made with a biscuit topping. The American original has remained popular for many years. This version takes advantage of the convenient canned pie fillings. The recipe serves 6.

You need:

1	tablespoon margarine
1	can blackberry pie filling
1	cup all-purpose flour
3	tablespoons sugar
1-1/2	teaspoons baking powder
1/4	cup margarine, softened
1/2	cup milk
	(*optional*) ice cream

What to do:

1. Preheat oven to 400°.
2. Spread 1 tablespoon margarine around the bottom and sides of a pie pan or baking dish.
3. Spread pie filling evenly across the bottom of the pan.
4. In a mixing bowl, mix flour, sugar, and baking powder.
5. Cut in margarine until mixture resembles coarse crumbs.
6. Add milk and stir until thoroughly blended.
7. Drop by spoon on top of pie filling in 6 mounds.
8. Bake for about 20 minutes or until top is golden brown.
9. (*optional*) Serve warm or cool with ice cream.

BIBLIOGRAPHY FOR THE WEST

Children's Nonfiction

Kent, Deborah. *America the Beautiful: Colorado*. Chicago: Children's Press, 1992.

Lillegard, Dee and Wayne Stoker. *America the Beautiful: Nevada*. Chicago: Children's Press, 1992.

McCarthy, Betty. *America the Beautiful: Utah*. Chicago: Children's Press, 1993.

Stein, Conrad R. *America the Beautiful: California*. Chicago: Children's Press, 1992.

Cookbooks

Editors. *Better Homes and Gardens Heritage Cook Book*. Des Moines, IA: Meredith Corporation, 1985.

Editors. *Heritage of America Cookbook*. Des Moines, IA: Meredith Corporation, 1993.

Pastimes and Tall Tales

Gintzler, A. S. *Rough and Ready Prospectors*. Santa Fe, NM: John Muir Publications, 1994.

Wade, Linda R. *California: The Rush for Gold*. Vero Beach, FL: Rourke Enterprises, Inc., 1991.

Social Studies

Bass, Herbert J. *Our Country*. Parsippany, NJ: Silver Burdett & Ginn, 1991.

Travel

Editors. *Mobil 1995 Travel Guide, California and the West*. New York: Fodor's Travel Publications, 1995.

Editors. *Mobil 1995 Travel Guide, Southwest and South Central*. New York: Fodor's Travel Publications, 1995.

GLOSSARY OF TERMS

adobe   a sun-baked brick made of clay used to make pueblos

antebellum   plantations that existed before the Civil War

Apache   group of American Indians of the Southwest noted for resisting white settlers; Geronimo was a leader

Appalachian   mountain range in the eastern part of the United States extending from Canada to Georgia

back country   thinly populated rural area along the Appalachian Mountain range

banjo   stringed musical instrument having a long neck and circular body that was probably first made in Africa

battle   extended struggle or controversy between two or more persons

bay   inlet off of a larger body of water

bayou   secondary waterway or any marshy body of water

Benjamin Franklin   printer, author, diplomat, and statesman who spent much of his life in Philadelphia, Pennsylvania

boom towns   large communities that quickly sprang up near mining camps during Gold-Rush days

breadbasket   a name given to the Middle Colonies because they raised and exported so much grain

Cajun   Acadian descendent from Nova Scotia

calliope   musical instrument with a series of steam whistles played like an organ; a popular form of music on riverboats

canyon   long, narrow, deep valley between high cliffs

cash crops   crops that are raised and sold for profit on the world market

charter   written agreement granting privileges from a sovereign country

chili   thick soup of meat and chilies; the national dish of Texas

claim   a tract of land that is staked out for ownership

cliff dwellers   bands of nomadic hunters who lived in caves in Colorado's mountains nearly 20,000 years ago

colony   settlement developed by a country beyond its borders

Conestoga   type of large wagon built by the settlers to carry goods along the road

Continental Divide   the ridge of the Rocky Mountains that separates rivers flowing toward the Atlantic Ocean from those flowing toward the Pacific Ocean

cotton   soft, white, fibrous material around the seeds of a plant grown for profit in the old South

covered wagon   wagon with a canvas top often used by pioneers for traveling

cowboy   person who tends cattle or horses on a ranch

Creole   person born of Spanish and French settlers located mostly in Louisiana

GLOSSARY OF TERMS (continued)

desert   dry, barren region that is largely treeless and sandy

drought   period of prolonged dryness to an area causing excessive damage to crops

economy   the concise use of resources for a specific region or country

expedition   journey taken for a specific purpose, such as to explore

explorer   person who travels in search of geographical information

fiddle   musical instrument that is a type of violin often played by pioneers

flatboat   raft-type of boat with a flat bottom that can travel through shallow water

forty-niner   one of thousands of men who set out for California in search of gold in 1849

freedom   the power of acting without restraint

frontiersman   person who lives or works on frontier land

fur trader   one who trades furs

ghost town   community abandoned by miners as soon as most of the gold was mined

gold fever   an obsessive desire to find gold

grain   the seeds of various food plants that produce food

Great Lakes   chain of five large lakes (Superior, Michigan, Huron, Erie, and Ontario)

Great Plains   region of the United States east of the Rocky Mountains and west of the Mississippi River noted for being flat

Hispanic   people who are descendants of the Spanish culture

homestead   the home and adjoining land occupied by a family

hornbook   wood shaped paddle that served as a tool for learning to read

House of Burgesses   colonial representative assembly in Virginia

hurricane   violent cyclonic storm with high winds accompanied by rain originating in the tropics

immigrant   person who leaves his or her country to live elsewhere

indentured servant   person who agrees to work for a certain period of time in return for travel expenses and keep

Indians   Native Americans who lived in America before the Europeans arrived

indigo   plant that produces blue dye; it was a cash crop in southern plantations

Jamestown   name of first English settlement in America

jazz   style of music developed in America from ragtime and blues

legislature   organized body of people having the authority to make laws

Lewis and Clark   the two men who led an expedition to explore the Northwest territory of the Louisiana Purchase

library   place where literary and reference materials are located

GLOSSARY OF TERMS (continued)

log cabin home made from logs and the most common type of dwelling built by the pioneers of the Midwest

long house communal dwelling of the Northwest Coast Indians often decorated with elaborate carvings

Louisiana Purchase a large section of land purchased by the United States in 1803 that extends from the Mississippi River to the Rocky Mountains

magnolia large, fragrant flowers that are white, pink, or purple growing on a tree; the state flower of Louisiana

Mayflower the small ship that brought the Pilgrims to America

Mayflower Compact an agreement made by the Pilgrims to consult each other about the laws of the Plymouth Colony

melting pot place where many cultures blend together

mesa smal, raised, flat-topped table land on top of a mountain or hill

mestizo people of mixed Spanish and Mexican Indian heritage

Midwest upper Mississippi Valley region that includes states around the Great Lakes

mill the process of grinding grain into flour

mission church and fort built by the Spanish in the early southwest and west

missionaries Catholic priests in the west and southwest who built missions and converted the natives to Christianity

Mississippi River mighty river that flows north and south from Minnesota to the Gulf of Mexico

Mormon member of the Church of Jesus Christ of Latter-day Saints, many of whom live in Utah

mother lode large region in California where much gold was found in the 1850s

mountain land mass that projects high above its surroundings and is bigger than a hill

mountain men the brave and hardy trappers and fur traders who lived and blazed trails through the Rocky Mountains in the 1800s

Native Americans first inhabitants of America

Navajo group of American Indians who live in northern New Mexico and Arizona, and are famous for making weavings

North Coast Indians the Indian tribes who live along the rugged west coast from Oregon to Alaska

Ohio River river that flows from Pennsylvania to the Mississippi River; was a major route followed by many pioneers

Oregon Country in the 1800s refers to the large area of land between the Rocky Mountains and the Pacific Ocean

Oregon Trail the trail pioneers followed in the 1800s that started in Missouri and ended in Oregon

GLOSSARY OF TERMS (continued)

paddle wheeler   steamboat propelled by a large wheel that has paddles

panhandle   strip of land resembling the handle of a pan, such as the northern extension of the state of Texas between Oklahoma and New Mexico

park   tract of land maintained in its natural state that can be visited by the general public

pass   narrow valley between mountains

Philadelphia   city in Pennsylvania founded by William Penn

piedmont   land that lies at the base of a mountain

pilgrim   person who journeys to a foreign land often for religious freedom

pioneer   person or a group of people who are the first to settle a new territory

plantation   large farm or estate worked by resident labor

potlatch   social event of the Northwest Coast Indians noted for feasting and gift-giving

prairie schooner   sturdy wagon with side boards, iron-rimmed wheels, and an arched canvas hood

printer   person who engages in the mass production of the written word

prospector   person who stakes and mines a claim by himself or with a small group of partners

pueblo   communal dwelling area consisting of flat-topped adobe houses in groups, sometimes several stories high

Pueblo Indians   group of American Indians in New Mexico who live in pueblos and are famous for making pottery

Puget Sound   a body of water that separates the Olympic Peninsula from the state of Washington

Puritans   group of protestants who wanted to purify the Church of England and founded the Massachusetts Bay Colony

Quaker   religious group who are also known as Friends of Society

racism   the belief that one race is superior to another

ranch   large farm for raising horses or cattle

reservation   land that is set aside for a specific group of American Indians to live

Rocky Mountains   great chain of mountains extending from Canada to New Mexico and bordered by Great Plains region

rodeo   contest where cowboys compete at a variety of riding and roping events using horses and cattle

Sabbath   day set aside for rest and worship

Sacajawea   Shoshone Indian woman who accompanied Lewis and Clark on their expedition

saguaro   the state flower of Arizona found on a type of tall cactus that bears white flowers and edible fruit

GLOSSARY OF TERMS *(continued)*

Separatists   group of people who wanted to separate from The Church of England; later called Pilgrims

silt   earthy material composed of fine particles of soil or sand suspended in or deposited by water

slave   person held in servitude or bondage

slave state   state in America in which ownership of a Negro person was legal

sod house   home built by pioneers of the Plains made from the thick, heavy soil of the region

sound   long broad passage of water generally parallel to a coast line

Spaniards   natives of Spain; a group of explorers from Spain who invaded Mexico in the 1500s

square dance   type of dance by four couples who form a hollow square

statesman   person who is actively engaged in conducting the business of government

steamboat   boat that is driven by steam power

Sutter's Mill   name of place near Sacramento, California where James Marshall first discovered gold in 1848

swamp   wet spongy land partially covered with water

territory   specific geographical region or area

Thanksgiving   holiday resulting from the Pilgrims' harvest celebration of 1621

tidewater   low-lying coastal land along an ocean

tobacco   plant cultivated as a major crop in Virginia and used for smoking

tolerance   the capacity to accept the beliefs or practices differing from one's own

totem pole   pole or post carved and painted with animals or objects made by the Northwest Indians that often tells a story

trapper   person who traps animals usually for the purpose of selling their fur

Willamette Valley   rich valley in Oregon and destination for many pioneers who traveled along the Oregon Trail

Williamsburg   colonial capital of Virginia from 1799–1870; has been reconstructed and is now open to the public

witch hunt   the searching out and persecution of those who hold unpopular views or practice witchcraft

yucca   the state flower of New Mexico that is a plant of the lily family with long leaves and white blossoms

THE FIFTY STATES

State	Date Entered Union	Order of Entry	Capital	Largest City
Alabama	1819	22	Montgomery	Birmingham
Alaska	1959	49	Juneau	Anchorage
Arizona	1912	48	Phoenix	Phoenix
Arkansas	1836	25	Little Rock	Little Rock
California	1850	31	Sacramento	Los Angeles
Colorado	1876	38	Denver	Denver
Connecticut	1788	5	Hartford	Bridgeport
Delaware	1787	1	Dover	Wilmington
Florida	1845	27	Tallahassee	Jacksonville
Georgia	1788	4	Atlanta	Atlanta
Hawaii	1959	50	Honolulu	Honolulu
Idaho	1890	43	Boise	Boise
Illinois	1818	21	Springfield	Chicago
Indiana	1816	19	Indianapolis	Indianapolis
Iowa	1846	29	Des Moines	Des Moines
Kansas	1861	34	Topeka	Wichita
Kentucky	1792	15	Frankfort	Louisville
Louisiana	1812	18	Baton Rouge	New Orleans
Maine	1820	23	Augusta	Portland
Maryland	1788	7	Annapolis	Baltimore
Massachusetts	1788	6	Boston	Boston
Michigan	1837	26	Lansing	Detroit
Minnesota	1858	32	St. Paul	Minneapolis
Mississippi	1817	20	Jackson	Jackson
Missouri	1821	24	Jefferson City	St. Louis
Montana	1889	41	Helena	Billings
Nebraska	1867	37	Lincoln	Omaha
Nevada	1864	36	Carson City	Las Vegas
New Hampshire	1788	9	Concord	Manchester

THE FIFTY STATES *(continued)*

State	Date Entered Union	Order of Entry	Capital	Largest City
New Jersey	1787	3	Trenton	Newark
New Mexico	1912	47	Santa Fe	Albuquerque
New York	1788	11	Albany	New York
North Carolina	1789	12	Raleigh	Charlotte
North Dakota	1889	39	Bismarck	Fargo
Ohio	1803	17	Columbus	Columbus
Oklahoma	1907	46	Oklahoma City	Oklahoma City
Oregon	1859	33	Salem	Portland
Pennsylvania	1787	2	Harrisburg	Philadelphia
Rhode Island	1790	13	Providence	Providence
South Carolina	1788	8	Columbia	Columbia
South Dakota	1889	40	Pierre	Sioux Falls
Tennessee	1796	16	Nashville	Memphis
Texas	1845	28	Austin	Houston
Utah	1896	45	Salt Lake City	Salt Lake City
Vermont	1791	14	Montpelier	Burlington
Virginia	1788	10	Richmond	Virginia Beach
Washington	1889	42	Olympia	Seattle
West Virginia	1863	35	Charleston	Charleston
Wisconsin	1848	30	Madison	Milwaukee
Wyoming	1890	44	Cheyenne	Cheyenne

NOTES

NOTES

NOTES

NOTES

NOTES